D1460377

A History of
WARRINGTON

ST.HELENS COMMUNITY LIBRARIES

3 8055 00876 8970

A *History of*
WARRINGTON

ALAN CROSBY

CENTRAL LIBRARY
VICTORIA SQUARE
ST. HELENS
WA10 1DY
TEL: 01744 456954/89

ST.HELENS COMMUNITY LIBRARIES	
A02	
Askews	
942.419	

 PHILLIMORE

2002

Published by
PHILLIMORE & CO. LTD
Shopwyke Manor Barn, Chichester, West Sussex, England

© Warrington Borough Council, 2002

ISBN 1 86077 222 6

Printed and bound in Great Britain by
THE CROMWELL PRESS
Trowbridge, Wiltshire

Frontispiece: Warrington town centre, from the first edition of the Ordnance Survey 25-inch to 1-mile map surveyed in 1893. This shows very clearly the intricate pattern of property boundaries, lanes and courts in the area of the medieval town, contrasting with the regularity of the more recent development around Cairo Street and Suez Street. The way in which a variety of industries impinged closely upon the town centre is also apparent. Large parts of this townscape have now disappeared, as a result of the closure of traditional industries and redevelopment of the town centre in the 1970s and 1980s.

CONTENTS

Twentieth-Century Warrington   **141**

ACKNOWLEDGEMENTS

The research for this book was most generously supported by sponsorship from firms and individuals within the Warrington area. We are extremely grateful to them all for their invaluable role in the success of the book itself, and for their contribution to this worthy and important project which benefits the people and community of Warrington. The sponsors of the project were:

    Warrington Borough Council
    English Partnerships (formerly the Commission for New Towns)
    The Greenalls Group plc (now the De Vere Group plc)
    Mr Harry Cunningham, JP, Freeman of the Borough
    Tinsley Wire (Warrington)
    The Locker Group plc
    Hancock and Wood Limited

In the research and writing of this book special help has been given by the following, and their assistance is acknowledged with thanks: the county archivist and staff of the Lancashire Record Office, Preston; the county archivist and staff of Cheshire and Chester Archives and Local Studies, Chester (with thanks to Mike Edison for help with photographs); Mrs Judith Baldry; and P.H.W. Booth. We would also like to thank Phillimore, the publishers of the book, for their skill with layout and design which has been so important in making this history of Warrington so attractive in appearance and 'feel'.

The book was conceived and created as a project of the Heritage and Archives section of Warrington Borough Council, and it has benefited from the continuing support of the borough and its officers. Sally Coleman, the former Heritage and Archives Manager, saw the need for an accessible, informative and attractive single-volume history of Warrington, which would provide an overview of the town's development and give readers suggestions and ideas for carrying on their own investigations and research. It is thanks to Sally that the book has come to fruition and her enthusiasm and encouragement have been invaluable. Particular mention must also be made of the Warrington Libraries and Information Service, and thanks expressed to Jo Unsworth (Senior Librarian) and Hilary Chambers (Archivist) for their help and patience. This book could not have been written without Janice Hayes of Warrington Museum, whose unrivalled understanding of the town's history and its source material, encyclopaedic knowledge of the photographic collections, and firm, fair and friendly criticism of the drafts of the text have made a world of difference. She is not, however, responsible for any failings, errors or inadequacies – those are mine alone!

ALAN CROSBY

ILLUSTRATION ACKNOWLEDGEMENTS

The majority of the illustrations in this book are from the large photographic and picture archive of Warrington Museum. I am especially grateful to Janice Hayes for her invaluable help with locating and identifying the material which has been used. The sources or location of other illustrations are as follows:

Items from the Warrington Library collection: the wanted poster (page 54); the sketches by Robert Booth (pages 57, 65, 69, 87); the plan of Stubs' works (page 79); poster for Monks Hall works (page 93); the photograph of Ship Canal navvies (page 100); the 1832 map of parliamentary borough boundaries (page 109); the Gas Committee advertisement (page 116); the cholera poster (page 123); and the photograph of laying the foundation stone of the Museum and Library (page 136).

Alan Crosby produced the maps, graphs and transcripts on pages 9, 11, 23, 31, 33, 34, 35, 40, 56, 62, 63, 66, 102, 108, 145, 146, 156, 157, 167, 171, 172 and 183, and also the photograph on page 168. The illustrations on pages 2 and 178 are reproduced by kind permission of Photochrome of Nottingham. The drawings of Winwick church and Warrington town (pages 10 and 17) are from the Burtonhead map in the Scarisbrick collection DDSc, Lancashire Record Office. The sketch of the encampment outside Warrington (page 44) is on the reverse of the 1818 Warrington land tax return, Lancashire Record Office QDF 2/18/71. The plan of earthworks on Mote Hill (page 12) is from *Victoria County History of Lancashire* vol.2 (1908). The photographs of the Warrington borough charters (pages 19 and 111) and of the Boteler Grammar School foundation charter (page 32) were supplied by Cheshire & Chester Archives and Local Studies and are reproduced with thanks for their help. Other credits, and kind permission for the use of material gratefully acknowledged, are:

Walter Simms and Cheshire Libraries, map of railways (page 75); the Greenall plc archives, Warrington Library, page 76 (both); Crosfield archives, Unilever plc, page 94 (both) and page 95; George Thornton: Peace Centre ceremony (page 185); Landscape Design Associates and Howard Ben Tré (Guardians of Warrington, page 185); Hancock and Wood (page 161); Aldon Ferguson and the Burtonwood Association: three photographs of Burtonwood Airbase (page 164); image by the late John Jenkins, courtesy of the Bewsey Old Hall Conservation Project (page 30). The Ordnance Survey maps reproduced throughout the book are taken from the 6-inch series of 1845; the 25-inch series of 1893; and the 50-inch series of 1850-1851.

Warrington before the Norman Conquest

1. Why Warrington?

Warrington has always been a key place on communications networks

This has been the most important factor in its growth and development

It originated at the lowest convenient crossing point on the Mersey

Streams of traffic on Thelwall Viaduct and complicated motorway junctions … IKEA and a huge Marks & Spencers … new industrial estates … a thriving shopping centre … these are some of the images that outsiders have of Warrington today. They reflect its present success, but behind them lies a long and fascinating history through which runs a common thread: Warrington is at a crossroads. Whenever we think about the way in which the town developed, its location is an ever-present factor, determining much of what it was in the past and is today. The axis of the M6, crossed by the M56 and M62, closely resembles the pattern of communications familiar to our Iron-Age ancestors three thousand years ago.

This aerial view of the Golden Square shopping centre, the heart of modern Warrington, also shows the crossroads at Market Gate which has been the focus of the town's development for over a thousand years. The ex-Cheshire Lines Railway and Midland Way (on the left of the picture) are more recent additions to Warrington's important transport network.

One of the main barriers to north-south movement in the region was always the Mersey valley. The river was wide and edged by extensive marshes and mosses, which in the past were difficult to cross. Below Warrington the Mersey widened rapidly to form the upper estuary (much of it reclaimed in recent centuries), and above it were the wetlands. At the head of the estuary, though, sandstone and gravels come close to the water and gave a drier approach. Here the river could be forded with comparative ease and this became a key point on a north-south routeway already in existence in the prehistoric period. The sprawl of the modern town has partly concealed the detail, but think of the long slope down Bridge Street towards the river, and the old geography will become clearer – this was the line of a convenient way to the water's edge thousands of years ago.

In the past there were fords and ferries across the river (the name Hollinfare, for example, means 'ferry by the holly-tree') but even today, apart from the two motorway viaducts at Barton and Thelwall, there is only one road bridge between Eccles and Warrington. This lack of alternatives concentrated traffic on Warrington crossing. The river was also crucially important. Above

Warrington it was navigable only for very small boats, so for most purposes this was the head of navigation. The town developed where the north-south land route met the east-west water route. These factors are similar to those identifiable in other places in north-west England, such as Preston, Lancaster and Carlisle. What is especially striking about Warrington is that its crossroads position is just as important now as it was to our distant forebears.

2. Before the Romans

In recent years archaeological investigation has revealed important evidence about the prehistoric period in the Warrington area. It was once thought that the Mersey valley was a wilderness, thickly-forested and scarcely populated, but it is now clear that there was extensive settlement in this district from the Neolithic period (4000 BC onwards). Detailed analysis of ancient pollen from pond muds and of the vegetation preserved in peat mosses indicates that about five thousand years ago people were beginning to clear the woodland to create farmland and sites for houses. They grew crops and domesticated animals. The landscape was changing and human activity was a key element in that process.

The creation of the new landscapes of agriculture and settlement was often interrupted and sometimes reversed, but over the centuries the woodland gradually disappeared. A growing population created new agricultural land and a network of tracks and lanes, exploiting the varied resources offered by the river, the tidal estuary, wetlands, woodlands, and drier slopes. Many prehistoric

People were living in the area of Warrington several thousand years ago

Archaeologists have found examples of their tools, pottery and other artefacts

Some of their settlement sites have also been identified and excavated

These people were farmers and fishermen; their activities began to change the local landscape

Polished stone axe head, from the Neolithic or New Stone Age, found at Orford. Possibly for ceremonial rather than 'everyday' use, the axe may have been lost at a ford on one of the channels of the Mersey

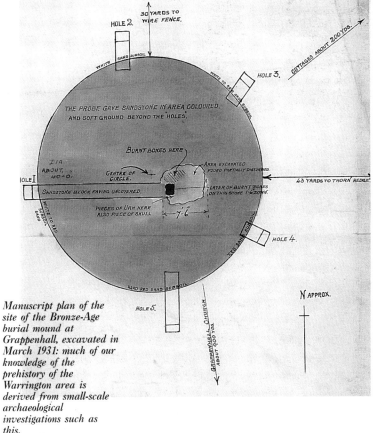

Manuscript plan of the site of the Bronze-Age burial mound at Grappenhall, excavated in March 1931: much of our knowledge of the prehistory of the Warrington area is derived from small-scale archaeological investigations such as this.

Bronze-Age cinerary urns, a quernstone [centre] and a food beaker [bottom right], from the Grappen-hall burial mound (see

plan, right): cinerary urns contained the ashes from the cremation of the deceased.

The excavation of the Bronze-Age burial mound at Southworth, in the early 1980s. The large circular shape of the mound is clearly seen. In the foreground are early Christian graves which were dug on the site when the mound was already 2,000 years old.

objects have been found in the Warrington area during the past two centuries: in 1985, for example, a perforated pebble hammer of the late Neolithic or early Bronze-Age (about 2500 BC) was discovered at Birchwood, and in 1931-1934 Bronze-Age urns containing charred wood, flints and bone needles were excavated in Chester Road, Grappenhall. Other important evidence of Bronze Age settlement includes the tumuli or burial mounds at Highfield Lane, Winwick, Southworth Hall, Croft and Grappenhall.

Aerial photography has also revealed many new pre-Roman settlement sites in the Mersey valley, while comprehensive excavation at Great Woolden Hall Farm, Glazebrook, showed that the site had been settled as early as the Neolithic period (about 5000 BC), with major activity during the late Iron Age (first millennium BC) and into the early Roman period. Much evidence for prehistoric and pre-Roman settlement in the Warrington area has been overlooked in the past, or destroyed by later development, but it is clear that when the Romans arrived they came to a land scattered with houses and farms, patterned by fields, and occupied by people who traded and used the fords over the Mersey.

FURTHER READING: Current thinking on pre-Roman settlement in the area is summarised in M. Nevell (editor), *Living on the edge of Empire: models, methodology and marginality* (Archaeology North West vol.3, 1998); see also D. Shotter, *Romans and Britons in North West England* (Centre for North West Regional Studies, Lancaster University, 1997)

3. The Roman occupation and its impact

The Romans occupied this part of Britain in the years after AD 69

Warrington lay where a key north-south 'trunk' road crossed the Mersey

Some archaeologists suggest that there may have been a fort at Warrington

It is also possible that Romans built the first bridge over the river

Before the coming of the Romans the Mersey was the frontier between two distinct British (Celtic) tribes. To the north were the Brigantes, whose heartland was around Ripon in Yorkshire, while to the south, in modern Cheshire, were the Cornovii, whose capital was at the Wrekin near Shrewsbury. The site of Warrington was on the border – the name 'Mersey' means 'the boundary river' – and it remained a frontier town for many centuries. In AD 43 the Romans occupied southern Britain but in the north-west the existing kingdom of the Brigantes was permitted to function as a 'client state'. Locally there was probably a small Roman presence but it was not until AD 69 that serious intervention took place. This was prompted by civil war in Brigantia and further unrest in north Wales. Recent evidence confirms that at this date a military road was constructed, running north-west from Middlewich to the river-crossing at Wilderspool, then heading north through Lancashire to Wigan, Walton-le-Dale and Ribchester. Another important early road linked the legionary fortress at Chester with York via Manchester, running along the Cheshire side of the river.

Warrington, halfway between Middlewich and Wigan, at a key crossing on the Mersey, and close to the Chester-Manchester road junction, must have been of strategic importance in the military campaign of AD 69 onwards, and for two centuries there has been speculation that a fort existed here. In the 1890s

Thomas May, one of Warrington's pioneer archaeologists, tried and failed to find one in the area of the modern town. The excavations at the Greenalls site in the 1990s encouraged the archaeologist Tim Strickland to revive the idea, and he argued that a fort may have been built in the early AD 70s overlooking the ford at Latchford, which he believed was the earliest Roman crossing-place. This must be speculation, but the possibility remains that there was a short-lived fort somewhere in the area.

By the end of the first century AD the northern frontier of the Empire had reached the line of Hadrian's Wall and the security threat was lifted. The north-south road became one of the main routes in northern England, and the Romans may have built a bridge over the Mersey close to the site of the medieval Warrington bridge. That, too, is as yet unproven.

FURTHER READING for sections 3 and 4: J. Hinchliffe and F. Williams, *Roman Warrington: excavations at Wilderspool 1966-1969 and 1976* (University of Manchester Archaeology Department, 1992); T. May, *Warrington's Roman Remains* (Warrington Guardian, 1904); T. Strickland, *The Romans at Wilderspool: the story of the first industrial development on the Mersey* (Greenalls Group plc, 1995)

BELOW *Thomas May, by profession a tax inspector but by inclination an enthusiastic and assiduous amateur archaeologist, was responsible for the first systematic investigation of the large Roman site at Wilderspool. In this view, taken in about 1900, he is shown drawing a section of recently-excavated Roman road surface.*

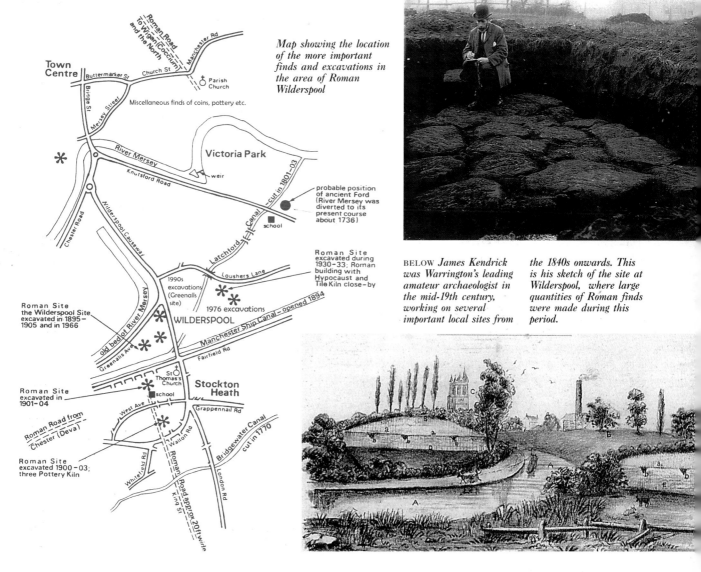

Map showing the location of the more important finds and excavations in the area of Roman Wilderspool

BELOW *James Kendrick was Warrington's leading amateur archaeologist in the mid-19th century, working on several important local sites from* the 1840s onwards. This is his sketch of the site at Wilderspool, where large quantities of Roman finds were made during this period.*

4. Wilderspool and its industries

There was a substantial Roman town at Wilderspool

It was an industrial and commercial centre, on the south bank of the river

Archaeological excavations since 1800 have revealed much about this town

Wilderspool declined in the third century AD and was eventually abandoned

It is certain that there was a major Roman site on the south bank of the river at Wilderspool, where a series of archaeological excavations in the past 200 years has revealed extensive evidence of Roman occupation lasting over three centuries. Much else was probably destroyed by the building of the railways and the Ship Canal, and by the shifting course of the river. At Wilderspool a large and regionally-important industrial centre developed after AD 80 where the north-south and east-west roads met the navigable upper estuary of the Mersey. It was this excellent accessibility which prompted industrial growth and made the place a major supply centre for the Roman armies further north, as well as for the civilian population of the region. Wilderspool became one of the leading industrial towns of Roman Britain.

The unique Roman actor's mask, discovered by James Kendrick near St Thomas' church, Stockton Heath, in the mid-1870s. The pottery mask, made from local clay, was described by Kendrick as 'the rarest and most precious object which excavations at Wilderspool have offered', and over 130 years later that judgment is still valid.

There was a substantial built-up area, with a network of streets and lanes extending from the bridge along the causeway to the edge of Stockton Heath, around Loushers Lane, and along the Manchester and Chester roads in the vicinity of the Ship Canal and Lower Walton. The industrial zone centred on the former Greenalls site, close to the waterfront and ideally placed for river and coastal shipping and road traffic to Wigan, Chester, Northwich and Manchester. Wilderspool was a wealthy place: archaeologists found large quantities of Samian ware, the high status pottery which indicates prosperous lifestyles.

> 66 [There were] some substantial and well-appointed stone buildings, with colonnades, hypocausted heating-systems, tiled roofs, glazed windows and painted wallplaster – sure indications of a sophisticated lifestyle for some of the occupants in parts of the Roman settlement 99
> Tim Strickland, *The Romans at Wilderspool*, p.29

Industries were many and varied. There was lead-working, using pigs of lead which came from Flintshire (where the lead was smelted and its silver extracted) and were brought by boat to Wilderspool. In the 16th century a group of lead pigs was found in the Mersey off Runcorn, possibly a cargo lost en route to Wilderspool 1,300 years before. The lead was reworked as water-pipes, coffins, weights, lamp-bases, toys such as model animals, and probably the large shallow pans used for evaporating brine at the Cheshire salt springs. Glass may have been made at Wilderspool, though the evidence is uncertain, and copper and bronze were certainly extensively worked, producing objects such as brooches, pins, medical instruments, mirrors, wire, nails, and bits of harness and military uniforms. The copper ore probably came from the mines at Alderley Edge, also worked in the Roman period.

One of the largest industries was iron-smelting and smithing. There were many furnaces, hearths and forges, some using coal from the Wigan area instead of the more usual charcoal. Wilderspool produced very large quantities of iron goods, sending them by sea along the west coast of Britain and overland by road. Tools and implements such as spearheads, knives, chisels, nails,

sickles, wheel-fittings, keys, hooks, bolts, trowels, chains and saws have been found during excavation. The variety of the goods manufactured suggests that this was a main north-western source of supply for basic military equipment, as well as domestic, agricultural and craft items.

Pottery was also made, especially in the vicinity of modern Stockton Heath. Cheap everyday wares were the mainstay, usually in a pinkish-orange colour and often with a cream or reddish *slip* or glaze. Because each pottery-producing area made items with distinctive characteristics – either unique designs or particular types of clays and glazes – it is possible to trace the distribution of these goods when they are found on other archaeological sites. Thus, the great *mortaria*, or grinding-bowls, produced at Wilderspool have been found as far away as Hadrian's Wall and the Antonine Wall in central Scotland.

Thomas May was careful to record the finds from his excavations, including their appearance as excavation progressed. This photograph shows part of the pottery kilns discovered at Stockton Heath.

The heyday of Wilderspool was the period from AD100-170. Thereafter it went into decline – its industrial revolution was succeeded by a post-industrial period in a way similar to that of the 20th century. After about AD175 the quantity of material found in excavations decreases very considerably, a pattern matched by the experience of other industrial sites in the north-west. Many of the metal-working trades of the town ceased, though the production of cheap pottery and small-scale smithing continued. Large sections of the town were abandoned and industrial dereliction set in. Wilderspool, having been one of the great industrial centres of Britannia, was now a small farming and fishing community. Why this dramatic change took place is unclear, but it was probably connected with the wider trends in the Empire: a variety of deep-seated and intractable financial and economic problems was associated with political disintegration, military insecurity and social turbulence. The mainstay of Wilderspool's industries – regional trade, military stores and local prosperity – all failed.

❝ following the end of Roman Britain we can imagine the more substantial buildings of the Roman settlement gradually becoming derelict and eventually falling into ruin, partially obscured by nettles, dockleaves and brambles. From the tenth century on the more substantial ruins would have been extensively robbed of stone for reuse in Saxon Warrington, across the river. Eventually, the surviving traces disappeared altogether as the area reverted to open-field agriculture and was ploughed ❞

Tim Strickland, *The Romans at Wilderspool*, p.51

5. After the Romans

Little is known about the area after the Romans had left

Its inhabitants continued their agricultural lifestyles as farmers

By AD 600 Warrington was on the frontier between Northumbria and Mercia

It is thought that in AD 642 one of the key battles of Anglo-Saxon England, Maserfelth, was fought just north of Warrington

In the late fourth century the last regular troops were withdrawn from north-west England and the effective control of Rome was at an end. To historians the next five centuries used to be known as the Dark Ages, because little detailed information was available and, although recent archaeological and landscape research has provided new evidence, there is much that is still uncertain about this period in north-west England. Some lengths of the main north-south road through Lancashire and Cheshire continued in use, and we know that there were agricultural communities in this district. It is also clear that population levels fell dramatically, probably as a result of a devastating plague or other epidemic in the late AD 530s. All over north-west England agricultural land went out of use and was replaced by secondary woodland and scrub.

The site of Warrington was probably occupied by a small farming community whose inhabitants could look across the river to the fast-disappearing remains of the old town of Wilderspool. These people spoke British or Cymric (a form of Old Welsh) and there was a small British principality occupying the area of Warrington and the Mersey valley northwards to Wigan, in the district known as Makerfield. South of the river Anglo-Saxon colonisation proceeded gradually during the sixth century: the Mercians (whose heartland lay around Lichfield and Tamworth) reached the Mersey by about the year AD 600. From the east the Northumbrians sought to extend their control across the Pennines into Lancashire and they had pushed south-west to the Mersey by the early seventh century. In AD 616 they defeated the Welsh in a major battle at Chester, but then came into conflict with the Mercians. In AD 642 at the battle of *Maserfelth*, probably somewhere north of Warrington, the Mercians and their Welsh allies defeated the Northumbrians.

Power blocks were emerging as a patchwork of separate tribes, both British and Anglo-Saxon, was swallowed up by these two large kingdoms. Cheshire was now definitely part of the Mercian territory, while south Lancashire was nominally Northumbrian. The Mersey was once again 'the boundary river' and Warrington lay exactly on the frontier.

FURTHER READING: The political development of the area between the end of the Roman period and the Norman Conquest is investigated in D. Kenyon, *The Origins of Lancashire* (Manchester University Press, 1991) and N.J. Higham, *The Origins of Cheshire* (Manchester University Press, 1993)

Line drawing of a detail from the Winwick cross. It has been suggested that this might depict the corpse of King Oswald of Northumbria being carried after his death in the battle of Maserfelth (642). This was probably somewhere nearby in the Makerfield area.

6. The early Church

In the late Roman period (perhaps about AD 300) Christianity came to this area and it may have survived during the Dark Ages. The name Eccleston, near St Helens, includes the British word *eccles* which means a church, and is usually held to denote a centre of Celtic Christianity. In the early seventh century the colonising Anglo-Saxons were converted to the new faith and adopted the *parish* system, the basic structure for organising the local church. The parish church was central to the existence of all local people, for here they were

Winwick church has important surviving sculpture from the Anglo-Saxon period. This attractive 19th-century drawing shows part of a richly-decorated cross head with its intricate pattern of interlacing – the sculpture probably dates from the ninth century.

baptised, married and buried; they paid a range of tithes and taxes to the church; and the annual cycle of its religious feasts and festivals was, with the agricultural year, the calendar which governed their lives. Ancient parish centres such as Warrington and Winwick therefore acquired a special significance.

In south-central Lancashire there were only five medieval parishes: Winwick, Warrington, Prescot, Leigh and Eccles. On the Cheshire side were two huge parishes, Great Budworth and Runcorn (which included the township of Thelwall). Historians have suggested that the original focus of Runcorn parish was at Daresbury or Preston on the Hill, both very ancient sites, and that a new church was founded at Runcorn in the early tenth century. All these parishes, sprawling across wide areas, included many separate local communities (later known as townships), so that each church was a 'central place' for the countryside around. There is little information about these early church buildings: they are undocumented, archaeological evidence is scanty, and only occasionally do clues survive in the structure itself. However, their dedications are informative. Winwick is dedicated to St Oswald, a heroic royal saint of the Northumbrian dynasty who was killed at the battle of *Maserfelth* in AD 642, and Warrington to St Elphin, an otherwise obscure Anglo-Saxon saint and a very rare dedication. This, together with the references to both in the Domesday Survey of 1086, makes it certain that they are among the oldest churches in the region, founded in the years after AD 620.

The parish church of St Elphin stood near the road from Latchford and was the original focus of settlement, but was later left isolated as the town centre shifted westwards. Nonetheless, it was many centuries before another church was founded in Warrington. The first church was probably wooden but by the 12th century had been rebuilt in stone: some of the carved stone capitals of that church have survived. As the focus of a large and increasingly prosperous parish the church was extensively reconstructed again in the 14th century: parts of this building still exist, though altered by the

There was Christianity in this area in the later Roman period

In the seventh century Warrington and Winwick became the centres of large parishes

St Elphin's, Warrington, and St Oswald, Winwick, were the 'mother churches' of the area

Several ancient legends concern the founding of Winwick church.

Ancient parishes and townships in the Warrington area. Although this map shows the position in the 1840s, most of the boundaries and divisions shown dated back to the period before the Norman Conquest. The large parishes each comprising several townships are clearly shown.

9

The earliest surviving drawing of Winwick church, taken from a manuscript map of about 1580. This was, with Warrington St Elphin, the oldest church in the district and was regarded as one of the 'mother churches' of south Lancashire. The living of Winwick, lavishly endowed with land and assets by its patrons over the centuries, was said to be the wealthiest in England.

Victorians. The crypt, spiral staircase leading from the crypt to the chancel, east and north walls of the north transept, and chancel (which has medieval windows and was built in the mid-1350s) are the remaining sections of Warrington's medieval parish church. Winwick parish church was possibly even older and like many ancient places became the subject of legends.

According to an old legend, Winwick was where St Oswald, king of Northumbria, was killed in battle. A church was to be erected nearby in a place, which had no name, but when the first foundation stones had been laid a pig was seen running around the building site, screaming '*Wee-ick, Wee-ick*'. It picked up a stone in its mouth and dropped it on the spot where the saintly king had fallen. The founders, seeing this as a sign, abandoned the earlier site and built their church instead on the place where the stone had dropped – and this was also how the place was named. Another tradition about Winwick church is less elevated in tone. A folk-rhyme recorded in the early 19th century says:

> The church at little Winwick
> It stands upon a sod
> And when a maid [virgin] is married there
> The steeple gives a nod
> Alas! how many ages
> Their rapid flight have flown
> Since on that high and lofty spire
> There's moved a single stone

FURTHER READING: W. Beamont, *Warrington Church Notes: the parish church of St Elfin's, Warrington and the other churches of the parish* (Percival Pease, 1878); see also A.G. Crosby, *Lancashire Dictionary of Dialect, Tradition and Folklore* (Smith Settle, 2000); the development of parish boundaries is summarised in D. Kenyon, *The Origins of Lancashire* (Manchester University Press, 1991) and N.J. Higham, *The Origins of Cheshire* (Manchester University Press, 1993)

7. *The Mersey frontier in the Scandinavian period*

During the time of the Viking invasions the Mersey was an important frontier

A defensive fort was founded by the Saxon Mercians at Thelwall in AD 919

It controlled the vital fords over the river, but all trace has now gone

By AD 900 a village was developing around Warrington parish church. However, these were troubled times. Viking raids on England were growing in intensity and penetrating further inland, and the very survival of the Anglo-Saxon kingdoms was in question. In AD 874 the Danes seized control of Mercia and in AD 893 attacked Chester, but fierce resistance from the men of Cheshire helped to turn the tide. By AD 900 Mercia had recovered its independence and reasserted control over the area. The main threat now came from the east as the powerful Viking kingdom of York tried to extend its control beyond the Pennines. In the early years of the tenth century the Mercians, borrowing a strategy used by King Alfred in Wessex, created a series of fortified strongpoints (known as *burhs*) along the Mersey to defend their frontier. The first involved refortifying the Roman walls at Chester (905) and it was followed by forts at Eddisbury (914), Runcorn (915), and Manchester – also reusing the Roman defences (919). In 919, too, a small defended *burh* was built at Thelwall.

Historians and archaeologists argue about the exact site of the *burh* at Thelwall, but clearly it protected the vital fords at Warrington, Latchford and Thelwall and helped to prevent a seaborne Viking attack up Mersey. The most likely location is next to the river close to the southern end of Thelwall viaduct, but the channels here have changed considerably over the last thousand years: the fort was possibly on an island which has now disappeared. These forts were required because of pressing military problems, but within a generation the insecurity had receded: a unified

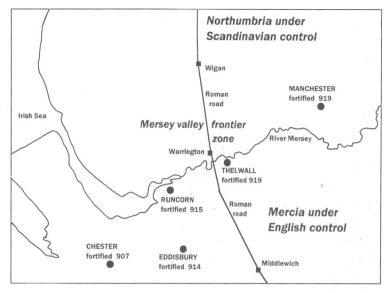

English state was created in the mid-10th century. The small *burh* at Thelwall (with its wet river-edge site) did not develop further and instead was superseded by the growing importance of Warrington, which lay above the key crossing place. During the medieval period Thelwall shrank into complete obscurity. Ironically its national fame came a thousand years later, when its new viaduct, another key river crossing, became a landmark of the motorway network and a familiar refrain on radio traffic reports.

FURTHER READING: An attractive introduction to the Viking period in the area is F.A. Philpott, *A Silver Saga: Viking Treasure from the North West* (National Museums and Galleries on Merseyside, 1990; see N.J. Higham, 'The Cheshire Burhs and the Mercian Frontier', in *Transactions of the Lancashire and Cheshire Antiquarian Society*, vol.85 (1988)

In the early 10th century the Mersey was not only the frontier between two kingdoms, Northumbria and Mercia, but also between two peoples, the Scandinavians and the English. To defend the English territories against Scandinavian incursions a series of fortified outposts was built along the Mersey axis in 907-920.

8. Before the Norman Conquest of 1066

Warrington was not only the centre of a large parish. It also became the political and military headquarters of the district in the years before the Norman Conquest and this helps to explain its growth into a small town by the end of the 12th century. At the time of the Domesday Survey [1086] south Lancashire was a no man's land, without a proper name: it was called simply *inter Ripam et Mersham*, meaning 'between the Ribble and the Mersey'. However, the lands on both sides of the river were already divided into *hundreds*, ancient divisions that served as the basic units for local administration. On the Cheshire bank the hundred of *Tunendune* extended from Weston Point to Thelwall, and Bucklow hundred from Thelwall along the river as far as Northenden and south towards Alderley Edge. The hundreds of south Lancashire were probably originally military districts defined in the years after AD 905 when Mercian control was being asserted. Two had been created by subdividing the old British territory known as Makerfield, one based on Newton-le-Willows, the other on Warrington.

This gave Warrington administrative, political and military significance. Its hundred was administered from a headquarters at Mote Hill, next to St Elphin's church, defended by ramparts and ditches. Within these earthworks

By 1066 Warrington was the administrative centre for a large district

This was known as the *hundred of Warrington*

There was a defended headquarters at Mote Hill, next to St Elphin's church

Domesday Book confirms that the king owned most of the land in the area

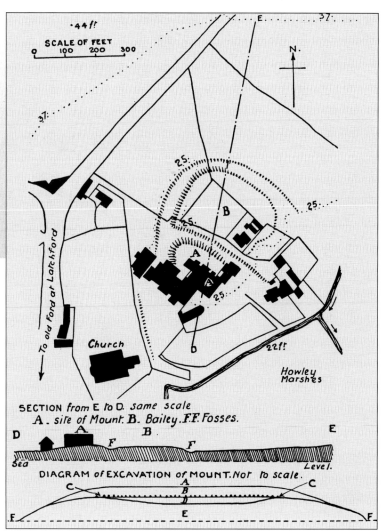

ABOVE *Two polished jet gaming pieces, discovered by the amateur archaeologist James Kendrick during his excavation of Mote Hill (next to St Elphin's parish church) in the mid-1840s. These pieces were probably chessmen and date from about 900. They indicate that the low hill above the Mersey was occupied by people of high class and considerable status: it was the military and administrative centre of the Warrington hundred.*

RIGHT *An early 20th-century plan and cross section of the earthworks and other buildings on Mote Hill, just north-east of St Elphin's parish church.*

stood a complex of wooden buildings, probably including the great hall from which the king's steward exercised his control over the district. As long ago as 1841 James Kendrick, Victorian Warrington's first great antiquarian, excavated on Mote Hill and found evidence of Anglo-Scandinavian occupation dating from the years around AD 900. Among his finds were two fine polished jet gaming pieces or chessmen, and this suggests that there was a sophisticated resident population, as befits a military headquarters. Most of the land in and around Warrington was in royal ownership – Domesday Book (1086) records that in 1066 it was held by Edward the Confessor.

FURTHER READING for sections 8 and 9: The Domesday Book entries for Warrington and other local communities are given in P. Morgan (editor), *Domesday Book: Cheshire* (Phillimore, 1978): this includes all of south Lancashire as well; J. Kendrick, 'An account of excavations made at Mote Hill, Warrington, Lancashire' in *Transactions of the Historic Society of Lancashire and Cheshire*, vol.5 (1853); J. Lewis, *The Medieval Earthworks of the Hundred of West Derby* (British Archaeology Research Series, no.310, 2000); D. Kenyon, *The Origins of Lancashire* (Manchester University Press, 1991); N.J. Higham, *The Origins of Cheshire* (Manchester University Press, 1993)

Medieval
Warrington

9. The Norman Conquest and its consequences

After 1066 the Normans built a small castle at Mote Hill

Its remains were deliberately demolished in the early 19th century

The castle served as the military headquarters for the district

There was an earth mound with wooden buildings and encircling ditches

All the history books tell us that the Norman Conquest took place in 1066. In fact in the north-west William I was not able to take full control of the region until 1070, following the merciless and brutal suppression of a large-scale revolt across the northern counties in the winter of 1069. In the aftermath of the rising total security had to be enforced, which meant replacing native landowners with tried and trusted Norman lords, whose power was based in military strongpoints controlling strategic places and keeping the local population under a tight rein. Mote Hill at Warrington, with its existing modest defences, was an obvious base for such a lord. After 1070 a small castle or similar structure was built within the older ramparts.

The typical castle of the immediate post-Conquest period was an earth mound (a *motte*) on top of which were wooden buildings and stockades. At its foot was a flatter enclosed area, the *bailey*, edged by large banks and ditches. Such motte and bailey castles are fairly common in Lancashire and Cheshire. Few were ever rebuilt in stone, and because they were made of earth they have often completely disappeared. The best example locally is the great mound of the castle at Newton-le-Willows. At Warrington there is some uncertainty about the exact form of the castle, because most regrettably it was deliberately flattened by developers in 1841-2. James Kendrick had excavated here in the 1830s and again just before its levelling. His descriptions and drawings are the only important record we have for the castle. They indicate an oval mound about ten feet high, with a water-filled moat about 40 feet across. This does not sound like a conventional castle and the archaeologist Jen Lewis has suggested that it was perhaps a *ringwork*, a large circular or oval rampart with ditches. This form of defence-work is now identified in large numbers from the Welsh borders and her explanation is perhaps more plausible, given that the site already had a complex of buildings. The Normans may simply have constructed new ramparts to encircle these, rather than building a completely new castle.

The Warrington entry from Domesday Book of 1086: the text is in heavily abbreviated Latin, but the name WALINTUNE *is clearly seen on the first line.*

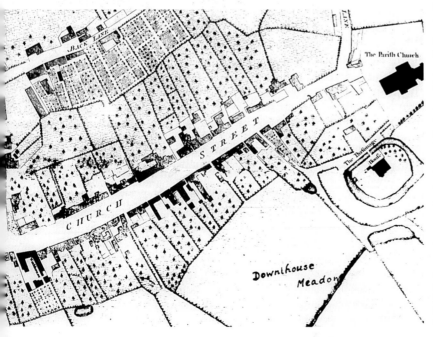

Donbavand's map of Warrington, drawn in 1772, shows that the old village of Warrington, a single street running west from the parish church, was at that time almost intact. The crofts and gardens behind the houses are carefully drawn and Back Lane (later School Brow) marks the edge of the village. Note, too, the circular moat around the old parsonage south of the church.

10. The lords and landowners of Warrington

One of the political strategies of the Norman kings, parallel with their military planning, was to create powerful local baronies to provide strong administrative control in difficult frontier regions. In Lancashire and Cheshire many such baronies were established and this helped to create the fortunes of great families who, in the succeeding centuries, held large estates in the two counties. Lands belonging to baronies could be anywhere: the barony of Warrington, probably created by Stephen, count of Mortain, in about 1118, included extensive properties in Lincolnshire, Derbyshire and Nottinghamshire as well as in south Lancashire. Stephen, grandson of the Conqueror, granted the barony to the de Vilars family, from whom it passed by marriage to the Botelers.

This family held the lordship of Warrington until the late 16th century and were by far its most important family (their name derived from that fact that relatives were hereditary butlers to the earls of Chester). The Butlers acquired extensive properties in the area, including the townships of Warrington, Great and Little Sankey, and Penketh, to which were added lands in Culcheth, Rixton with Glazebrook, much of the Leigh area and other scattered estates in Lancashire from the Ribble down to St Helens.

Until the 1280s their main seat or residence was at Mote Hill, but in the late 13th century they moved to a more desirable country property, their hunting lodge at *Beau see*, the 'beautiful place', whose name was eventually modified to Bewsey. They were there by 1294 and from that time this was Warrington's seat of government: the old and doubtless uncomfortable buildings of the castle, already fire-damaged, were abandoned. The house was extended and a new deer park had been created by 1313. Bewsey (Old) Hall appears to date mainly from the early 19th century, with some surviving fabric from around 1600, but the medieval and Elizabethan house, now almost entirely demolished, was very much larger, with a complex

The barony of Warrington was created in about 1118

It was held by the de Vilars family and later by their relatives, the Botelers

The Botelers were lords of Warrington for 400 years until the late 16th century

In the late 13th century they moved to Bewsey Hall, which they rebuilt and extended

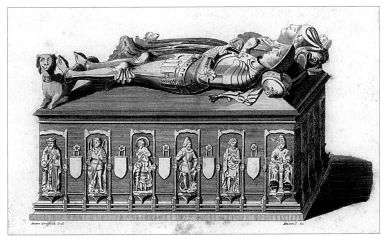

LEFT *A mid-19th-century engraving of the tomb of Sir Thomas Boteler and his wife, in St Elphin's parish church, Warrington. For over 300 years the Botelers of Bewsey Hall were the leading family in the district. They were lords of the manor of Warrington, owners of the market, patrons of the friary and the most powerful and prosperous landowners.*

ABOVE *Seals of members of the Boteler family and of their maternal ancestor, Richard Pincerna. Wax seals such as these were normally affixed to official documents in the early medieval period, when even many important people were unable to read or write.*

RIGHT *Bewsey Old Hall and the surrounding landscape, from the Ordnance Survey 25-inch map of 1893. Despite the impact on its original setting caused by building the St Helens Canal in the 18th century, the* medieval hall was clearly a building of major importance. It was surrounded by a large moat and with a gatehouse, gardens, extensive outhouses and farmland.*

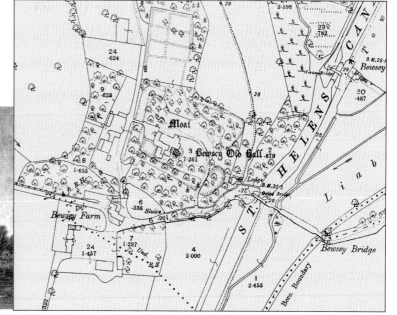

ABOVE *An 18th-century engraving of Bewsey Hall, emphasising its attractive and peaceful wooded setting.*

series of outbuildings. It was encircled by the great moat and associated ditches and fishponds and these, with the timber-framed gatehouse and 'stronge drawebridge', must have created a very impressive approach to the house for visitors from the Warrington direction.

FURTHER READING: W. Beamont, *Annals of the Lords of Warrington and Bewsey* (Charles Simms & Co., 1873); J. Hayes, *Bewsey Old Hall* (Lancashire History Quarterly, vol.1 no.1 March 1997) [also gives a great deal of information about the lords of Warrington]

11. *The shape of the town and the role of the bridge*

Warrington was developing into a small town by about 1200

The original centre was next to St Elphin's church at the bend in Church Street

In the 13th century a new bridge was built over the river

Bridge Street became the main road and the centre of the town shifted to what is now Market Gate

The bridge, frequently rebuilt, was the key to Warrington's prosperity

By 1200, its importance boosted by its role as administrative headquarters for the district and with its market and trading functions growing, Warrington had become a small town. Changes in the road network encouraged the relocation of the commercial centre, which shifted from the old site, around the parish church, to the vicinity of the present market place. At the time of the Norman Conquest the ford at Latchford was more important than that at the bottom of Bridge Street. The church and castle stood next to the old road, which today is Howley Lane. By the end of the 11th century (and perhaps earlier) a market was being held outside the parish church. The widening of Church Street outside St Elphin's, so distinctive on the older maps and still detectable even today, is therefore the location of Warrington's first market.

During the 12th century the direct road which is now Wilderspool Causeway and Bridge Street started to return to favour. In the years after 1200 Ralph, Earl of Chester, allowed the local Boydell family to levy tolls on fords and ferries across the Mersey between Runcorn and Thelwall. This implies that no bridge then existed, but one is mentioned in a document of 1285, so sometime before the early 1280s the ford had been replaced. Thereafter most traffic used Bridge Street, rather than Howley Lane, and this became the main artery. The street market by the church was now out on a limb, served only by a secondary road, and the commercial focus of the town shifted to the crossroads above the bridge where it has been ever since. It is reasonably clear that in the later 13th century a new market place was laid out near the crossroads in response to this shift. The reason why the market place lies behind the main roads of the town centre is that it was created *after* the roads and building lines around Market Gate had been defined, using vacant backland to allow a more spacious and convenient layout. This move enhanced the potential of the market and Warrington began to rise through the ranks of north-western towns, recognised as one of the main market centres of the region.

The rights to the bridge-tolls were granted to the Boteler family, which produced decades of legal argument. The Boydells were understandably aggrieved because the bridge diverted traffic from fords and ferries and so reduced their toll income, but the Botelers were more powerful and their rights were reiterated in 1310 and 1321. The Boydells retaliated by blocking roads leading to the bridge from Cheshire. As late as 1364, when a replacement bridge was being constructed, Sir John le Boteler, Geoffrey de Warburton, Matthew de Rixton and their workmen were given royal protection against their enemies, suggesting that the Boydells were still intent on revenge. The 1364 bridge was made partly of stone (masons are referred to in the documents) and when it was completed by 1369 a friar, Brother John of Lichfield, was licensed to hold services in a chapel at the bridgefoot. Such little chapels were common in medieval England though only a handful now survive. Travellers could pray for safety on their journey, and the situation on a bridge

The first contemporary view of Warrington is this sketch, drawn in about 1580. It shows a small town of half-timbered houses, dominated by [left] the tower of the Jesus church (the former friary, pulled down in the 17th century) and [right] the tower of St Elphin's church. The fine stone-arched bridge over the Mersey, rebuilt in 1495 at the expense of the 1st Earl of Derby, seems out of proportion. This, however, symbolises its central role in Warrington's well-being and prosperity.

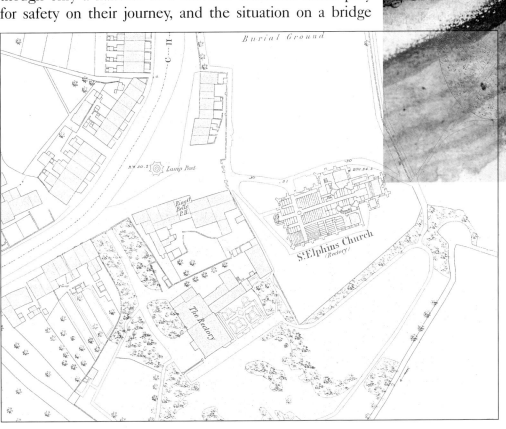

The parish church of St Elphin, on the superb 1850 Ordnance Survey 1:1056 survey of the town. The wider section of Church Street at the churchyard gate was Warrington's first market place. The long curve of the churchyard and rectory garden may mark the outer edge of pre-Conquest defensive earthworks.

guaranteed plenty of passers-by throughout the year and a useful income from alms and donations.

Yet within fifty years this bridge was in a sorry state: in 1420 the son of Sir John le Boteler left 20 marks (£16.66) for its repair but by the early 1450s it had collapsed and Warrington was bridgeless. Fords and ferries were again the only way of crossing what in 1453 was called 'the great and rapid water of the Mersey'. In that year an indulgence was granted by the archbishop of York and the bishops of Carlisle and Durham to all who contributed to a rebuilding fund but the 1466 survey of the town mentioned the place 'where the bridge of Warrington formerly stood'. Not until 1495 was the third bridge constructed, paid for by Thomas Stanley, 1st Earl of Derby, and built as a matter of urgency ready for the royal visit of King Henry VII and Queen Elizabeth to Lancashire that July. The king and queen crossed the new bridge and passed through Warrington en route to Bewsey, to spend the night with the Botelers. When he died in 1502 the earl left the huge sum of 800 marks (£667) to provide a fund for the upkeep of the bridge and to buy out the toll rights, so that thereafter the crossing was free. This fine stone bridge is shown as the most prominent feature of Warrington in the first known picture of the town made in about 1580.

FURTHER READING: For roads in the area in general, A.G. Crosby (editor), *Leading the Way: a history of Lancashire's roads* (Lancashire County Books, 1998); G.A. Carter, *Warrington Bridges 1285-1985* (Cheshire Libraries, 1985); see also G.A. Carter, 'Roads in Grappenhall, Thelwall, Legh and Colsweynok in 1328', in *Cheshire History* no.9 (Spring 1982); the background of urban history in the area is covered in R.A. Philpott, *Historic Towns of the Merseyside Area* (National Museums and Galleries on Merseyside, 1988) and A.G. Crosby, *The towns of medieval Lancashire: an overview* (Bulletin of the Centre for North West Regional Studies, Lancaster University, 1994)

12. *The medieval borough*

By the end of the 13th century Warrington was a borough

This gave special privileges and more freedom from the lord's control

The Botelers later regretted this and took back some powers over the town

They remained the real rulers of Warrington until 1815

By 1292 Warrington had become a borough, a special and privileged status which could only be granted by the Crown after the issuing of a charter. In a borough the townspeople enjoyed what were known as 'liberties', such as a 'free court' (that is, one controlled not by the lord of the manor but by the citizens) and the more fortunate people of the town enjoyed a special and generous form of landholding which was known as 'burgage tenure'. The date of the original charter for Warrington is not known because the document has been lost for many centuries, but during a legal inquiry in 1292 it was claimed by townspeople that William le Boteler I (the first Boteler lord of the manor, who died in 1233) had secured borough status for Warrington. The alleged charter was produced in court, though there is no reference to it in the charter rolls, the Crown's own record of such grants. It is, however, a plausible story: many comparable places obtained such charters in the century after 1150, a time of economic expansion and population growth in England.

In 1292 William le Boteler III, grandson of the borough's founder, obtained another charter which, while confirming some of the privileges of the town, sought to deprive the citizens of their own courts and to return control firmly into the hands of the lord. There was a protracted and bitter legal dispute over

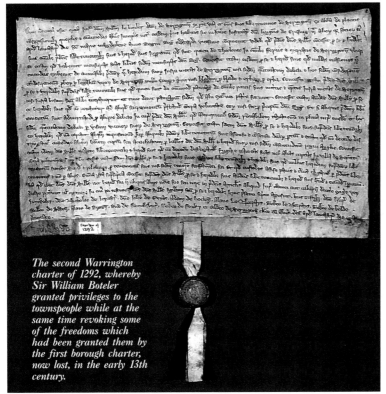

The second Warrington charter of 1292, whereby Sir William Boteler granted privileges to the townspeople while at the same time revoking some of the freedoms which had been granted them by the first borough charter, now lost, in the early 13th century.

In this extract from the 25-inch to 1-mile OS map of 1893, the long and very narrow plots on the east side of Bridge Street and on both sides of Buttermarket Street are clearly shown. Though they had long since been built over, these plots were the 'fossilised' remains of the distinctive medieval pattern of burgages, the main property divisions of the ancient borough which had been laid out in the 13th century.

these actions, but in 1300 the people were finally forced to concede. They renounced their right to a free court so that, although Warrington remained technically a borough, the most important element of that status, legal freedom from the lord, was removed. This prevented any further moves towards civic independence during the next five hundred years, and precluded the evolution of a town council. Warrington's people had no direct voice. They did not control the town, its streets, markets, or basic administration. The lords of the manor were the real rulers of Warrington from 1300 to 1815, when the Police Commissioners were established as the town's first modern local government body.

FURTHER READING: G.A. Carter, 'The Free Borough of Warrington in the Thirteenth Century', in *Transactions of the Historic Society of Lancashire and Cheshire*, vol.105 (1953); A.G. Crosby, *The towns of medieval Lancashire: an overview* (Bulletin of the Centre for North West Regional Studies, Lancaster University, 1994)

13. Trade and markets

The importance of the market in the life of the town cannot be overestimated. Much of the profit from its trade went to the Boteler family but for Warrington as a whole it was central to well-being, bringing direct benefits and generating spin-off trade for craftsmen, carriers, and street vendors: the people who came to the market bought goods in shops, ate fast food, and had their horses stabled. This was one of the most important markets in north Cheshire and south Lancashire, its 'border' location being turned to advantage because the products of Cheshire and its rolling acres could be sold and exchanged for the

Warrington's medieval success depended on its market

This was one of the largest in the north-west and drew trade from a wide area

The town also had lively and busy fairs held twice a year

A charter to hold a market was granted to the Boteler family in 1277

They drew valuable income from market tolls, stall rents and fines levied on traders

Country people in Warrington market. This engraving was made in 1830, but although the costumes differ somewhat the scene is otherwise very similar to that of five hundred years before. As one of the leading markets in the north-west, Warrington drew its trade and custom from long distances and its market trade extended across much of the region.

goods of already-industrialising Lancashire. Adding to Warrington's strength as a market town was its position as the focus of routes which fanned out from the bridge, like tentacles extending into the two counties, feeding its market with traders and their commodities, and purchasers and their full purses.

The market was formally established in 1277 in a charter granted by the Crown to the lord of Warrington, William le Boteler, permitting him to hold a market on Fridays, and to levy lucrative tolls and other charges. It is certain, though, that the market had actually been held long before the date of its formal beginning. Here, as in other towns, the lord of the manor took control of (and seized the financial benefit from) an existing market – in 1292 a local jury claimed that the market had in fact been held from time immemorial. In 1288 William le Boteler was empowered by a second charter to switch the market day from Friday to Wednesday, which was presumably thought to be an even better commercial prospect.

Warrington also had fairs (at which cattle from the rich pastures of south Lancashire and Cheshire were a speciality) since 'time immemorial', and here, too, the Boteler family successfully acquired the rights. In 1255 William le Boteler obtained permission from Henry III for an annual fair of three days at the Feast of the Transubstantiation of St Thomas the Martyr (6-8 July) and the 1277 market charter authorised a pre-Christmas fair on the eve of St Andrew and for one week afterwards (29 November to 6 December). In 1288 the summer fair was extended to cover a full week from 6-13 July.

14. Fair time in Warrington

The *Ballad of Warrikin Fair* is the oldest known Lancashire verse

The fair was often unruly and drunkenness was commonplace

The fairs survived to the end of the 19th century: William Beamont wrote a detailed description of them

He also recorded the ceremonial opening and closing of the fair

The Fair was known far and wide, and is the setting for the oldest known Lancashire poem, *The Ballad of Warrikin Fair*. The exact age of the ballad is uncertain, but as it refers to Randle Shay, the steward of the Boteler family during the reign of Edward VI (1547-1553), it is likely to be at least 450 years old. Not written down until the early 19th century, when it was transcribed in Lancashire dialect, it tells the story of Gilbert Scott, who was cheated by a purchaser when selling his mare at Warrington Fair, and whose wife Grace not only got her own back but also took the money. It is an ancient tale. Were the characters based on real people, and the story on an actual episode? We will never know. What is clear, though, is that the Fair was a great event, sung about in alehouses and taverns across the county. It was lively and tumultuous. We have no medieval descriptions, but the atmosphere remained largely unchanged for centuries. In July 1633 a local man called Oliver Gerard overdid things at the fair:

    66 where unadvisedly being abroad in the streets in the night time was taken with [by] the watch, and being somewhat overtaken with drink, as men are

apt in that case to give evil speeches ... was carried before Mr. Ireland one of his majesty's justices ... who finding him faulty and worthy of punishment committed your petitioner to the House of Correction, where [since] he hath remained to the overthrow of his poor wife and two young children besides his sorrow and grief for his offence and hard fortune "

In the late 19th century William Beamont wrote down his memories of the fairs of his youth sixty years before, in a vivid description which gives a good impression of how the scene must have been in the medieval period as well:

“ a bazaar where might be seen piles of broad cloth from the West of England, and equal piles of narrow cloth from Yorkshire, with flannels and knitted stockings from Wales, cutlery and hardware from Sheffield and Birmingham, linens from Ireland, and toys, eatables, comestibles, confectionery, and sweetmeats from everywhere. Each trader had his own compartment, and politely invited customers to view his wares ... the frequenter of these stalls would hear many a dialect besides his own, but none, I think, that would surpass in beauty and expression, the Lancashire "

He recalls how the fair was opened. Again, the sense of excitement, colour and ceremony was undoubtedly the same six hundred years earlier. A procession headed by the town crier, staff in hand and wearing his liveried costume, silver badge on his arm and silver-laced cocked hat on his head, went around the market area and the central streets. He was followed by the leading citizens, the four constables of the manor of Warrington and their deputies, and in the rear came the steward of the manor. Even in Beamont's youth the lord

The Church Street fair in Warrington survived just long enough to be captured on one of the first photographs of the town. The fair was discontinued in 1859, partly because 'scenes of riot and dissipation' which were a 'disgrace to the age and country' were alleged to have been commonplace, but what we see in this exceptional early image (taken in 1855) seems very decorous and calm.

of the manor owned the market rights and his officials oversaw the conduct of trade, using the formal ceremony to impress everybody watching with their authority. The procession stopped in the accustomed places, the town crier called three times 'O Yes', and the steward read the proclamation for the opening of the fair and the rules for its proper conduct.

> 66 No sooner was the fair declared to be open than the Corn Market and the streets adjoining it were filled with cows of all sorts and ages, ranged along the streets in rows, with their cowmen and owners standing by them and inviting customers 99

Horses were sold on the second day and then came the fun-fair, medieval in style, with showmen and strange curiosities and wondrous exhibits:

> 66 The noise and the hubbub and the shouts of the showmen continued throughout the fair, and would have disturbed the least nervous of men; but to these were added the continuous blare of brazen trumpets, the clashing of cymbals and the beating of drums 99

FURTHER READING: The ballad of Warrikin Fair is given in full in several works, including B. Hollingworth (editor), *Songs of the people: Lancashire dialect poetry of the Industrial Revolution* (Manchester University Press, 1977); Beamont's descriptions are from his *Walks about Warrington* (1887)

15. The friary

Medieval Warrington had an Augustinian friary

Friaries are an indicator of the commercial importance of a town

Warrington friary was founded in the third quarter of the 13th century

It survived for 150 years after the Dissolution of the Monasteries

No trace can now be seen above ground

A sign that Warrington was a prosperous community with a thriving economy and plenty of trade was the founding of a friary in the late 13th century. By the 1220s many people were disillusioned with the ostentation of the Church and the lavish lifestyles of many clergy. In Italy new monastic orders, the *friars* (from the Latin word for 'brother') were founded and quickly spread across Europe. Represented most famously by the Franciscans, but also including the Augustinians, Dominicans and Carmelites, they returned to Christ's own ideals of poverty, charity and helping others. They lived in modest circumstances, did not have large estates or opulent churches, and collected alms to be redistributed to the poor, sick and needy. They begged on street corners or walked through towns and markets asking for donations. The presence of a friary was an indication of the commercial importance of a place, because trade meant people and people meant money in the collecting-cup. At Warrington the river crossing and the road network brought many traders and travellers who would give alms.

The Augustinian friary was founded sometime between 1261 and 1292 by William le Boteler. Landowners frequently sponsored religious houses as an act of piety: William was eventually buried in the friary church, a position of honour representing a special 'nearness to heaven'. The friary was carefully-placed between Bridge Street and Friars Gate, close to the bridge and the main road in a situation giving maximum potential for obtaining alms from good Christian folk. William Beamont, in the 1840s, used his historical imagination:

An artist's impression of a scribe at Warrington Friary, writing a document ready for the signature of Friar Penketh, head of the English chapter of the Augustinian order and the only Warrington man mentioned by Shakespeare (in Richard III).

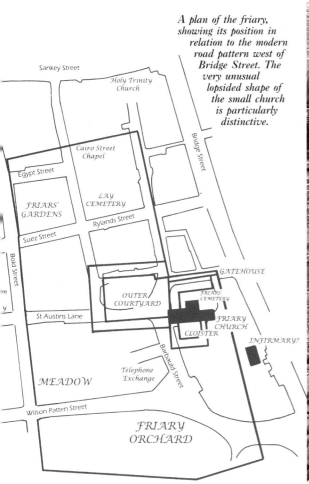

A plan of the friary, showing its position in relation to the modern road pattern west of Bridge Street. The very unusual lopsided shape of the small church is particularly distinctive.

Sankey Street

Holy Trinity Church

Cairo Street Chapel

Egypt Street

LAY CEMETERY

FRIARS' GARDENS

Rylands Street

Suez Street

Bold Street

Bridge Street

GATEHOUSE

OUTER COURTYARD

FRIARS CEMETERY

St Austins Lane

FRIARY CHURCH

CLOISTER

INFIRMARY?

Barbauld Street

MEADOW

Telephone Exchange

Wilson Patten Street

FRIARY ORCHARD

The 1930 friary excavations attracted large crowds. Here they gaze not only at the camera but also at the foundations of the nave and chancel of the church, which were uncovered and plotted before being buried once more beneath Barbauld Street.

> ❝ Let us for a moment imagine ourselves passing along the narrow but picturesque streets of ancient Warrington, and meeting at some sudden turn one of the cowled brethren, or the prior himself, hurrying on his way, in sombre robes, to discharge some errand of charity or business, and giving, as we meet, the passing *Benedicite* ❞

The friary had an uneventful existence and little detailed information on its history has survived. As befitted an order dedicated to poverty, the church was modest. When its site was partly-excavated in 1886 (during the widening of Bridge Street) and subsequently, it was found that the church was of an odd lopsided shape, with a short wide nave, a north transept of almost equal size, no south transept and a narrow off-centre choir. There were other buildings, such as an infirmary and domestic accommodation for the friars, of which almost nothing is known.

It was flourishing in 1520, when Sir Thomas Boteler left money for its improvement, but in 1539 the friary was dissolved by Henry VIII and the site sold to Sir Thomas Holcroft, a notorious land-dealer who acquired many former monastic properties. Local people wanted to retain the church for their own use, because it was much more conveniently sited than St Elphin's, and for some decades services were held there – it was popularly known as the Jesus Church. By the middle of the 17th century, though, it was falling into disrepair and decay and was demolished: by 1700 only the arch of one gateway survived. Today there is no visible sign of the friary or its associated buildings, although street names such as St Austin's Lane remind us of its location.

FURTHER READING: W. Beamont, *The History of Warrington Friary* (Chetham Society Old Series vol. 83, 1872); W. Owen, *Warrington Friary and the recent discoveries there* (Transactions of the Historic Society of Lancashire and Cheshire, vol.41, 1890); G. Owen and F.H. Cheetham, *Warrington Friary: the discoveries of 1931* (Transactions of the Historic Society of Lancashire and Cheshire, vol.88, 1937)

16. *The 1466 survey: the town and its landscape*

In 1466 Sir Peter Legh, one of the largest local landowners, commissioned a survey of his estates

This gives a unique view of the layout of late medieval Warrington

The town was small and set among the fields and meadows

The survey records the names and properties of many Warringtonians at the time of the Wars of the Roses

It also describes the agriculture, fields, commons and woodlands of the district

In the later medieval period much property in the Warrington area was owned by a branch of the Legh family of Lyme in Cheshire. The mother of Sir Peter Legh (*c.*1387-1460) was the heiress of Gilbert de Haydock and she brought her south Lancashire estates into the family. This branch of the Leghs settled at the moated manor house of Bradley in Burtonwood and in 1466 Sir Peter commissioned a comprehensive survey of his estates. This gives a remarkably detailed picture of many Warrington properties and allows a relatively full reconstruction of the geography of the late medieval town – Warrington is unique among the towns in the region in having such a detailed record. The Latin survey was transcribed and translated by William Beamont in 1849. It describes each property in terms of its tenancy and rent, its area and land use, and its exact location.

Medieval Warrington was small. We do not have population figures, but in the 15th century it had only a few hundred people – no more than a moderately sized village today. There were four main streets: Bridge Street (also known as Newgate Street), Sankey Street (Sankeygate), Church (or Kirk) Street and the Horsemarket, together with a warren of lanes and yards. The centre of the town was divided into *burgages*, plots of land held by leading citizens (the burgesses) with a favourable type of tenure which in some ways resembled modern freehold. The burgages were long and narrow, the short face fronting the street and a long plot stretching back behind. This maximised the number of properties with valuable street frontages and on these plots the wealthier townspeople built their houses, inns, and shops. The distinctive pattern of burgages was still very clear in the 19th century and even today (for example, on the east side of Bridge Street) can still be discerned:

66 RANDAL son and heir of Matthew de Rixton holds … four burgages lying together, in which Alan Walton, John Dychefeld, and John Pulforthe now dwell and inhabit, which burgages are situate between an empty burgage formerly of Geoffrey Werburton of Newcrofte on the north, and another empty burgage of Thomas Dawne … on the south, and extend in length from the king's highway of Newgate on the west as far as the appleyard of Henry Byrom 99

Almost all houses in Warrington backed onto gardens, fields, woods, lanes and mosses – the edge of the heath was only just north of the market place. Many properties had barns, stables and outbuildings, orchards were everywhere, and animals were kept in the very heart of the town. The first

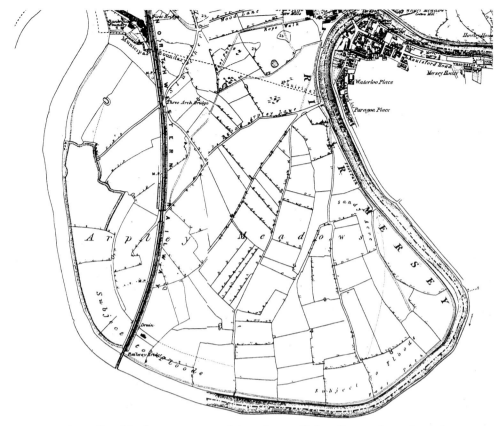

The Ordnance Survey 6-inch map of 1845 recorded the town and its surroundings just after the first railway came and just before the great mid-Victorian industrial boom. The meadows at Arpley, within the great bend of the river, still survived as open countryside as they had been in 1466 when the Legh estate survey was made. Note the series of long narrow fields in the centre, which though hedged and enclosed were the last survivors of the strip fields of the medieval town.

property described below was roughly where Cairo Street is today, the second on the site of the Town Hall.

> ❝ ROGER HOLBROKE holds of the said Peter Legh, knight, one new messuage [property] in the town of *Weryngton*, with a new barn and seven gardens inclosed with hedges and ditches, containing two acres of arable land, with one oven, which oven is situate and lying near to the house and church of the Augustinian Friars in the aforesaid town; which messuage, barn, and garden lie and are situate in the king's street called *Sonky-yate* … and extend in length from the king's street … on the north, as far as a garden with trees growing therein, which belongs to the said Augustinian Friars of the aforesaid town on the south … **also** he holds five acres of arable land inclosed with hedges and ditches … called Stanefeld … extending in length from the aforesaid street called *Sonky-gate* on the south, as far as *Weryngton* heath on the north … ❞

A commercial centre was starting to appear, adjacent to the market place, with shops and craft workshops. Everybody lived above the shop. As in other medieval towns the finest houses (several described in the 1466 survey as 'fair' or 'newly built') were at the very centre of town. People did not yet live away from work, and it would be another 300 years before wealthier citizens preferred to reside on the outskirts:

> ❝ PETER LEGH, knight, hath a certain small fair hall with a high chamber and two shops, situate at the corner of the western street leading from the market place of *Weryngton* towards the high church of the said town, and in the western side of the said street, in a place called *le Markethyate*, where four streets of the said town meet together in the form of a cross … ❞

The townspeople put their animals on the common lands to graze. The most important such area was Warrington Heath, north-west of the town centre in the area of Froghall Lane and Dallam Lane. On the edge of the heath, in one of the highest places in Warrington, was what the 1466 survey calls *molendinum ventricium* – the town windmill. Close to the river were the meadows at Howley, which were communally managed. Their hay crop was vital as winter feed for the town's animals, and individual tenants of the Botelers had rights to cut and use hay, subject to strict controls over when they could mow and how much they could take. After the second hay-crop had been cut in late August the meadows were grazed for a couple of months: the dung from the cattle and sheep which fed there enriched the soil and helped to ensure a good hay crop next year. By 1466 these meadows were being 'privatised', divided into separate sections and let to individual tenants, so that the communal exploitation of that resource was on the wane.

The medieval moated manor house at Bradley in Burtonwood township had close associations with the Boteler and Haydock families, but in the 15th century passed into the hands of the Legh family of Lyme. This view, taken by Thomas Davies in the mid-1850s, shows the remains of the medieval stone gatehouse and bridge over the moat.

At Arpley and Howley there were areas of arable land, in 1466 still managed as open fields in which tenants of the manor – the townspeople of Warrington – had their separate strips, unfenced and unenclosed. We know the names of some of these great fields: at Arpley there was *le Warthe* and *Weteakyrs* [Wheatacres], and nearby was *Stanfelde*, which lay on either side of Sankey Gate where Bank Quay railway bridge is now. The 1466 survey records pieces of land in the open fields:

> **❝** JOHN FULSHAGH of *Weryngton* holds of the said Peter [Legh] … four acres of arable land lying together in the great field called Arpley, lying upon the shore of the water of Mersey on the west side of the said field … JOHN HARDEWAR of *Weryngton* … holds nine small butts [short strips] of land lying together in the place called *Le Warthe* in Arpley field … ROGER HOLBROKE … holds five acres of arable land lying in the open field of Arpley … JOHN SMYTHE of *Weryngton* … holds two acres of land lying together in the field called Howley **❞**

But the survey also shows that a lot of the better-quality land around the town had already been enclosed – that is, divided into smaller separate fields, hedged and ditched, and let out to individual tenants of the manor for their private use. Many entries specifically refer to such properties: for example

> **❝** ROGER HOLBROKE … holds five acres of arable land inclosed with hedges and ditches in the aforesaid place called *Stanefeld* … WILLIAM FLETCHER of *Weryngton* … holds four acres of arable land in Arpley inclosed with hedges and ditches lying outside the [open] fields and nearer to the town of *Weryngton* **❞**

FURTHER READING: W. Beamont (editor), *Warrington in 1465* (Chetham Society old series, vol.17, 1849) [the survey was actually in 1466]

Warrington
1500-1700

17. The sixteenth and seventeenth centuries: an overview

Between 1500 and 1700 Warrington experienced many far-reaching changes

Most buildings were reconstructed and the town acquired fine examples of black-and-white architecture

Trade expanded as Lancashire and north Cheshire experienced population growth and economic development

Some Warrington people became very prosperous, with comfortable lifestyles

The survey of 1466 is a uniquely-detailed glimpse of a small late medieval town, and shows us a community on the verge of large-scale change. The 16th century was a crucial time in the development of north-west England, as population began to grow, towns expanded more rapidly, and industry emerged as a significant element in the local economy. Nowhere was unaffected by these developments, but change was greatest in south Lancashire and north Cheshire, from Liverpool along the Mersey to Manchester and the Pennine foothills. Warrington was still small by later standards, but its position ensured that it reaped the benefits of these developments. Its market, already one of the largest in the region, was well-placed to serve the growing population, and the increase in trade brought extra traffic across the bridge and through the streets of the town. True, this added to congestion, but it also meant major economic benefits. The role of the town as head of navigation meant that it took advantage of the growth in coastal shipping: goods brought by road were transhipped to vessels, and imported commodities were brought upriver to Warrington.

Warrington underwent considerable physical change in this period, a harbinger of more extensive rebuilding in the following two centuries. The gradual disappearance of the friary buildings after 1539 was the greatest single change, but during the early 17th century (and especially after destruction during the Civil War) small and modest urban properties were reconstructed on a more ambitious and architecturally-impressive scale. Characteristic of this period was elaborate half-timbering, the 'black and white' buildings which were once found in all the towns of south Lancashire. Warrington retains a few examples, of which the *Barley Mow* is the most

ABOVE *Warrington and its hinterland, from the first county map of Lancashire published by Christopher Saxton in 1577. The large capital letters in which the town's name is written reflect its regional significance as a market centre and crossing place on the Mersey. Note the circular dotted lines which indicate the great deer parks at Bewsey, Bradley and Newton-le-Willows.*

LEFT *The oldest house in Warrington (until its demolition in 1936) was this superb medieval building at Cockhedge. The view, taken by Birtles in 1905, shows on the left the great hall and on the right the short wing which was the parlour. The house, dating from the early 15th century, was constructed of wattle and daub.*

impressive, but older engravings and descriptions demonstrate that this was once typical of the more important buildings in the town centre. The poor continued to live on the outskirts, in single-storey thatched dwellings, but the confident wealth of the town merchants was quickly translated into fashionable new houses and substantial inns and shops.

Not only the appearance but also the life of the town changed. The expanding trade of the region was reflected in the availability of new foodstuffs, luxury items and imported goods, while the foundation of the Boteler grammar school meant that Warrington was an early beneficiary of the interest in educational provision identifiable in the region as a whole. Warrington was becoming less self-sufficient, more integrated into the wider world. In 1580 the first surviving picture of the town was made, a small coloured sketch on a map of the Burtonhead estate near St Helens. It shows a town of half-timbered buildings, the towers of the parish church and the friary and, most prominently, the bridge over the Mersey. Its vital role in Warrington's prosperity and success is emphasised by its pre-eminence in this little image. And, to add to our knowledge of the appearance and plan of the town and its economic life, we for the first time begin to have documents which tell us about individual people. The inventories taken of the goods and possessions of Warrington's wealthier citizens from the late 16th century onwards show us how they lived. We can find out about their domestic comfort and luxury items, furnishings and stock in trade. They become real people, not just names and dates.

The Barley Mow, now one of the most important of the town's old buildings, is a fine example of late 16th-century half-timbering, though it has frequently been altered and restored over the past 400 years. To the left is the late 18th-century town house which was the office of William Beamont, the town's first mayor and most important local historian of the 19th century.

FURTHER READING: J.H. Hodson, *Cheshire 1660-1780: Restoration to Industrial Revolution* (Cheshire Community Council, 1978); a useful background to the architectural history of the 16th and 17th centuries in this area is given in L. McKenna, *Timber Framed Buildings in Cheshire* (Cheshire County Council, 1992)

18. *The inventory of Sir Thomas Boteler, 1579*

One well-documented individual, the richest man by far in Elizabethan Warrington, was Sir Thomas Boteler of Bewsey who died in September 1579. A month after his death a full inventory was made of his property, including the furnishings and household goods at Bewsey Hall. It testifies to the great wealth of the estate and the importance of his family. There were, for example, 54 pigs and swine, and 23 horses (all individually described), and many dozen acres of barley and wheat. Among the items listed are 60 great cheeses, produced on the estate; wax and honey, and bees in hives; leather and hides; and huge quantities of sawn timber, with the extraordinary figure of 232 'timber trees' felled in the park at Bewsey and now ready for turning into

Sir Thomas Bewsey of Warrington was the richest man in Warrington

When he died in 1579 a superb inventory of his goods was made

This gives a clear picture of the high level of luxury enjoyed by the Botelers

A computer-generated image which shows a possible reconstruction of the appearance of Bewsey [Old] Hall in the late 17th century. As with many houses of its type and period, the building grew organically. Although the details remain unclear, it is likely that the late medieval timber-framed black-and-white section (dating from the heyday of the Botelers) was extended in the late 16th century by Edward Boteler, with a two-storey brick wing and projecting porch. This was in turn extended by Thomas Ireland, perhaps just before James I's visit in 1617, with a third gabled storey.

boards and planks, which perhaps suggests that a major rebuilding project was under way.

Everything speaks of rare levels of luxury: the lifestyle of the Botelers was far more sophisticated than that of any of their neighbours. The inventory records a silver toothpick, water-glasses, cases of table knives, and elaborately decorated and gilded pottery. The family plate included a heavy engraved silver ewer and basin, a nest of covered silver tureens, a silver salt-cellar, and a dozen silver spoons. There was a clock (an unusual item in this period) and pictures decorated the walls, including one of Christ and – to demonstrate the loyalty of this Protestant family – a portrait of the queen. Another sign of their adherence to the new religion was an 'Englysshe Bybull'. The soft furnishings were ostentatious: green silk quilted bedcoverings, painted wall-cloths in the great hall, and huge piles of linen sheets, pillowcases, towels, table cloths, and napkins.

Yet this world of wealth and splendour fell apart on the death of Sir Thomas. His only son and heir, Edward Boteler, had incurred enormous debts when living in London and in the previous year had been disinherited in favour of his sister Elizabeth. On their father's death a bitter legal battle was waged for control of the estate, a battle complicated by the intervention of Edward's patron, Robert Dudley, Earl of Leicester. Eventually Edward's two sisters and widowed mother were forced to relinquish their claims to the property. Leicester, using his immense power and influence, compelled Edward to cede control to him so that in 1586, when Edward died, the Boteler estates fell into Leicester's hands. In 1588 he also died and in 1597 his illegitimate son, Robert Dudley, sold the estate to two purchasers. Sir Richard Bold, Leicester's steward and one of the manipulators of the whole episode, acquired the manor and estates of Burtonwood. The Bewsey and Warrington properties were bought by Thomas Ireland of Childwall, who became the lord of the manor. His son sold the manor of Warrington in 1625, but his remote descendants owned Bewsey until the early 1970s.

FURTHER READING: W. Beamont, *Annals of the Lords of Warrington and Bewsey* (Charles Simms & Co., 1873); J. Hayes, *Bewsey Old Hall* (Lancashire History Quarterly, vol.1 no.1 March 1997); the inventory of Sir Thomas Butler is published in G.J. Piccope (editor), *Lancashire and Cheshire wills and inventories from the ecclesiastical court, Chester vol.ii* (Chetham Society Old Series, vol.51, 1860)

19. Thomas Allen, woollen-draper (died 1592)

Over in the town, meanwhile, lived a wealthy woollen draper, Thomas Allen, who had a large and very comfortable house close to the market place, at the heart of the town's commercial and social life. The property had at least seventeen rooms, some with delightful names such as the Lion Chamber, the Swan Chamber, the Rose Chamber and the Raven Chamber (these indicated the themes of the decorations, perhaps wall-paintings or hangings). This was a very large household. When Thomas died in 1592 he had no fewer than 28 beds, including several 'four-posters'. In the Lion Chamber his inventory records a 'standing bed with a tester [canopy] with curtains belonging to the same … featherbed, two mattresses, one bolster, one pillow, two blankets, one caddow [quilt] and one covering [bedspread]'. The servants had less luxury: one was accommodated in what was graphically described as 'the highest roof', a tiny garret under the eaves containing one truckle bed (a low bed of very basic construction), while another slept in 'the hayloft' where there was 'a pair of bed-stocks' (a wooden-frame bed which could readily be assembled and taken to pieces … a forerunner of IKEA perhaps!), a chaffbed (straw mattress), a bolster, two sheets, a blanket and a coverlet.

There was a buttery, with pewter, brass pots, wooden utensils, glasses and bottles and a meat-safe, but the other cooking equipment was fairly basic: seven spits of different sizes (for birds, big pieces of meat or game), two frying pans and two dripping pans (to go under the spits to catch fat and juices), and a gridiron for grilling. Food was preserved and stored: five huge flitches (sides) of bacon, tubs of salted beef, three mugs (earthenware jars) of eels, caught in the creeks of the Mersey and 'put up' in salt and fat; four mugs of goose-fat for cooking and medicinal use; and plenty of malt and brewing equipment for making the beer which was one of the staples of life.

Evidence such as this inventory helps us to build up a picture of the townspeople and their lifestyles, and it tells us a good deal about Warrington. The costly furnishings demonstrate that a merchant in this relatively small country town could enjoy a high standard of living. The prosperity of Warrington and the expanding trade which it supported was such that real wealth could be acquired by some of the citizens. But most lived more humble and much harsher lives: of them we know almost nothing.

FURTHER READING: The will of Thomas Allen is in the Lancashire Record Office (WCW 1592, Thomas Allen of Warrington)

Thomas Allen was a wealthy draper of the town who died in 1592

He had a large house near the market place

His domestic furnishings and other goods are recorded in an inventory

His lifestyle reveals the prosperity of the town's leading merchants

In the Name of god Amen the xi[th] daie of November anno domini 1592 I Thomas Allen of Warringtone in the countie of Lancaster Woollendraper beinge at this present sicke in bodie but of goode & perfecte memorie (god therefore be praised) do institute ordeine & make this my laste Wille & testament … First I commend my soule toe thandes of almightie god, trustinge that by the merrittes of the death & passion of Christ Jesus my only lorde & saviour I shall bee in the number of them toe whom noe sinne shall bee imputed, but taken & accepted for righteous … I give toe the reparacion of the parishe churche of Warrington toe bee bestowed att the discrecion of the parsone there, x[s] … I give toe the mendinge of the highewayes abowte this towne x[s]

A transcript of part of the will of Thomas Allen, one of Warrington's most prosperous late Elizabethan citizens. His expressions of religious faith and hopes for eternal life and resurrection are followed by charitable gifts to good causes in the town.

20. The Boteler Grammar School

The grammar school was founded by the will of Sir Thomas Boteler (died 1526)

It was one of the earliest and wealthiest such schools in north-west England

The school educated local boys in Latin, Greek, mathematics and religious instruction

By the 19th century it had fallen on hard times and had a bad reputation

Wealth might in some circumstances lead to a sense of civic duty or devotion to charitable causes. In the Middle Ages pious prosperous people could pave the way to heavenly salvation by giving money to monasteries or churches. By 1500 this route to eternal life was less popular and instead charitable bequests for more practical causes gained favour. Money might be given to the poor and needy, or to education. When Sir Thomas Boteler died in 1526 his executors recorded that he had long intended to found a free school for boys in Warrington, and he bequeathed a large endowment for this purpose. In this enlightened gesture the Boteler Grammar School originated.

The new foundation was given many valuable properties in north-west England – more so than almost any other school in the region. It had houses at Tyldesley; burgages in Warrington; arable land near Wigan; over 800 acres at Arrowe in Cheshire; 75 acres at Goosnargh and Chipping near Preston; and another 75 acres at Hulse and Stubleach near Northwich. In 1607 several descendants of Sir Thomas (wanting to get their hands on its assets) challenged the title of the school to its extensive lands and raised legal objections to the way the charity was run. New regulations and a clear legal title were confirmed in 1610. The lands were let to tenants on a long-term basis and the rents used to fund the school. In 1825 the income, about £800 per annum, meant that it was one of the richest schools in the north-west.

The school provided a classical education (for boys only) with Latin, Greek, religious instruction and mathematics as the main subjects. A house and land in Back Lane were provided by the trustees for Richard Taylor, the first schoolmaster, and his successors. The boys were educated free of charge, apart from nominal quarterly payments of a few pence for 'extras', and they attended divine service at the parish church on Sundays, Wednesdays and Fridays. The infants were taught 'a b c', learned from primers, by two of the senior boys. Yet despite its wealth, by 1800 the school was in a sorry state, with poor academic standards and an average attendance of only twenty pupils. There followed a very un-savoury period when the headmaster and the trustees were at loggerheads and, at enormous expense, fought a protracted legal battle which culminated in a settlement in 1820. The trustees agreed to pay the master the prodigious sum of £300 a year, with a free house and large garden. The assistant master or usher was to be paid between £60 and £100 a year, and the writing master £40 to £60.

Grammar schools such as this

The 1526 foundation charter of the Boteler grammar school in Warrington, with its splendid array of seals affixed to the bottom edge of the parchment. The grammar school was one of the earliest in the region and among the wealthiest, thanks to the lavish generosity of its founder, Sir Thomas Boteler, and his executors.

were founded (though usually with far less money) in many Lancashire towns between 1500 and 1650, but Warrington was, with Bolton and Manchester, one of the very first. They began life with honourable aspirations and for decades did excellent work, but later sank into decay and legal squabbling. The experience of the Boteler foundation was far from unusual.

FURTHER READING: H. Lievesley, *Boteler Grammar School, Warrington, 1526-1976* (1976); see also the *Further Report of the Commissioners for inquiring concerning Charities* [the Charity Commissioners] for Lancashire, 1825, [Warrington parish] for a full discussion of the origins and endowments of the Boteler Grammar School and other Warrington educational and social charities

21. *Regulating the town and the market*

An increasingly busy, prosperous and more sophisticated town needed higher standards of administration, though to achieve that ideal was an uphill struggle. In 1617 a set of byelaws for the government of Warrington was drawn up by the manorial steward and approved by a jury of townspeople. The rules covered many aspects of life, seeking to introduce order and ensure that inappropriate behaviour was punished. Some dealt with the general public interest: thus, to tackle fires, all prosperous citizens were to have a ladder and a hook for pulling burning thatch from roofs; no animals were to roam uncontrolled in the streets; no vagabonds were to be sheltered; and illegal gaming, dice, cards, and bowls were forbidden, particularly on the Sabbath Day. Townspeople were not permitted to build muckheaps in the streets, or to leave open holes after they dug clay for building, or to gather brushwood or rushes within the park at Bewsey. Animals were not to be grazed on the commons except in approved numbers and at permitted times, and gates, hedges and ditches were to be properly maintained. Other rules related to the market and its trade. Weights and measures were to be accurate, prices were controlled, and there was much concern over false measure and adulteration of foodstuffs:

Part of the 1617 regulations for the government of Warrington, listing the standard weights and measures. These were kept by the manorial stewards at the court house in the market place, and used for checking the quantities and quality of goods offered for sale in the market and shops of the town.

66 No man bringe anie corne to the market to sell but if it be not as good under as it is at the top of the sacke and like windowed [winnowed i.e. no chaff to be included], uppon paine to forfate to the lord 3s 4d, or the corne soe found to be distributed amonge the poore folke of the towne … noe manner of person nor persons shall set or sell no manner of vitell [victuals], neither of fishe nor fleshe not other vitall, except [it] be marketable 99

The goodes belonging to the lord of the towne of Warrington and of the markett. To remaine in the towne howse or Cort howse of Warington.

Imprimis one Iron yard made by the Standard at Lancaster
Item Brasen Weightes, vizt. one of viij li waighte, another of 4, the third of 2 pound, the 4 of 1 li, the 5 of half a pound, the vj a quarter, the vij towe ounces, the eight an ounce, and 3 other lytle ones all of them conteyning half an ounce, with a paire of Brasen scales to waighe in
Item a Statute book remayninge in the stewardes handes
Item a Winchester Bushell made by the Standard and hanged in a Cheyne in the Cort Howse
Item a halffe Bushell made and hanged in like manner
Item a pecke in licke maner
Item an halffe pecke
Item an Ale Quarte of Ashe wood
Item A sealing Iron for the yard
Item a sealing Iron for the Measures
Item an Iron Stampe for weightes
Item 2 burninge Irons with the kinges Crowne and name
Item one Chest bond with Iron with locke and kay to kepe the yarde, the quart and the weightes in together with the pecke and halffe pecke
Item an Iron with 2 letters on, vizt., T.I., being for the name of Sir Thomas Ireland, nowe lord of Warington

The town was governed by the manor court, which passed byelaws

A complete set of regulations from 1617 gives extensive detail about the administration of Warrington

Among them, regulations for the conduct of market business are prominent

Traders were not to *forestall*, or wait outside the market, buy cheaply the goods arriving for sale, and then re-sell them at a profit. Neither were they to sell goods outside trading hours, which were indicated by the ringing of the market bell. The regulations reveal some of the main commodities sold in the market: butter, eggs and cheese (known as 'white meats'); various grains; fish and meat; cattle and horses; hemp, flax and yarn; hosiery and stockings; and boots and shoes. We might suspect that because these rules were thought necessary implies that such unsociable or questionable activities were rife. We may also doubt that they had any real effect!

FURTHER READING: The early 17th-century Warrington byelaws are transcribed in full in R. Sharpe France (editor), *The Statutes and Ordinances of Warrington 1617*, in Record Society of Lancashire and Cheshire vol.109 (1965), pp.21-30

22. *Population in the sixteenth and seventeenth centuries*

Parish registers give information about the people of the town from the end of Elizabeth's reign onwards

Life was precarious, with outbreaks of plague and other pestilence a recurring hazard

The surviving parish registers for Warrington begin in 1596 and they provide a record, even if a brief one, of ordinary people – not just the wealthy but also the poor and the humble. We can use them to calculate statistics of population changes. For instance, the graph shows the annual number of burials at St Elphin's church between 1600 and 1632. In a normal year there were around 85, but numbers fluctuated. A good harvest meant that people were better-fed and less susceptible to malnutrition or disease. A severe winter meant more deaths from hypothermia. Similar fluctuations occur today, but what is striking is that occasionally there were what historians call 'crises of mortality', when the burial figures increased dramatically. Such crises are hardly known in modern Britain.

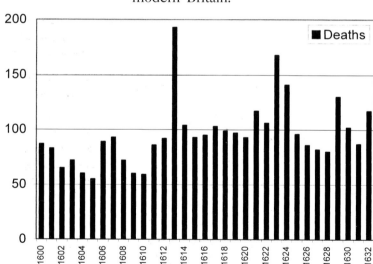

The graph of annual totals of burials in the parish of Warrington reveals sharp fluctuations, the result of epidemics and other 'mortality crises'. The plague of 1613 and the epidemic and famine of 1623-4 are particularly prominent.

The year 1613 was catastrophic, with 193 burials, well over twice the usual rate. In one year perhaps 10 per cent of the population died, equivalent to perhaps 19,000 extra deaths in the modern borough. What caused this devastating event, which did not affect other parishes in the area? The parish registers do not say, but there can be little doubt that it was a visitation of plague, the most feared of all diseases. Plague was usually found in towns because it was there that the black rats lived, scurrying through wooden houses and insanitary yards and carrying the fleas which harboured the plague bacillus in their gut. When the fleas bit humans the terrible infection was passed on. Plague usually died away within a year, and the pattern of the Warrington outbreak is characteristic.

A decade later the town was again hit by a crisis, but this time one which affected all north-west England from the Scottish border to Cheshire. The cause of the exceptional mortality in 1623 and 1624 was probably famine, resulting from the disastrous failure of two successive harvests, but malnutrition was exacerbated by typhus. This crisis, even worse than that of 1613, lasted two full years and in Warrington the death rate doubled. There cannot have been a family in the town unaffected. Houses were left empty, trade collapsed, and solemn funeral processions, the tolling clang of the mourning bell, and the haunted faces of the poor must have been the overwhelming images for many months. Plague came again in 1647, when infected people were housed in 'isolation units', wooden cabins hastily-constructed for the purpose on Warrington Heath, well away from the town. In 1652 it reappeared in Sankey and Latchford. During the 16th and 17th centuries there was a general air of growth and expansion, but events such as these were an all-too-frequent reminder of human weakness and the perilous insecurity which was the lot of most people. For plague no real remedy or solution was available. There was no means of escape.

> **The Humble Petticion of the Inhabitants of Gret Sankey in the Countie of Lancaster**
>
> That about the beginninge of August last it pleased god to vissit Towe familys in the seide towne with the Contegius diseasse of the Plauge which seide howses by order from Mr Ireland & Mr Bold have beene shut upe ever since And one of the familys beinge apoore tradsman a taylor whoe lived by his trade & deprived of his libertie, the towne hath beene forced to mentayne him and his famyly beinge five in nomber for most part which hath put the Towne to exterordinerie cost & altogether undon the poore man: & the rest of the poore inhabitants beinge that they have beene deprivd of goinge to markett at Warrington or else wheare, Now your petticioners humbly desire this honerable bench to consider thire Condition & take some Course whereby they may bee Releivd in grantinge them some allowance for thire Charges: or that thire proporsian of the Ley alredy gatherd for the poore of Liverpoole which yet remayne in the hands of thire Constable as alsoe another Ley for the poore of the parish of Prescott, may by your order granted for the reliff only of the said famyly, & the rest of the poore inhabitants ...
>
> an accompt to bee made of the charge & Certifyed upon oath to Mr Aspinwall

The petition of the inhabitants of Great Sankey to the justices of the peace for Lancashire, 1652, asking for financial help to defray the costs and expenses of local people afflicted by plague.

FURTHER READING: The printed volumes of the Warrington parish registers are published by the Lancashire Parish Register Society: volumes 70, 95 and 125 cover the period 1591-1706 for baptisms, marriages and burials. The original registers (available on microfilm) are at the Cheshire & Chester Archives & Local Studies in Chester. The mortality crisis of 1623-1624 is discussed in A.B. Appleby, *Famine in Tudor and Stuart England* (Liverpool University Press, 1978)

23. Warrington in the Civil War

These were natural disasters, but twenty years after the famine came a man-made calamity. In September 1642 civil war broke out between King Charles I and Parliament. The north-west was a key area of military operations during the war and Warrington, because of its vital location at the lowest bridging point on the Mersey, was prominent in the strategies of both sides – indeed, Charles nearly made his declaration of war here. The town saw action even before hostilities officially began: on 20 June 1642, in a pre-emptive strike, the Royalists seized the arms magazines. Partly to secure this asset, in October 1642 they established a headquarters at Warrington and fortified the town with hastily-constructed ramparts and ditches. Its unwelcome role as a military headquarters ensured that it would be in the front line and during the spring of 1643 fighting moved

The Civil War between king and parliament lasted, with intervals, from 1642 to 1651

Warrington, because of its strategic position, was often involved in fighting

In 1643 the town was besieged by parliamentary forces and bombarded by cannon from the vicinity of the parish church

There was extensive destruction in the siege and the fire which followed it

The Civil War was one of the most traumatic events in Warrington's history

James Stanley, 7th Earl of Derby: a 19th-century engraving of a formal portrait now at Knowsley Hall.

This house in Church Street, now the Marquis of Granby, was used by James, 7th Earl of Derby, as his headquarters during the siege of Warrington in 1643. During the siege, and as a result of Derby's decision to set fire to the town, many properties were destroyed.

back and forth in the area between Warrington, Leigh and Wigan.

On 3 April the Royalist leader, Lord Derby, won a minor battle at Stockton Heath and five days later defied a Parliamentarian attempt to capture the town itself. Yet he could not take advantage of this opportunity, and at the end of May Parliamentary forces stormed and entered Warrington. During April 1643, when Derby was conducting his campaign from lodgings in Church Street, Parliamentary forces headed for Warrington from all directions and their cannon bombarded the town from Mote Hill, just east of the parish church. Derby, panicking, ordered the town to be set on fire and it was said to have burned for three days. The final assault in the last week of May involved more bombardment and street-fighting. Subsequent Royalist campaigns to recapture the area met with failure and in June 1645 the king's armies were decisively defeated.

In the summer of 1648 war broke out again. Remaining Royalists, allied with a large Scottish army, moved south through Lancashire in a great ill-disciplined force strung out over many miles. On 16 August the cavalry reached Wigan but the infantry, still in Preston, were attacked and put to flight by Oliver Cromwell's army. The desperate Royalists and Scots fled panic-stricken through Wigan and on to Warrington, where people must have been fascinated and appalled by the sight of thousands of terrified soldiers streaming into the town. Cromwell gave hard chase, and many Royalists were killed in another engagement at Winwick. At Warrington on 19 August what remained of the Royalist and Scottish armies surrendered to him: they are said to have been imprisoned in what is now known as Scotland Road.

The king was executed in January 1649 but a year later war erupted again in Scotland. In August 1651 Prince Charles, proclaimed as Charles II, came south through Preston and, joined by many Lancashire Royalists, arrived in Warrington on 16 August. Here he reviewed his position and instead of heading for London chose to go down the Welsh borders, on a campaign which led to shattering defeat by Cromwell and his armies at Worcester. The fateful decision taken at Warrington on that August day ushered in nine more years of republican government. And finally, in 'Warrington's last act'

The 1901 statue of Oliver Cromwell, which commemorates his role in the events of 1648 when in the aftermath of the battle of Preston fighting took place in and around the town of Warrington.

during these bitter times, the town was the scene of an abortive rising by Sir George Booth of Dunham Massey, a former Parliamentarian totally disenchanted with the regime. He planned a large-scale insurrection and chose Warrington as the mustering place for the rebel troops of Lancashire and Cheshire. They met here on 1 August 1659 and the next day marched unhindered to Chester, seized the city and on 7 August, numbering 4,000, came back again en route to Manchester. On 19 August, though, the rebel army was defeated by government troops near Northwich.

What it did all this mean for Warrington and its people? According to contemporary accounts (disputed by some historians) when the smoke of war cleared much of the town lay in ruins and many properties had been destroyed. Numerous townspeople had lost their livelihoods and an unknown number their lives. To some historians the events at Warrington were just a side-show – the great battles were fought elsewhere and the town only receives a footnote in books about the war – but that should not make us think that it did not matter. At no other time in the past thousand years has such extensive devastation and terrible suffering come to this town. Civil war was not romantic: it was brutal and bloody. Of that the people of Warrington were left in no doubt at all.

FURTHER READING: A useful introduction to the main campaigns is given in P. Newman, *An atlas of the English Civil War* (Croom Helm, 1985); for local studies see J. Kendrick, *An account of Warrington Siege AD1643* (reprinted edition with introduction by H. Wells, pub. H. Wells, 1996); see also G. Ormerod (editor), *Civil War Tracts* [relating to military events in Lancashire], Chetham Society Old Series vol.2, 1844

24. *Lawlessness and misbehaviour in the seventeenth century*

Everyday life could be pretty rough, too. In the 17th century crime such as theft and vandalism was rife and violent death was common. The records of the quarter sessions courts demonstrate that in Warrington, as elsewhere, people took the law into their own hands to solve grievances and pay back grudges, while the temptation to steal was great because the security of houses and shops was minimal. We have no crime statistics for the reign of Charles I but the evidence in court cases tells its own story and gives a flavour of life in Warrington before the Civil War. Most crimes remained unsolved: there was no police force or forensic science. Suspects and witnesses were taken to a magistrate and cross-examined before the case was dropped for lack of evidence or sent to the quarter sessions.

A typical case of suspected theft was examined by the leading local magistrate, Thomas Ireland, in 1627. Thomas Harper of Warrington, bread-baker, claimed that on 20 February at about 8 p.m. in the entrance hall of his house he found Thomas Stopford, yeoman, carrying a woman's gown. Harper said that it was his wife's and had been taken from their bedchamber. He seized Stopford by the shoulder and the arms, and during the struggle the gown was thrown into the street. A witness, William Russell of Warrington, ironmonger, confirmed the story. Magistrates found it almost impossible to judge such cases: positive evidence was almost always lacking and the accused

Lawlessness was an everyday occurrence in the 17th century

Records of the quarter sessions courts give information about crime and punishment

The court records are a valuable insight into everyday life 300-400 years ago usually claimed to have received the stolen goods innocently. This case was dropped. There were, though, many more serious problems of criminality, including violence and bodily harm. In November 1627 Margaret Browne, spinster, claimed that Alice, wife of James Eaton of Warrington, had …

> **❝** wounded her in the face with a knife and [threatening] to cut her throat hath cut her band [neck-cloth] therewith and also that she stands in bodily fear of her life, for … Alice Eaton hath threatened to kill her [and is] a woman suspected to be of lewd and evil behaviour **❞**

Two years later Katherine, wife of Thomas Parr of Warrington, butcher, alleged that Thomas Barnes, a shoemaker, tried to enter her house and break down the inner door, and made threats against her. Subsequently, at about one o'clock in the morning, he thrust his head in at the kitchen window (why was she there at that time?) and told her he would fetch her out and 'reviled her with uncivil words calling her whore'. Her husband got out of bed and with a stick threatened to hit Barnes, saying that these continual abuses were insufferable.

There was fraud and deception. In July 1629 Robert Vaughan confessed that on a Wednesday in June he and John Walkden sold beans for their master, Mr. Bolton, in Warrington market, for 16s. 6d. a bushel. They agreed to claim that a bushel had only fetched 15s. 6d., and to pocket the difference. Walkden, frightened by what they had done, admitted the offence. People might be prosecuted for offences which would seem to us quite harmless. There were laws against play-acting and frivolous pursuits on Sundays: in May 1632 Gregory Harrison, an alehouse keeper, told Thomas Ireland that the previous Sunday at about midday nine young men came to his alehouse and asked to go into the loft. He allowed them to do so (why he agreed to this strange request is not clear) and expected that 'they would have stayed [no] longer than for the drinking of a Can or two of ale', but that they remained for an hour or two. The young men were arrested by the constables and churchwardens of the town, because this was during the time of divine service and they had been 'acting of a play' called *Henry the Eighth*.

Slander was frequent and was regarded as particularly objectionable if the victim was somebody in authority. These cases give us especially colourful examples of 17th-century language. In 1632 Randle Barnes, constable of the town, was abused by John Fisher, an itinerant pedlar, 'in the open street at Warrington'. Fisher called him 'an idle fellow … with many other reproachful sayings against the said constable, in the hearing of the market people'. Much more juicy was the case in April 1633 when a local magistrate, Edward Bridgeman (brother of the bishop of Chester) claimed that he had received extremely abusive language from James Preston of Warrington, a piper, who declared that 'he cared not a fart of his arse for me' and who later repeated this, adding for good measure that the same applied to 'any Bridgeman in England'.

Conviction was relatively rare, but punishment presented its own problems. In the 17th century the death penalty, later widespread for even minor crimes,

The justices of the peace were the mainstay of the law and order system. They were county (or more rarely, town) gentlemen who acted on behalf of the Crown, dispensing justice and maintaining a watchful eye on the administration of the area. Here, in 1633, Thomas Ireland of Bewsey and Edward Bridgeman, brother of the bishop of Chester, sign a document recording their examination of a witness in a case of theft.

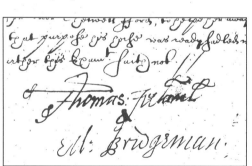

was relatively uncommon, while in the whole of Lancashire there was only one prison, Lancaster Castle, together with a House of Correction at Preston and a few local lock-ups. It was difficult to sentence criminals to imprisonment – there was no space to house them – and so corporal punishment, fines or cautions, were used instead. In January 1630 Thomas Alexander attempted to rape Elizabeth Lowton in the backyard of her father's house in Warrington, throwing her down upon a pile of wood and breaking her arm. His punishment was that:

66 for that the said Elizabeth's arm was broken by him ... he the said Alexander shall pay for the care of her arm, and for his present corporal punishment we [the magistrates] have ordered that the said Smith shall be immediately whipped through the town of Warrington, where he did the said offence, whereby his punishment may be an example to others who may so offend in the same kind. 99

FURTHER READING: The documents quoted in this section are all in the quarter sessions records held at the Lancashire Record Office, Preston [reference QSB, covering the 1630s: the courts which met alternately at Ormskirk and Wigan dealt with cases from the Warrington area]

25. *Joshua Abraham of Warrington, died 1680*

Thus, 17th-century Warrington was (like everywhere else) a mixture of sophistication and roughness. The growing wealth went side-by-side with poverty, violence and human misery. But it is striking that the town seemed to recover quite quickly from the disasters of the Civil War, its commercial and trading importance unaffected by the devastation. We can measure the growing quality of life for the better-off citizens in various ways. Their houses were rebuilt in up-to-date styles, they could take advantage of business opportunities, the first signs of industrial growth appear, and the shops of the town were offering new and exotic commodities.

In 1680 a wealthy trader died. Joshua Abraham was a grocer and the inventory of his possessions includes the goods in his warehouse, cellar and shop. His total assets, excluding property, amounted to £766 – perhaps £200,000 in modern terms. Using his inventory we can appreciate the great diversity and range of products available, at a price, to Warringtonians by the late 17th century. Some historians see this period as the beginning of 'the consumer age' and it is now recognised that the provincial towns of England, such as Warrington, were becoming more sophisticated. In Warrington's case access to luxury goods, exotic foodstuffs, and specialist items was made easier by its location near Liverpool, which was rapidly cornering the transatlantic trade and the import of spices and luxuries.

In the shop were all sorts of spices and imported foods. There were huge quantities of raisins, currants, aniseed (a favourite remedy for indigestion and flatulence), turmeric and cloves, pepper of many varieties, ginger, different sorts and qualities of sugar, candies and comfits (little sugar-coated spiced sweets). He sold tobacco and pipes and *aqua vitae* (a powerful whisky-like spirit). His shelves had boxes of dyestuffs – logwood, indigo, redwood and

The rise of Liverpool as the focus of the transatlantic trade brought many changes to life in the area

Merchants and grocers had access to a far wider range of imported foodstuffs, spices and luxury goods

The inventory of the possessions of Joshua Abraham, a Warrington grocer who died in 1680, is a very valuable source

It conveys the powerful impression of an Aladdin's cave of exotic and fragrant herbs, spices and imported and expensive goods

Many tradesmen in the later 17th century issued their own tokens, because of a severe shortage of small change. These are examples of tokens produced by Warrington shopkeepers in the 1660s.

others – because people wanted more colourful and newly-fashionable textiles. He had the ingredients for ink – galls, alum and lamp-black – and he had paper. The ladies of Warrington would have enjoyed visiting his shop to buy ribbons and lace, inkle (decorative tapes for lacing garments) and yellow satin. They could also have bought hour-glasses, sealing-wax, playing cards, starch and needles, thimbles and beeswax. The shop must have smelled wonderful.

The evidence of a grocer's shop like this in a town such as Warrington tells us that, although the place may still have been small, its citizens (and the country people who came to town on market days) had access to the spices of

Part of the inventory of the goods of Joshua Abraham of Warrington, salter [grocer], died 1680

In the warehouse

Four Gallons of Linseed oil att	00-12-00	
one barrell of Tarr att	00-18-00	
Four Gallons of Traine oil att	00-10-00	[whale oil]
Six hundred pound of rosin att	03-00-00	[resin]
five hundred weight of Chalk att	00-08-00	
Thirty pounds of punning stone att	00-04-00	[pumice]
In Barrells Casks & other odd things	00-08-00	

In The Shop

Loafe shugar att	07-13-00	
Brown sugar bastard att	00-17-00	[unrefined]
Black & Brown thred att	02-13-02	
Inkle & phileting att	01-05-02	[lace and tapes]
one hogshead of Sugar	10-04-00	
White poudered sugar att	03-17-00	
Crown sope att	00-05-00	
Anell-seeds one hundred & 6 pound att	03-00-06	[aniseed]
One runlet of anell-seed water att	01-17-00	[small barrel]
Aqua vitae att	01-02-00	[spirits]
Coliander seeds att	00-12-00	[coriander]
Cariwes-seeds att	00-11-00	[caraway]
one Runlet of anell-seed water & the runlet att	01-19-00	
Two runlets att	00-01-06	
Pipes two gross	00-01-00	
Packthred	00-02-00	
Figgs att	00-06-00	
Rice att	00-09-06	
one barrell of Allome	05-02-00	[alum]
one Hogshead of Treacle att	05-05-00	
Treacle att	02-00-00	
Currans att	14-00-00	
Anell-seeds att	00-04-06	
Raisons att	03-15-00	
Gumarabeck att	00-15-10	[gum arabic]
Brass & iron wier att	00-19-03	
Pepper att	06-03-02	
Resin att	00-08-10	
Turpentine	00-12-06	
Black sope att	00-01-00	
Stone Pitch att	00-03-00	
Three barrells of Lamb black att	00-01-03	[lamp-black]
Sallett oil att	00-03-04	[salad oil]
Asneck att	00-06-00	[arsenic]
Gunpowder att	00-00-10	
Tallow att	00-04-00	
Red & yellow oker att	00-04-05	
Shott att	00-10-00	
Umber att	00-04-00	

the East and the dyestuffs of the New World, to fancy goods and consumer luxuries. For Warrington, the times were changing and people's lifestyles were altering too. For those who could afford it there were new goods in plenty to be bought, and for those who could not there were all sorts of luxuries to which they might aspire: imagine them thinking, 'One day we will be able to go to Mr. Abraham's shop and buy just what we want'.

FURTHER READING: For background to this period, P. Borsay, *The English Urban Renaissance: culture and society in the provincial town 1660-1770* (Oxford University Press, 1991); the will and inventory of Joshua Abraham are in the Lancashire Record Office [reference WCW 1680, Joshua Abraham of Warrington]

26. *Reclaiming the mosslands*

Growth did not only affect the town itself. In the surrounding rural townships of south Lancashire population increase from the late 16th century began to put pressure on agriculture. There were more mouths to feed and demand for food rose continuously. Agricultural practices were still basic and yields from existing farmland could not easily be increased. Demand could only be met by extending the land under cultivation, by draining mosses or enclosing areas of heathland (previously used as rough grazing) and turning them into improved pasture or arable. During the reigns of James I and Charles I this process gathered pace and the landscape around Warrington changed as ditching and hedging divided up open mosses and heaths. The conversion from communal land to private estate was not without opposition, for the ordinary people felt, with reason, that they were being excluded and saw ancient rights extinguished. Sometimes they tried to retaliate. In the autumn of 1628

Population growth in the 17th century put pressure on local agriculture

Farmers needed to grow more, so improvements were made to farmland

These included draining mossland and enclosing commons and wastes

Many locals were hostile to such changes, which disrupted farming tradition

Landowners, though, won the day because of their superior power

William Yates's map of the county of Lancaster, 1786, shows that there were still large tracts of unreclaimed mossland east of the town. In earlier centuries the mosses had been much more extensive, stretching in a broken arc through Dallam, Burtonwood, Sankey and Penketh.

41

Thomas Ireland of Bewsey ordered that Graystone Heath, in Great Sankey and Penketh, should be enclosed and hedged. On 14 March 1629 William Barrow of Bewsey, his tenant, went to the heath and found:

> 66 one Thomas Rothwell of Great Sankey … husbandman and Richard Farrer in the same town … husbandman, [pulling] down the hedge and ditch, whereupon [he] wished the said Rothwell and Farrer that they would give over that work … but they refused to do so [and] Rothwell in a most deriding manner did say that he would come and put the said hedge down and not be forbidden by any for he would come to Bewsey gates and there shout that Ireland might hear him [and] that he cared not for Ireland nor never a man that he keeped [employed] 99

FACING PAGE, LEFT
Gleaning at Arpley: this haunting image dates from about 1900, when the last meadows and fields beside the river were about to be swallowed up by industrial sites and railway yards.

FACING PAGE, RIGHT
This extract from Peter Burdett's 1772 map of Cheshire shows that south of the river the countryside was almost entirely rural. It remained so for another century, though by the 1860s suburban development and industry were creeping over from Warrington, and railways had threaded their way through the fields and villages.

Comparable examples of opposition to the actions of the manorial lord can be found in other local communities. People also resented the deliberate closing-off of roads and tracks which had been used for many generations. In 1632, for example, the people of Burtonwood complained that Ireland's men had blocked the ancient highway from their village through Dallam to Warrington. Other enclosures were the work of individual tenants, who with the approval of the lord of the manor fenced off 'intakes' from the moss or heathland. In 1627 it was said of what is now Harpers Road and Crab Lane that:

> 66 the Common or Waste groundes called Fernhead Comon … is latelie inclosed and the kinges higheway betwixt Warington & Culcheth [is] become verie fowle & almost impassable [because] severall Inhabitantes there have made Inclosures upon the said Common 99

FURTHER READING: The documents quoted in this section are among the quarter sessions records in the Lancashire Record Office, Preston [reference QSB, for the 1630s]

27. *Agriculture and market gardening*

On newly-improved lands it was possible to grow a wide range of new crops

Market gardening developed, supplying urban markets

Warrington market was famed across the region for its fruit and vegetables

The expanding output of local farmers generated further business for Warrington market. There were no immediate local competitors except Lymm market, which was very much smaller: the markets at Prescot, Knutsford, Northwich, Altrincham, Leigh and Wigan were all a good few miles away, so Warrington served a large geographical area, but its reputation was such that people would travel many miles to attend. It was particularly well-known for its fruit and vegetables: in 1633 a Bolton woman, Alice Smyth, testified that …

> 66 on 22 August she came unto the Town of Warrington to buy Apples, having used Warrington Market 22 years for that commodity … and that day bestowed 8s 6d in good money in pears 99

We know of this because the magistrates were involved: Alice's husband gave her the enormous sum of six shillings to spend on fruit, as well as two shillings in farthings for other goods, and this money proved to be counterfeit. But it is a revealing snippet of detail, given that in the 1466 survey the orchards of Warrington were an important feature, while in 1795 a leading local writer noted how the town was the source of much of the fruit and vegetables

sold in Manchester, Bolton and other manufacturing towns. The growth of market gardening, later so important in the mosslands of south Lancashire and north Cheshire, can be dated to the early 17th century. Substantial areas of newly-won farmland were used for this profitable business. In 1632, for example, Thomas Salmon of Warrington was said to have drained, cleared and dug land close to the town, and 'converted to gardening … one acre and a half & thereon sowed diverse garden seeds and set some roots, namely cabbages, carrots, parsnips, radishes, onions and some others' for sale in the markets not only at Warrington but also at Manchester, Leigh, Wigan, Prescot, Bolton and Knutsford. There were many other such small entrepreneurs in the district, and during the 17th century their efforts added greatly to the diversity of local agriculture.

Country people at Warrington market, 1830. As the town grew, and as the great cities of south Lancashire provided a fast-growing demand, market gardening became a major activity on the reclaimed mosslands of the Mersey valley. Warrington market was noted for its locally-grown fruit and vegetables.

FURTHER READING: The case of Alice Smyth is among the Lancashire quarter sessions records QSB 1/126/67; Thomas Salmon's activities are noted among the records of the diocese of Chester [Cheshire & Chester Archives & Local Studies EDC5, 1632]

28. The cloth industry

Other aspects of agriculture had a direct link with the town's early industrial economy. The damp riversides and wet lowlands of south-west Lancashire were ideal for growing flax and hemp, the raw materials for the production of linen and canvas respectively. Throughout the district in the Tudor and Stuart period these two textiles were woven in large quantities, supplying local demand but also a wider market as economic activity expanded. Warrington was a main centre for their production and the linen trade of the town was noted from the 16th century. John Worthington, a Warrington linen and woollen draper who died in 1598, sold his goods as far afield as Berkshire and

Agriculture provided the raw materials for the main industry of the town in the 16th and 17th centuries

Warrington was a centre for the weaving of sailcloth, canvas and linen, made from locally-grown flax and hemp

The weaving and cloth trades were the subject of comment from travellers, impressed by the large volume of sales on the market

Warrington was the major supplier of sailcloth to the Royal Navy during the 18th century

other textile merchants of the town had similarly wide contacts.

By the 1570s, though, Warrington was beginning to specialise in the production of canvas, and particularly in what were then known as 'poldavies' or sailcloth. In 1586 16 'hempyards' were recorded in and around the town and, as the linen and woollen trades dwindled and contracted, eclipsed by the better organised textile businesses developing in south-east Lancashire, canvas and sailcloth retained their importance. Producers capitalised on the dramatic rise of Liverpool as a port in the second half of the 17th century. This gave a huge new market, reinforced by Britain's increasing involvement in foreign wars – every naval campaign meant potential business for the Warrington sailcloth manufacturers, so that by the middle of the 18th century it was said that the district provided the sails for half of the Royal Navy. Equally, peace meant possible hardship: in 1749, when John Robinson of Warrington feared bankruptcy as a result of the end of the War of the Austrian Succession, it was said that he employed 5,000 people in the area. He was a sailcloth merchant who followed the standard practice of 'putting out', whereby hemp yarn was distributed to local people, woven on handlooms in their cottages, and the

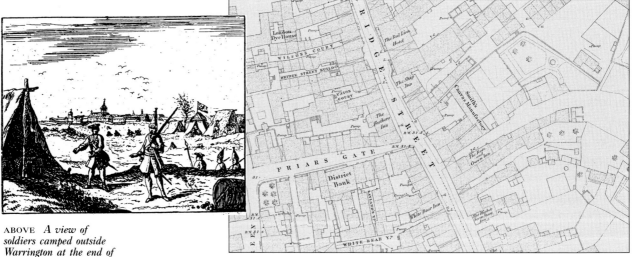

ABOVE *A view of soldiers camped outside Warrington at the end of the Napoleonic Wars. The cupola of Holy Trinity can be seen in the distance. The prolonged war with the French from 1793 to 1815 generated a huge demand for sailcloth for the Navy, making this the last great boom period for the earlier Warrington textile industry.*

RIGHT *The large-scale Ordnance Survey plan of 1850 recorded 'Smith's Canvas Manufactory' in a yard off the east side of Bridge Street. This was the last survivor of a large number of weaving sheds which in the later 18th century had produced sailcloth and canvas.*

finished cloth collected by the merchant via middlemen. At this time, though, the rise of the factory system was foreshadowed. A Warrington sailcloth 'manufactory' advertised for sale in 1759 included a weaving shed, in which there were 19 looms, as well as spinning and dressing mills, a warehouse, and bleaching equipment.

The linen and canvas industry, with its army of experienced domestic spinners and weavers, and its well-organised system of 'putting-out', underlay the development in Warrington itself, and in adjacent villages such as Stockton Heath and Lymm, of the fustian trade which is first documented in the early 18th century. Fustian (a cloth with a cotton and linen mixture) and cotton were destined to replace sailcloth as the mainstay of the local textile industry in the early 19th century.

FURTHER READING: I. Sellers, *Early modern Warrington*, gives a very useful summary of the cloth industry and its development in the 17th and 18th centuries; see also E. Roberts (editor), *A History of Linen in the North West* (CNWRS Lancaster University, 1998)

Eighteenth-Century Warrington

29. Warrington 1700-1800: an overview

Population figures help us to trace the growth of Warrington after 1700

Its expansion was slower than that of Liverpool and Manchester

It was one of the most important industrial and commercial towns in the region

After 1801, when the first national census was taken, accurate statistics are available for the population of each town and village. Before that date we can work out the changes which took place only roughly, using sources such as parish registers and tax returns. In the mid-seventeenth century the population of Warrington was probably about 2,000, which is very small by today's standards (it is about the size of Croft village or Appleton Thorn). In comparison, Liverpool had not many more inhabitants at that time – perhaps about 3,000 – and Manchester with about 5,500 was Lancashire's largest town. During the next hundred years those two places grew very rapidly indeed and Warrington, though it increased steadily in size and population, was left far behind. By the mid-1770s, when relatively reliable figures can be calculated, Liverpool (with its booming maritime trade) probably had about 50,000 and Manchester about 40,000 people. Warrington, in contrast, had perhaps 8,000 inhabitants. The 1801 census showed that Warrington had been far outstripped: in that year Liverpool had a population of 84,000, Manchester 77,000, and Warrington only 11,000 – but that meant that even so it was about the same size as Preston, Wigan or Macclesfield.

Some historians have argued, partly on the basis of figures such as these, that Warrington in the 18th century was a failure when compared with the other towns of the region. Clearly that was not the case. It was not an overnight 'boom town' like St Helens and Widnes in the early 19th century. Its new industries, river trade, and market did not attract floods of migrants in the way of Liverpool and Manchester, but it was generally recognised by contemporaries as a substantial and important place. Warrington lacked some of the key advantages of the great new industrial centres – there were few raw materials and no local fuel supplies, since it was not on the coalfield and its streams

The 1772 plan of Warrington shows that the previously compact country town was beginning to expand across the fields and gardens behind the main streets, as population grew and the first industries *appeared. Nonetheless, the prevailing impression, after half a century of steady growth since the opening of the first river navigations and turnpike roads, was still that of a market town.*

were of little value for water-power. Furthermore its port was relatively small and had little potential for major growth as ships became too large to navigate the upper estuary easily. But its geographical location gave it crucial significance and was incontestably to its benefit: all sorts of industries did develop in and around the town, and it comfortably held its own. Nobody has claimed that 18th-century Preston or Wigan were failures, but their size and rate of population growth were very similar to those of Warrington.

Thus, the development of the town was steady though unspectacular, and that in the long run was firmly to its advantage. Warrington acquired a diverse range of industries, many of them arising from local initiative and local roots, and was not dangerously reliant on a single trade as (to their eventual cost) were the cotton towns. Its economic base was associated, as it always had been, with its convenient location and its good communications, factors which help to explain the cluster of industries at or near Bank Quay. And, above all, its fortunes continued to rely to a considerable extent upon the time-honoured role which it played as the market and social centre for a wide tract of countryside and gradually-industrialising villages on both sides of the river. For north Cheshire and south-central Lancashire Warrington was the local metropolis, and in that it had no rivals. Industry was not everything – the stalls in the market and the stables behind the coaching inns, the lawyers' offices and the drapers' shops were as much a part of the town's economic well-being as files and fustian, glass and soap.

Donbavand's painting of the town of Warrington, 1772. This is the first detailed and accurate image of the town, and it emphasises not only the beginnings of industrialisation (the Bank Quay glassworks, for example, at the left edge) but also the sense of a pleasant country market town with some fine buildings (most notably, the newly-built Bank Hall, now the Town Hall) and the tower and cupola of Holy Trinity church.

FURTHER READING: Useful statistics on population sizes are given in C.B. Phillips and J.H. Smith, *Lancashire and Cheshire since 1540* (1994) and Ian Sellers, *Early modern Warrington* (1998)

30. Visitors' impressions

The comments made by visitors give some idea of what Warrington was like

Its narrow streets and busy market were two of the most noteworthy features

Others reported on the lively trade of the town as a whole

ABOVE *The postboy crossing Warrington bridge, the 'logo' of the Warrington Advertiser, which was published by Eyres' Press and was the town's first newspaper.*

RIGHT *William Yates's 1786 map, like Donbavand's painting, reveals a country town, still quite small, where industry was starting to make its presence felt: he marks the glass and copper works at Bank Quay. The importance of the north-south road and Warrington bridge is also clear.*

From the 16th century onwards there are descriptions of Warrington in the diaries, journals and letters of visitors to the town, or those who passed through. John Leland, an antiquarian and traveller who toured England in the mid-1530s, noted (in modern transcription) that 'Warrington, on the Mersey in Cheshire, is also a paved town. It has one parish church, right at the end of the town, and an Austin friary by the bridge. The town is of considerable size, and it has a better market than Manchester'. He also felt that Wigan, though the same size, had better buildings than Warrington, and despite his comments on its market he was very impressed with Manchester. Later opinions of

Warrington seemed to vary, with the narrowness of the streets seemingly a matter of particular note. William Blome in 1673 suggested that Warrington was 'a very fine and large town, which hath a considerable market on Wednesdays for linen cloth, corn, cattle, provisions and fish', and Daniel Defoe in the early 18th century commented on a 'large, populous, old-built town, but rich, and full of good country tradesmen. Here is particularly a weekly market for linen'.

In contrast, Judge Curwen in 1777 was very rude: 'streets narrow, dirty and ill-paved; like many other towns, with a gutter running through the middle, rendering it inconvenient passing through the streets' – but then he was rude about everywhere else as well. Edward Mogg in 1822 considered Warrington to be 'a large town, situated on the northern bank of the Mersey, over which there is a handsome stone bridge; it, for the most part, consists of long narrow streets, made up of ill-built houses, but some of them, however, are wide, and contain many handsome modern erections, besides the church, in which there are several good ancient monuments'. Neither of these later observers felt it necessary to comment on industry or pollution, for despite the increase in manufacturing during the later 18th century there was as yet nothing in Warrington comparable with the forests of chimneys or the great mills of the cotton towns.

31. Governing Warrington in the eighteenth century

Throughout the 18th century the town was controlled by its manorial lords

The court house in the market place was the forerunner of the town hall

Each township in the area was a separate local authority, with its own powers and officials

Although the town was growing steadily it was still administered, as it had been for several centuries, under the medieval manorial system. There was no local council, so that power over what happened in the town rested largely with the lord of the manor. In 1625 the lordship of Warrington had been sold to

This enlargement from Donbavand's 1772 painting shows, just to the left of the impressive tower and cupola of Holy Trinity, the lower tower on the old manorial court house in the market place.

William Booth of Dunham Massey and it was owned by his descendants until 1769. In that year Mary, Countess of Stamford, daughter of the last of the Booths, disposed of the manor to a rising local figure, John Blackburne of Orford, and the Blackburnes continued as lords of the manor until the new borough council bought out their rights in 1851. These two families, the Booths and then the Blackburnes, exercised their authority through the manor courts, which met on a regular basis at the court house in the market place.

> 66 The building, which was square and looked venerable with its crumbling red stone, had a tower at its south corner, and was approached by a flight of stone steps on the outside. Its date probably went back to the end of the fifteenth century; and the lower had some carvings upon its outer walls, among them a pair of shears such as are used in sheep shearing, with the letters T.B. [Thomas Boteler] in text hand beside them … The tower contained the town bell, which was rung in case of fire … [here] Sir Thomas Boteler, the founder of our free school, and his successors, lords of Warrington, held their manor courts 99
>
> Beamont, *Walks about Warrington*, 1887

A remarkable early photograph, showing the demolition in 1854 of the old court house in the market place. This was one of Warrington's most interesting buildings, but Victorian ideas of progress demanded that it be swept away. In this view the dressed stone columns, which were 'recycled' from the medieval Warrington friary during the early 17th-century reconstruction of the court house, can clearly be seen.

The courts dealt with two main types of business, all of it organised and 'stage-managed' by the steward of the manor. First, the court controlled the tenancies of the many Warrington people who lived in properties owned by the lord, approving new leases and terms of rental, including the services of manual labour which the tenants had to perform for the lord. Second, it transacted all sorts of minor administrative business which helped to keep the town in good trim: ordering tenants to clear ditches, remove obstructions in the highways, maintain their buildings, cut back overhanging hedges, and ensure that animals did not roam free in the streets. The manor, most importantly in financial terms, also controlled the market which generated a very substantial income from fines, tolls and charges.

Parallel with this was the pattern of townships. Every separate community was a township in its own right, so that in the Warrington area places such as Poulton-with-Fearnhead, Orford, Grappenhall, and Houghton, Middleton and Arbury were completely independent and had no connection with Warrington at all. Each of these townships was responsible for important aspects of local government, forming a separate miniature bureaucracy for each community. In 1554, for example, parliament legislated to compel townships to take over road maintenance and highways, so every one of them nominated its own highway surveyor. Under Acts of Parliament of 1598 and 1601, each township was a separate poor law authority and appointed an overseer of the poor from among the ratepayers. Each had a constable, who had the thankless task of trying to maintain law and order, and – even worse – going around the houses to collect the rates in cash. The overseer, highway surveyor and constable were unpaid, served one-year terms of office, and had no training apart from knowledge and experience. They kept basic accounts and paperwork, much of which survives today in Warrington Library's archive section.

Warrington town was in official terms simply another township, but its problems were vastly greater than those of the rural communities around. It had a much larger population, a far larger built-up area with streets, houses and yards, and was beginning to industrialise. During the 18th century the problems of managing a growing and busy town became too great for the manor and the existing ancient system of local government. By 1800 many people were convinced that Warrington needed a new and more dynamic form of administration to tackle the growing difficulties of an inadequate infrastructure, serious law and order breakdown, poor roads and worsening public health.

FURTHER READING: W. Beamont, *Annals of the Lords of Warrington and Bewsey* (Charles Simms & Co., 1873); W. Beamont, *Walks about Warrington* (1887)

32. *Managing the poor*

Archives give us a very detailed picture of the lives of the 18th-century poor

The town had a large number of paupers and treated them relatively well

Individual cases can be traced using the surviving records

The apprenticeship system, payments to the poor, assistance in kind and other help were administered by the overseer of the poor

The overseer of the poor was a key figure in every community. In his hands was the well-being – in some cases the life or death – of a large sector of the population. In late 18th century Warrington about 20 per cent of the people could be classed as paupers, despite the less-than-generous standard used at the time. Money was raised from the rates and then distributed to help the poor. The overseer assessed the merits of each case and determined whether an individual or family should receive assistance and, if so, how much and how often. He took into account not only their circumstances, but also their honesty, whether they had been a burden on the community in the past, or had moneyed relatives who could support them, or whether they were just being greedy.

For Warrington we are especially fortunate because the survival of the records has been very good, while 18th-century record-keeping in this area was unusually efficient. We thus have a clear and detailed picture of how the poor law affected the lives of local people. Assistance was given only to the 'deserving' poor – the very old and very young, physically-disabled, wives abandoned by their husbands and left with young children to maintain, or

those who had suffered because of disease, illness or loss of goods in fire or
flood. Listed below are some typical payments made by the Warrington
overseers. The people lived in their own homes and most were paid weekly.
They had to appear before the overseer each Thursday or Saturday to plead
for more help, for only a few, usually the long-term disabled, received payment
on a continuous basis.

Saturday 5th August 1769

Alise Pucell	1 wk	0-1-0
George Bate	1 wk	0-1-0
Widdow Longshaw	1 wk	0-0-9
Ailse Heyes	1 wk	0-0-6
William Gorstage	1 wk	0-0-6
Bettey Meason	1 wk	0-0-6
Marget Allcock	2 wk	0-1-0
Alise Pickrin	1 wk	0-0-6
Widdow Linney	1 wk	0-2-0
Nancy Jackson	4 wk	0-1-0
Marget Smith	1 wk	0-1-1
Mary Nickenson	1 wk	0-0-6
Hannah Jones	1 wk	0-0-6
Jane Richardson	1 wk	0-0-6
Marget Tomson rlf	1 wk	0-1-6
Sarah Ballshaw	1 wk	0-0-6

In this table the values are in £sd, in which 1s 0d equals 5p

The sums paid were modest. Most people received only sixpence a week
(2½p in modern currency): the wage of a labourer was about 3s. 6d. a week at
the time, and a generous estimate of the modern value suggests that 6d. is
equivalent to about £7. Warrington's poor were not treated generously, though
they were saved from starvation. The system allowed payments for other
purposes: below are some examples from 1770, typical of those throughout the
18th century:

2 Jan	Ann Stubs for Burial of a Child	0-2-0
9 Jan	Given Ailse Morriss for taking Care of John Banks	0-1-6
16 Jan	Given George Mooss to Beurey his Wife	0-7-0
13 Mar	For a Chield that was Left in the town Beurial	0-5-0
26 May	Ester Hobson for Looking after Bettey Ainsworth Lying in	0-3-0
29 May	for a Coffin for Marget Smith Chield	0-4-0

If paupers had trades but were unable to find the resources to set themselves
up with equipment or tools, the overseer might help out. Thus in September
1770 Catherine Pollitt was given 4s. 0d. (20p) to have two wheels on her cart
mended, and in January 1770 Jonathan Walklet was lent 4s. 0d. 'to buy Twigs':
he was a basket-maker and needed the money to buy raw materials. Pauper
children, whose upkeep was a charge on the township, would be put out as
apprentices at the age of eight or nine, often in distant towns, and a payment
of £1 or thereabouts made to the master to take the child. These are examples
from 1770:

20 Jan	Pd Richard Dutton for taking Martha Barns Son Prentice Thomas Barns	1-0-0

| 30 Jan | Pd William Breeanridge For Taking Thom. Smith Printice Wigan | 1-0-0 |
| 27 Feb | Richard Bozston taken Joseph Chaddock prentice Chapel Lain Wigen Linnin Weaver | 1-1-0 |

Sometimes the overseer helped people from another township and reclaimed the money from his opposite number there. Sometime he might even have felt real humanity towards the forlorn individuals who came before him:

24 Jan	A Woman from Shakerly Reliefed	0-2-0
26 Jun	Jane Brown Relieved She Does not belong to this town	0-1-6
10 Jul	Jane Brown Relief Belong to Burton Wood	0-1-6

The number of paupers receiving help varied from month to month as the weather changed and seasonal trades began and ended. In 1771, for example, the number of cases 'on the books' in Warrington ranged from 87 in January to 54 in August. In the summer and autumn, agricultural work was readily available, the weather milder, and food supplies more abundant. The harshness of winter and scarcity of cheap food in spring, in contrast, meant hard times and humiliating appearances before the overseer to plead for help. Warrington's overseers were thorough in keeping their accounts, so that we can chart the outgoings and see how their finances worked. There were bad years, with severe weather, epidemics, or trade depressions. In 1770, for example, the town's overseers paid a total of £285 to paupers in their homes, yet in 1772 the sum was only £204. There were costs in maintaining the workhouse, and administrative expenses, but even so the ratepayers had a bargain. Annual expenditure was about a shilling (5p) per head of the population, which even in 1770 was a pretty small sum. Whether it was enough, and whether the town's paupers received a 'fair deal', is another matter entirely.

FURTHER READING: The information in this section and the next is mainly derived from poor law records (to be found at refs. ms 101-219) in the archive section of Warrington Library: ref. ms 120, the book detailing 'Payments to the Out Poor' was the main source used to provide statistics; file on the workhouse [Warrington Museum]

33. *The workhouse*

Paupers might also be sent to the workhouse

This was opened in Church Street in 1728

It was run relatively humanely and the original set of rules survives

Instead of giving assistance to the poor in their homes the overseers of Warrington could also, in some circumstances, send people to the township workhouse in Church Street (opposite the Fennel Street turning) which had been opened in 1728. The workhouse could hold up to about a hundred people, and was in theory managed by a committee of three men (one of whom was always a member of the Patten family) although the actual work of running the institution was the responsibility of a governor or master who had a small 'flat' on the top floor. The workhouse was intended mainly for paupers who were, for various reasons, unable to help themselves – the disabled and chronically sick, the very old and infirm, orphaned children, and deserted wives or widows left with very young children to maintain. It was, by the standards of the time, a humane and well-run establishment, managed quite efficiently and probably with some sympathy. As the name suggests, inmates were to be put to work if they were capable of employment: spinning and preparation of cotton, hemp and flax, and weaving of cloth for sale, were the main tasks. There were strict rules of behaviour, drawn up in 1729, and these can be summarised as follows:

- all inmates were to wear a badge on their sleeve
- none to leave the building without permission (the possible penalty being corporal punishment or loss of meals)
- nobody in the workhouse to steal any goods, such as food, clothing, coals or material
- none to swear, curse, shout or quarrel, or to be drunk
- fires only to be allowed in the bedchamber [dormitory] for the warming of the sick, women lying-in, or for cooking and heating washing water
- all healthy people to rise at 6 a.m. in the summer and 7 in the winter, and to go to bed at 9 p.m. in summer and 8 in winter, and no smoking in bed
- the beds to be made by 9 a.m., the rooms swept by 10 a.m., the bedrooms washed twice weekly in summer and once in winter, and the kitchen and dining room washed daily: dishes to be washed twice a day
- all children to be clean and combed by 7 a.m. in summer and 8 in winter, ready for morning prayers
- children under six years to be taught to read, and those over six who cannot read to be allowed one hour a day for learning
- all inmates to go to the parish church twice on Sundays, without loitering or wandering
- all to attend the morning and evening prayers in the workhouse
- all persons who are put to work are to do so at the appointed times and for the required hours
- inmates to receive one penny for every shilling that they earn by their labour
- no inmates to beg from visitors, and money put in the donations box is to be spent on helping the sick and diseased among the inmates

An enlargement of Webster's 1855 photograph of Church Street, showing the old Warrington town workhouse (the large building on the right) which had been closed four years earlier. To its right is the old Bull's Head *public house.*

34. Law and order

As Warrington's old-fashioned system of local government creaked and strained to cope with the demands of a changing world, so the exercise of law and order was an increasing problem. By the end of the 18th century the town was acquiring an unenviable reputation for rowdiness and drunkenness, particularly among its young working men, and this was accompanied by a generally high level of petty crime and misdemeanour. The usual public punishment for minor offences was to be put in the stocks or the pillory. Most communities had a set of stocks, in a prominent position: at Grappenhall, for example, they stood by the churchyard wall and the pub, at Lymm at the foot of the village cross. The Warrington stocks, like those of Latchford, were on wheels so that they could be moved to the scene of trouble: the customary places were outside the bridewell in Church Street or in the market place, the latter being especially favoured because it was particularly public. Warrington had a certain undesirable fame because it was one of the last places where the brank, or

The growth in population presented problems of law and order

The town had no police force and crime prevention was very difficult

Offenders might be put in the stocks or forced to wear the scold's bridle

Two robberies of the Royal Mail were the most sensational crimes in late 18th-century Warrington scold's bridle, was used: in 1856 it was said that it had been employed 'almost within living memory' [that is, in about 1770]:

> " Cicely Pewsill, an inmate of the workhouse and a notorious scold, was seen wearing this disagreeable head-gear in the streets of Warrington, for the space of half-an-hour or more. One can hardly conceive a punishment more degrading to the offender, or less calculated to refine the spectators "

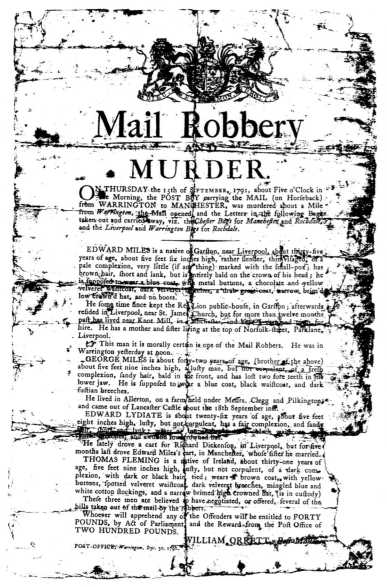

Mail Robbery
AND
MURDER.

ON THURSDAY the 15th of SEPTEMBER, 1791, about Five o'Clock in the Morning, the POST BOY carrying the MAIL (on Horseback) from WARRINGTON to MANCHESTER, was murdered about a Mile from *Warrington*, the Mail opened, and the Letters in the following Bags taken out and carried away, viz. the *Chester* Bags for *Manchester* and *Rochdale*, and the *Liverpool* and *Warrington* Bags for *Rochdale*.

EDWARD MILES is a native of Garston, near Liverpool, about thirty-five years of age, about five feet six inches high, rather slender, thin visaged, of a pale complexion, very little (if any thing) marked with the small-pox; has brown hair, short and lank, but is entirely bald on the crown of his head; he is supposed to wear a blue coat, with metal buttons, a chocolate and yellow velveret waistcoat, dark velveret breeches, a drab great-coat, narrow brim'd low crown'd hat, and no boots.

He some time since kept the Red Lion public-house, in Garston; afterwards resided in Liverpool, near St. James's Church, but for more than twelve months past has lived near Knot Mill, in Manchester, and kept a very good team for hire. He has a mother and sister living at the top of Norfolk-street, Parkland, Liverpool.

☞ This man it is morally certain is one of the Mail Robbers. He was in Warrington yesterday at noon.

GEORGE MILES is about forty-two years of age, (brother of the above) about five feet nine inches high, a lusty man, but not corpulent, of a fresh complexion, sandy hair, bald in the front, and has lost two fore teeth in his lower jaw. He is supposed to wear a blue coat, black waistcoat, and dark fustian breeches.

He lived in Allerton, on a farm held under Messrs. Clegg and Pilkington, and came out of Lancaster Castle about the 18th September inst.

EDWARD LYDIATE is about twenty-six years of age, about five feet eight inches high, lusty, but not corpulent, has a fair complexion, and sandy hair, short and lank; wears a ... black waistcoat ..., and a round low crowned hat.

He lately drove a cart for Richard Dickenson, in Liverpool, but for five months last drove Edward Miles's cart, in Manchester, whose sister he married.

THOMAS FLEMING is a native of Ireland, about thirty-one years of age, five feet nine inches high, lusty, but not corpulent, of a dark complexion, with dark or black hair, tied; wears a brown coat, with yellow buttons, spotted velveret waistcoat, dark velveret breeches, mingled blue and white cotton stockings, and a narrow brimed high crowned hat, (is in custody.)

These three men are believed to have negotiated, or offered, several of the bills taken out of the mail by the robbers.

Whoever will apprehend any of the Offenders will be entitled to FORTY POUNDS, by Act of Parliament; and the Reward from the Post Office of TWO HUNDRED POUNDS.

WILLIAM ORRETT, Postmaster.

POST-OFFICE, *Warrington*, *Sept.* 30, 1791.

Warrington's most famous WANTED *poster. A reward of £240, an astonishingly large sum, was offered for the arrest of the alleged murderers of James Hogworth, the postboy, at Woolston in 1791.*

By far the most celebrated local crimes, though, were the two robberies upon the Royal Mail in the late 18th century. In March 1788 the post-boy James Archer was robbed of his mailbag between Stretton and Higher Whitley, on the road to Northwich. He escaped but was imprisoned at Middlewich for suspected complicity in the attack. Three years later his assailant, William Lewin of Great Budworth, was hanged for a series of mail robberies. In September 1791 James Hogworth, aged 24, was carrying the mails from Warrington to Manchester when he was attacked in the early hours of the morning at Woolston. He was tied up, stabbed and thrown into a brook. His murderers were eventually apprehended and executed at Lancaster in March 1792. The body of one, Edward Miles, was gibbeted at Woolston, close to the scene of the crime, and left to rot and disintegrate as a warning to others.

> " there his body still continued to hang at the beginning of this [i.e., 19th] century, to the terror of the belated foot passenger, who hastened his footsteps at nightfall to be out of the hearing of the chains creaking and clanging in the night breeze "

While this sensational murder, and its equally sensational aftermath, attracted a great deal of attention, it was not representative of crime in general. It was the day-in, day-out problem of trying to maintain law and order, control the streets, deal with drunken rowdies and apprehend petty thieves, which caused so many difficulties. One of the most pressing problems for the new century, and one of the most controversial, was the need to establish a police force and give the town a proper law and order agency for the first time. That

LATCHFORD STOCKS

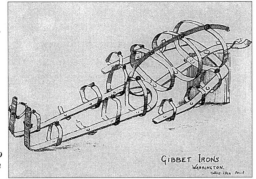

GIBBET IRONS
WARRINGTON.

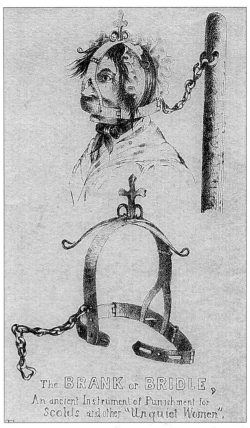

The BRANK or BRIDLE,
An ancient Instrument of Punishment for
Scolds and other "Unquiet Women".

Three Warrington punishments, drawn in 1872 from the examples which had been preserved by the town. They show the 'mobile stocks' which were once owned by the township of Latchford; the gibbet iron on which Edward Miles, the murderer of the Warrington postboy, was hung in 1791; and the notorious scold's bridle or brank, a 'cruel and unusual punishment' said to have been used in the town as late as the 1770s.

might seem a very obvious policy to follow, but many Warringtonians were fiercely opposed to the idea because it would, inevitably, cost money. That meant higher rates, and that was very unpopular.

FURTHER READING: C. Madeley, 'Obsolete modes of punishment' in the *Proceedings of the Warrington Literary and Philosophical Society*, 1888-1889; Beamont, *Walks about Warrington* (1887); file on the Postboy Murders [Warrington Museum]

35. *Religion in the eighteenth century*

Although the Reformation in the 1530s and 1540s in theory imposed a single national religion to which all people belonged, the reality was more complex. In south-west Lancashire and to a lesser extent west Cheshire there remained a substantial section of the population who continued, with varying degrees of openness, to believe in the 'Old Faith', Roman Catholicism. From the late 16th century, too, dissent within the Anglican Church produced movements such as the Puritans and eventually the nonconformists, Protestants who stood outside the Church of England (they would not 'conform' to the rules of the Church). Both groups were persecuted for their faith during the 17th century, though the Puritans took control of the nation during the Civil War and Commonwealth period (1645-1660). However, in the late 17th century, for political reasons, the Protestant dissenters were granted freedom of worship.

In 1662 Robert Yates, the Puritan rector of Warrington, was ejected from his living as the Church was purged of dissenters within its ranks – Samuel Mather at Burtonwood was similarly expelled. Yates became the leader of the town's

The nonconformists or Puritans enjoyed mixed fortunes in 17th-century Warrington

After 1689 they had freedom of worship and Cairo Street chapel was founded in the early 18th century

Catholics had no such freedom until the late 18th century

In 1709 Holy Trinity became the first new Anglican church in the town after the Reformation

To their Majesties Justices of peace at the Quarter Sessions at ormeskirke the 23rd July 1689

Whereas by an Act of this present parliament entitled an act for exempting their Majesties protestant subjects dissenting from the Church of England from the penalties of certaine lawes The places of meeteing for their religiouse worshipp are required to be certified to the generall quarter sessions of the peace for the County City or place where such meeteing shall be held

In pursuance whereof Peter Aspinall minister in holy orders preacher or teacher of a congregacion of Protestants dissenting from the Church of England haveing taken the oaths & made & subscribed the declaracion in the said act appointed on behalfe of himselfe & his congregacion doth certify that a certaine Edifice or barne in Warrington called Ecclestons barne of late belonging to Lawrence Eccleston deceased being within this County of Lancaster is intended & appointed for a place of meeteing for an assembly or congregacion of Protestant dissenters And doth humbly desire the same may in pursuance of the said Act be recorded at this Quarter Sessions

Peter Aspinwall

ABOVE *The petition presented to the county magistrates in the summer of 1689, which sought approval for the licensing of a nonconformist meeting house in Warrington. The town's first official place of worship for the dissenters from the Church of England, it was the predecessor of the Cairo Street Chapel.*

BELOW *St James's Church, Latchford, was built in 1777 and its tall spire, shown here, was a notable local landmark. It was later removed following damage during an earthquake, and the church itself was eventually relocated on Wilderspool Causeway. This engraving dates from the 1790s.*

nonconformists and during a brief period of toleration in 1672-1673 he was authorised to use the Court House in the market place for 'Presbyterian' services: that he could do this was a reflection of the Puritan beliefs of the Booth family, lords of the manor. When freedom of worship was granted by Parliament in 1689 the town's nonconformists began to hold services publicly again, using Eccleston's Barn near the market place in Sankey Street. In 1703 they obtained land close by, on the south side of Sankey Street, and there built a meeting house, simple and plain in its architecture. Records for 1717 suggest that several hundred worshippers regularly assembled here and it soon became inadequate to cope with the numbers, so in 1745-46 this building was replaced (on the same site) by the present Cairo Street Chapel.

The nonconformists were a powerful element within Warrington's economic and social life from the early 18th century, though politically they were hampered – as they were everywhere else – by the fact that the Anglicans had a tight hold of the reins of local and national power. With the exception of the Booths, most of the leading families of the area (including the Blackburnes and the Pattens) were loyal to the Church of England. The Anglicans were in a mess in the early 18th century. The church of St Elphin was inconveniently distant from the town centre, too small for the growing population, and had been badly-damaged during the Civil War siege back in the 1640s. It was not repaired properly until the Reverend Samuel Shawe (rector 1690-1718) oversaw the demolition of the damaged steeple and its replacement by a tower, and refitted the interior. During the 1720s and 1730s further alterations were made, cramming wooden galleries into the body of the church in order to accommodate as many extra worshippers as possible. Later in the 18th century this continued, with the nave being enlarged in the late 1760s and a further gallery built.

Just as important in the long run was the decision by Peter Legh of Lyme, the owner of extensive lands in the Warrington area, to finance the construction of an entirely new church, the first new Anglican place of worship in the town. He claimed that the inconvenience of St Elphin's was an important factor and in 1709 the new chapel of Holy Trinity, in the very centre of the town, was consecrated. A new schoolroom and schoolhouse was opened next door for the Bluecoat School (see below).

The Reverend Shawe was highly displeased, because any new church reduced the influence and role of St Elphin's, but there was little that he could do apart from make every possible difficulty for the curate of the chapel. Holy Trinity was rebuilt in 1760, and is today a particularly attractive feature of the town centre. Its reconstruction coincided with the increasing tendency of leading families to patronise this church rather than St Elphin – in other words, it had acquired the inestimable advantage of being fashionable.

The distinctive and decorative mid-18th-century tower and cupola of Holy Trinity church are prominent in this 1830 sketch by Robert Booth, showing Warrington town from the north.

Other churches and chapels began to appear in new suburbs and outlying areas. St James, Latchford, was built in 1777 and quickly became known as the centre for the evangelical 'low Church' wing of the Anglicans. John Wesley came to Warrington in 1755, though there were already Methodists in the town before that date, and he visited on several later occasions (the last, as a white-haired 87-year-old, in 1790). By 1779 the Methodists had built a new chapel and minister's house in Bank Street, and were enjoying bad relations with the longer-established Unitarians of Cairo Street. The Roman Catholics, who after 1750 were able to worship, if not openly at least without real fear of persecution, started holding masses at a building behind the *Feathers Hotel* in Bridge Street and at a house in Dallam Lane: in 1778 the first Catholic chapel was opened at the south end of Bewsey Street. In 1784 there were 70 Catholic communicants in Warrington (though in the rural townships around they were more numerous – 215 in Croft, for example) and by the early 19th century they had become a significant force in the religious life of the town.

FURTHER READING: Ian Sellers' book *Early modern Warrington* has a particularly comprehensive coverage of the religious history of the town during the late 17th and 18th centuries; see also W. Beamont, *Warrington Church Notes: the parish church of St Elfin's, Warrington and the other churches of the parish* (Percival Pease, 1878)

36. Education and the Warrington Academy

Throughout the North-West the 16th and 17th centuries had seen a growth in literacy, as educational opportunities expanded for the middle classes and at least some of the relatively poor, and as printed works were more widely disseminated. In the 18th century the increasing population threatened to end this improvement, because existing schools could not cope with the rising number of children. The problem was especially acute in the larger towns, where many poor children had no education of any sort. However, philanthropic motives encouraged some individuals, and a few existing charities, to enter the field of educational provision: as yet the state and local government played no part. Attempts were made in Warrington to provide a limited education for the lower orders. The Bluecoat School, originally located in the schoolroom next to Holy Trinity Church and from 1782 in new premises

The Boteler Grammar School educated only a small minority of the children of the town

The Blue Coat School sought to provide free schooling for poorer children

Despite this, in the early 19th century only seven per cent of Warrington children received any proper education

Warrington Academy was a centre of intellectual and cultural life

It had the potential to become a university but left the town in 1786

Joseph Priestley, one of the greatest scientists of the 18th century, was the most famous and influential figure to have taught at Warrington Academy. His international reputation drew many students and academics to the town, but the would-be university of which some people dreamed never came to fruition.

in Winwick Street, arose out of a charity established in the 1670s to help poor children:

> It was ... thought necessary in order to Rescue Such poor Children from Ignorance and Vitious courses of living & to make them fit for Apprenticeships to bring them under good Discipline first by putting them to the Charity School, there to learn the knowledge & Practice of the Christian Religion as profest in the Church of England ... to make them good Servants to God and their Masters, Good and Serviceable in their Generation

This school was generally regarded as more 'deserving' than the wealthy Boteler Grammar School and by 1825 had attracted no fewer than 73 separate charitable legacies from local people, totalling over £2,300 (perhaps £500,000 in modern money). These bequests had been invested in property, giving the school an annual income of over £200. The school was run more economically than the Grammar School, with lower overheads, and so was able to help many more children. In 1825, 14 boys and 10 girls were boarders, who were educated and clothed with the blue uniform from which the school took its name, while a basic schooling was given to another 120 day boys and 30 day girls. The curriculum was simple: reading, writing and arithmetic, with needlework for girls. Despite its modest aims, some argued that the school gave considerably greater benefit to the town than its older and more superior rival. In the late 18th century a variety of other schools were established, including private academies for children of middle-class Warringtonians, and a few dame schools for poorer children, of which almost nothing is known. Despite this, it was estimated in 1818 that only seven per cent of children in Warrington received any sort of elementary education (better than, for example, Ashton-under-Lyne with a mere two per cent, but not as good as Blackburn with nine per cent).

Although for the population as a whole this was less than satisfactory, the second half of the 18th century saw Warrington playing a perhaps unexpected role, as the location of what some have seen as a would-be university. In 1757 Warrington Academy was founded to act as a centre of nonconformist and dissenter learning, the driving force behind its establishment being the Reverend John Seddon, the minister at Cairo Street chapel. Its meteoric rise and high reputation gave Warrington a shining reputation as 'the Athens of the North'. The Academy, originally at Bridge Foot and later occupying purpose-built premises in Academy Place, 'stood forth as a centre of scientific and literary activity, and a citadel of religious and political freedom'. There were comparable academies in a few other towns, but Warrington had a special importance and attracted some of the greatest teachers and educationalists of the day, people who because of

The purpose-built premises of Warrington Academy, in Academy Place, was in the 1760s and 1770s the focus of what might, but for a turn of fate, have become England's third university.

The Bluecoat School in Winwick Street, 1906. The headmaster, Edward Rose, is shown with 15 boys and 15 girls who wore the distinctive blue uniforms of the original foundation, though by this time there were several hundred other pupils who did not wear this special costume.

their nonconformity were unacceptable to the two reactionary and elitist universities, Oxford and Cambridge, which banned them from teaching. Among the great names who came to Warrington and worked here were John Holt, one of the leading mathematicians of the period; the Reverend Gilbert Wakefield, classicist and theologian; Dr John Aikin, literary scholar; and above all Joseph Priestley, the greatest scientist of the mid-18th-century world.

The Academy became a centre for intellectual, scientific and cultural debate and learning, over 400 students being educated there during its 30-year life. The money for its support was subscribed from as far away as the American colonies, but it derived much of its strength from the influential nonconformist community in and around Warrington itself, and from dissenters in other northern towns for whom it was a beacon of freedom and opportunity. It was a way of escaping from the oppressive restrictions of the Church of England and gave nonconformists an exciting new voice. In 1786, though, the staff and students of the Academy moved to Manchester, in part because the orderly and efficient management of the institution had broken down and there were problems of ill-discipline and squabbling. Warrington was left with a great gap in its cultural life, and a 'might have been': had the Academy survived into the 1830s there is a good chance that it might have become a university in its own right. What would Warrington have been like today if it had become the site of England's third university?

FURTHER READING: P. O'Brien, *Warrington Academy 1756-86: its predecessors and successors* (Owl Books, 1989); P. O'Brien, *Eyres' Press 1756-1803: an embryo university press* (Owl Books, 1993); H. Lievesley, *Boteler Grammar School, Warrington, 1526-1976* (1976); the *Further Report of the Commissioners for inquiring concerning Charities* [the Charity Commissioners] for Lancashire, 1825, gives information about the endowments of the Bluecoat school; W.B. Stephens, *Adult education and society in an industrial town, Warrington 1800-1900* (University of Exeter Press, 1980)

37. *The market and the trade of the town in the eighteenth century*

Warrington flourished as a market town in the 18th century

Fish, shellfish, fruit, vegetables, dairy products and cloth were among the main commodities traded on the market

Market gardening and fruit-growing continued to be locally important trades

Almost all 18th-century visitors to Warrington who noted their impressions referred to the market, one of the most prominent features of the town. There is no doubt that it was among the largest and busiest in all north-west England, far more so than the size of the Warrington alone could support, and this confirms that it drew its trade from a great area of Lancashire and Cheshire. It was held, as it had been for centuries, in the very heart of the town, but the

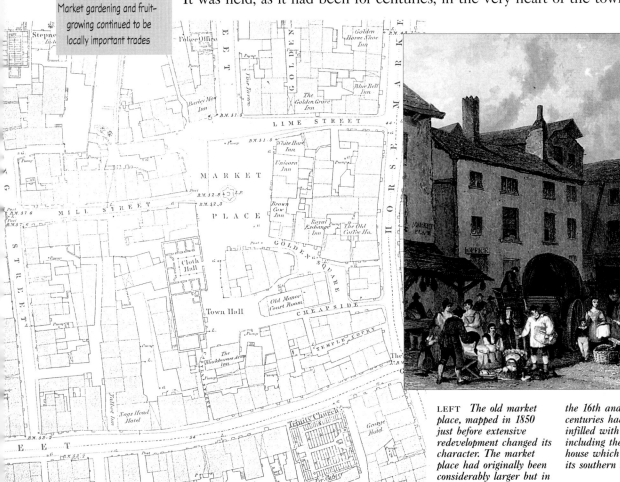

LEFT *The old market place, mapped in 1850 just before extensive redevelopment changed its character. The market place had originally been considerably larger but in* the 16th and 17th centuries had been partly infilled with buildings, including the manor court house which is shown at its southern side.

This 1790s engraving of the Mersey from Latchford gives interesting detail of the fishermen netting for shoals of sparling (smelts). The river was an important source of fish until the early 19th century, when increasing levels of pollution began to reduce stocks. The picture also shows a Mersey flat, the typical sailing barge of the river; the old water-powered cornmill at Howley; and three churches, St James Latchford, Holy Trinity, and St Elphin.

market place itself was becoming seriously inadequate. Not only was the trade growing, and so putting pressure on the available space – too many stalls in too small an area – but also the market place was inconveniently cluttered with buildings. Stalls and traders now spilled out along the neighbouring streets, impeding the free movement of traffic and giving the manorial steward a headache, for stalls along the streets were very much harder to regulate and control.

The business of the market was extremely varied. Warrington had important fisheries in the as-yet-unpolluted Mersey and its creeks and sandy flats: in 1720 it was reported that the town sold 'sturgeons, mullets, sand eels, prawns, lobsters, oysters, shrimps, and the largest and best cockles in England', while salmon, smelts and herring were also landed in large quantities. In 1698 Thomas Patten wrote to Richard Norris of Speke, referring to the over-fishing of the 'River Mercy' by the men of the Warrington stretch of the river:

> 66 vast numbers of salmon trout are taken, so as to supply all the Country, and Market Towns 20 miles round, and when the Country is cloyed [full up] or when they cannot get sale for them, they give them to their Swine .. they take all summer long great numbers of Kippers [herring] which have come up the river to spawn and come down in the summer, poor, lean and unwholesome towards the sea … our Mercy fishermen have mercy on none they can catch, for all are fish that come to the net and none safe they can lay their hands on 99

Warrington market place in 1830. This well-known illustration conveys the lively atmosphere of the market, just before it was increasingly subject to official control and regulation. It also emphasises the fine half-timbered architecture of the Barley Mow and adjacent buildings. Perhaps, though, the newly-erected gas lamp has pride of place?

Cloth was a major item of market trade, commented on by many travellers: Defoe in 1720 refers to a local speciality, huckaback, which was a sort of linen used for tablecloths, napkins and towels. He reported that about £500-worth of this cloth was sold each market day (equivalent to perhaps £125,000 today).

The market at Warrington was celebrated not only for its fruit and vegetables but also for cattle and livestock. This 1794 engraving of 'a Lancashire cow' shows the sort of beast traded in large numbers in the town. The cattle not only provided meat for Warrington butchers' shops, but also the hides that were the mainstay of the important leather and tanning trade which expanded rapidly in the second half of the 18th century.

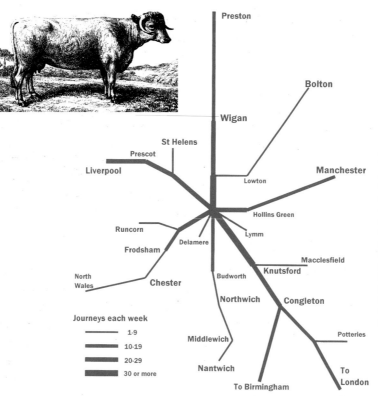

Carriers' routes from Warrington, 1828. Carriers' carts were the heavy road freight vehicles of the day, transporting a wide range of commodities on inter-urban journeys and also serving villages and country areas along the way. They were a key element in the transport network, and this diagram shows how the town was not only a focal point on the regional system but also had long distance links to London, the Midlands and Wales.

The rich and fertile agricultural lands of south Lancashire and north Cheshire supplied the market with butter and cheese, which were sufficiently important to have special areas given over specifically for their sale (hence the street-name Buttermarket). Warrington was also noted for its fruit and vegetables: in 1795 John Aiken, as well as noting that the fisheries were declining because of over-use and pollution, wrote that

> 66 quantities of fruit and vegetables grown around the town are sent away for the supply of Manchester, Bolton and other parts in the manufacturing districts … the land around Warrington consists of rich meadows bordering on the river, and occasionally flooded, and of pasture and garden ground. It is noted for its gooseberries which are superior in size, and of greater variety of kinds, than in most parts of the kingdom. A very fine kind of damson is common here. Potatoes are raised in large quantities and thirty or forty thousand bushels (about 1,250 tons) have been shipped at Bank quay in a year 99

FURTHER READING: J. Aiken, *A description of the country from thirty or forty miles round Manchester* (1795); T. Heywood (editor), *The Norris Papers* (Chetham Society Old Series vol.9, 1846); D. Defoe, *A Tour through the Whole Island of Great Britain* (1724: Penguin edition, 1976)

38. *The river and canals*

As we have seen, communications were always a central element in Warrington's development and help to explain its economic and commercial success. During the 18th century the north-west of England underwent a 'transport revolution', which was inextricably tied in with industrialisation and

The improvement in transport helped to reinforce Warrington's role as a market and trading centre

The Mersey and Irwell Navigation (built 1724-1736) was the first major project

Other local waterway schemes included the Sankey and Bridgewater Canals

Warrington's trade benefited considerably from the improved accessibility the growth of towns. Warrington shared fully in these changes and by the early 19th century had emerged as one of the key transport centres not just of the region but of the country as a whole, a position it has retained ever since and which has reinforced and strengthened its economic base for two and a half centuries. The 18th-century changes were built around two new and inter-related transport networks: one was the expansion of the waterway system, first by making rivers navigable and then by constructing entirely new canals; the other was the creation of a system of improved roads, the turnpikes, designed for faster and easier transport of industrial and agricultural produce. For both, Warrington was of major importance.

The Mersey and Irwell Navigation was the first large-scale project to affect the town and its vicinity. The idea of making the river properly navigable above Warrington was already being aired in 1660s, though the priority was to clear the Mersey below the town of the many obstacles to efficient navigation – weirs, sunken vessels, sandbanks and shallows. In the early 1690s one of Warrington's greatest merchants, Thomas Patten, had the fishweirs and other obstructions below Bank Quay removed and a modest trade to Liverpool developed, but Warrington remained the effective head of navigation. However, the commercial and trading importance of Manchester continued to grow and existing overland routes became quite inadequate to deal with the increased trade. In 1712 the engineer Thomas Steers proposed to make the river navigable up to Manchester by building locks and short new cuts across the longest loops. Eight years later (things moved as slowly then as they do now!)

'Old Billy' was a famous local character in the early 19th century. Foaled in 1760 at Woolston, the horse worked for many years pulling barges on the Mersey & Irwell Navigation, then became a gin-horse working for the Navigation Company. He died in 1822, aged 62, and still holds the record for the longest-lived horse ever recorded. In 1820 he took part on Manchester's celebrations for the coronation of George IV, as a celebrity in his own right.

The commemorative medullion issued for the official opening of the Liverpool and Manchester Railway in 1830. It shows, in a symbolic representation of the triumph of the new mode of transport over the old, a train speeding over the great Sankey Viaduct while a boat drifts lazily along the canal below.

Canals and river navigations of the Warrington area, 1720-1850. The Mersey & Irwell Navigation and the Bridgewater Canal provide competing routes between Manchester and the sea, while the access northwards into the Lancashire coalfield guaranteed major traffic for these concerns and the Sankey Navigation.

a group of Manchester and Liverpool merchants adopted his plans, made large financial contributions, and in the following year obtained an Act of Parliament for the improvement of the river from Bank Quay to Hunts Quay in Manchester.

Work only began in February 1724 and it was 12 years before the navigation was open, with a new wharf and warehouses at Bank Quay and other wharves at Atherton's Quay just downriver and at Great Sankey. But although it was said in 1739 that 'boats pass and repass upon the river, with large quantities of goods from Warrington and Liverpool', trade was slow to build up and competition from turnpike roads soon made further improvements necessary – in the 1760s long new cuts were made at Woolston and Howley.

The old way and the new: this famous view, engraved in 1835, shows the Sankey Navigation or St Helens Canal just south of Newton-le-Willows, spanned by the magnificent new viaduct of the Liverpool and Manchester Railway.

This coincided with the beginning of a new age of water transport, for in 1755 an Act of Parliament authorised the making of a navigation along the Sankey Brook, from the Mersey to St Helens. Within a year its promoters decided instead to build a separate waterway, rather than use the existing stream, and England's first true modern canal was completed in 1759. The Sankey Navigation, passing along the valley east of Warrington, revolutionised the industrial and commercial potential of the waterway network, though it diverted some of the trade that hitherto transferred to the river at Bank Quay. In 1759 the much more famous Bridgewater Canal was authorised. It was opened in stages from 1761, and, although it had little immediate impact upon the Warrington area, keeping to the higher ground south of the river, the canal was a potential disaster for the Mersey & Irwell Navigation. In 1779, just three years after the Bridgewater was finished, the Navigation was bought for a mere £10,000 by a consortium of Liverpool and Manchester businessmen. They had it dredged and cleared and, by 1788, 24 vessels were regularly working the river above Warrington, and a steady dividend of five per cent was paid.

In the 1790s a series of substantial new cuts was built across the longer meanders, including those at Butchersfield below Hollins Ferry, Woolston and Howley. Attention turned again to the river below Warrington, where tides and silting still caused delays. A bypass canal on the south shore, from Latchford to Runcorn, opened in 1803 and a year later was extended round the Runcorn Gap to Hempstones. The canal was three miles shorter than the river but bypassed Warrington, although the old channel remained navigable. In January 1811 long-distance carrier services to Bolton and Bury were started and in August 1806 special boats had begun carrying passengers from Manchester to Runcorn (for the Mersey ferries). The journey took eight hours with a

Warrington stop originally at Black Bear bridge (later moved to Warrington bridge where passengers could transfer to the Liverpool stagecoach). After 1810 the Navigation entered a prosperous period, paying very large dividends: 20 per cent in 1816 and 40 per cent in 1829. In 1819 a new Woolston Cut, 1¾ miles long, bypassed the older cut and the original river and in 1822 the lock at Runcorn was rebuilt to take sea-going vessels. Traffic rose from 93,000 tons in 1816 to 133,000 tons in 1823.

> **❝** Warrington's river in 1824: 'the communication between Liverpool and Manchester ... is incessant, and the brick-dust coloured sails of the barges are seen every hour of the day on their passage, flickering in the wind **❞**

In 1825 the Navigation had 64 vessels, with a carrying capacity over 2,000 tons, and Warrington had a busy river trade, but threats now came from two directions: the Liverpool and Manchester Railway scheme, and a plan for a ship canal from the Dee via Lymm to Manchester. Local voices, such as the owners of the Mersey Mills at Warrington, strongly opposed the ship canal project, which eventually failed, but competition from roads and railways ate into the profitability of the company during the 1830s. It could not afford the heavy investment to turn itself into a ship canal and, although in 1835 about 7,000 flats a year still came to Warrington, it was reported that 'the trips are at present made with difficulty owing to the shallow water and narrow channels combined with the number of vessels grounded each tide betwixt Runcorn and Fiddlers Ferry'. Dividends began to fall though tonnage rose to 220,000 in 1841, but then railway competition was really biting and the golden years were over.

FURTHER READING: C. Hadfield, *The Canals of North West England* (2 vols) (David and Charles, 1970); J. Corbridge, *A Pictorial History of the Mersey and Irwell Navigation* (E.J. Morten, 1979); P.A. Norton, *Railways and waterways to Warrington* (Cheshire Libraries, 1984)

39. *The turnpike roads and the bridge*

Although in other parts of Lancashire and Cheshire long stretches of new road were built in the later 18th century, in the Warrington area the turnpike road network was almost entirely made up of existing routes which were taken over and improved by private profit-making trusts, the costs of the work (and the profits) being met by charging tolls on users of the roads. Turnpike roads were invented in the 1660s but did not reach the North-West for several more decades. The first road from Warrington to be turnpiked was what is now the A49 through Winwick to Wigan (1726), and this set the pattern – each of the seven turnpike roads which led to the town (from Prescot, Wigan, Manchester, Altrincham, Knutsford, Northwich and Chester) was a major regional trunk road, so that, although Warrington was an important traffic centre and an objective in its own right, an equally relevant consideration was that it lay at the junction of a network of key routes that were

By 1800 a network of turnpike roads focused on Warrington bridge

The town became one of the main route centres on the national road system

This meant through-traffic and increased prosperity

Warrington had many coaching inns, stables and hotels

Robert Booth's 1830 sketch of the tollgate on the Warrington and Wigan turnpike road at Winwick

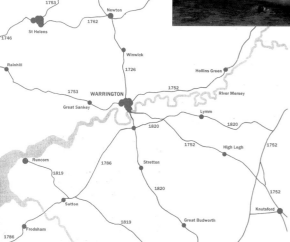

A late 18th-century drawing of the old Warrington bridge (constructed in 1495 and rebuilt in 1746, after the Jacobite rising, with a central watchtower and guardhouse). The lower window in the central pier was a small cell or dungeon.

The turnpike roads of south Lancashire and north Cheshire, showing the dates of the authorising Acts of Parliament.

From Liverpo.	Marton, *Davenport Arms*	From London
40¼	Marton, *Davenport Arms*	165¾
39¼	Siddington 🖃 Turnpike	166¾
	2¾ m. farther,	
	To Macclesfield 4½ m.	
	Forward to Wilmsloe 5 m.,	
	thence to Manchester 12¼ m.	
34¼	🖃 to Chelford	171¾
	🖃 to Holmes Chapel 6 m.	
31¼	Ollerton Gates	174¾
29¼	* KNUTSFORD, M.H.	176¾
	🖃 to Newcastle under Lyme,	
	by Holmes Chapel, 24 m.	
	to Northwich 7 m.	
26¾	Mere	179¾
	🖃 to Northwich 7 m.	
	To Altringham 5 m. 🖃	
24¾	High Legh	181¾
20¾	Duke of Bridgewater's Canal	185¾
19	Latchford	187
	¾ m. farther,	
	🖃 to Chester 20 m.	
	Cross the 🖃 river Mersey,	
	and enter Lancashire.	
17¾	* WARRINGTON, entrance, Lancashire	188¾
	Forward to Newton 5 m.	
	To Manchester 18 m. 🖃	
16¾	🖃 to Sankey Bridge	189¾
	Cross the 🖃 Sankey Navigation	
	¾ m. farther,	
	🖃 to Liverpool, by Penketh, 14¾ m.	
15¾	Sankey	190¾
11	Rainhill	195
8	* PRESCOT, Church	198
	To St.Helens 3½ m.; thence to Wigan 10½ m. 🖃	
4	Knotty Ash	202
	A little farther,	
	🖃 to Warrington, by Penketh, 14¾ m.	
	* LIVERPOOL	206

Road traffic increased rapidly as turnpikes improved the roads themselves, and carriages and coaches became faster and more comfortable. This extract from a national guide to road travel published in 1822 emphasises that long-distance passenger traffic and light freight business was now feasible. Places such as Warrington, at key junctions in the national network, derived much trade from the coaching business.

upgraded to cater for long-distance inter-urban movements. This created a large and surprisingly efficient system, which focused on one single point: the Mersey bridge at Warrington itself, which by 1810 had became one of the busiest locations anywhere on the national road system.

Throughout the 18th century the bridge across which all this traffic poured was still that built in 1495. It stood for over three hundred years, although in 1745, when the Jacobite armies were coming down from Scotland, it was made unusable to prevent the rebels from crossing: the two centre arches were demolished to water level. In May 1746 the contract for rebuilding specified that the new work should include a watchtower, with a small dungeon beneath, on the downstream side of the central stone pier. However, this partial demolition and reconstruction, as well as its great age, meant that the bridge was structurally unsound by the end of the century. That, together with its narrowness and the congestion resulting from the volume of heavy traffic which crossed it daily, meant that its replacement became imperative. In 1816 it was demolished, having been paralleled for the previous three years by a new wooden bridge.

The road traffic had a profound impact upon Warrington itself, for all vehicles had to pass through the very heart of the town (a problem for which solutions only began to appear at the end of the 19th century) and this created congestion and traffic nuisance on an unprecedented scale. It also meant that stables, hostelries and inns became a significant element in the town's economy. Already by 1658 there were three coaches a week between London and Warrington, and by the end of the 1660s the network had grown considerably as routes extended further north into Lancashire. Warrington was a recognised place for over-night stops, as travellers from, for example, Liverpool (which did not have regular through coaches to London until the mid-18th century) awaited the London coach. In the early 18th century the Chester churchman Henry Prescott, who had family in the Upholland area, records in his diary on dozens of occasions that he stopped, either over-night or for dinner, at Warrington en route from Wigan to Chester. By the 1750s the improvements in roads and the expansion of traffic brought the town into much closer contact not only with London but also with other provincial centres. The journey to London had taken a week in the 1660s, but faster roads and better coaches meant that by 1760 it was down to three days (though the single fare, at two guineas [£2.10] for inside travel, was horribly expensive – perhaps £500 in modern terms). Warrington was also the post town for a vast area. The first records of a post agent in the town appear in the 1640s but after 1663, when the General Post Office was established, it chose Warrington as its main regional office. There was a fast postal service to London six days a week by 1700, when letters were collected from and distributed to the entire south of Lancashire (including Liverpool, which was a sub-office of Warrington). The new Royal Mail depots at Dallam and Westbrook have a long and illustrious ancestry!

FURTHER READING: J. Whiteley, 'The Turnpike Era' in A.G. Crosby (editor), *Leading the Way: the history of Lancashire's roads* (Lancashire County Books, 1998); K.W.L. Starkie, 'The evolution and development of the turnpike road in Cheshire', in *Cheshire History* no.39 (1999-2000); G.A. Carter, *Warrington Bridges 1285-1985* (Cheshire Libraries, 1985); J. Addy (editor), *The diary of Henry Prescott LL.B., deputy registrar of Chester diocese*, vol.1 (Record Society of Lancashire and Cheshire vol.127 [1987])

40. Developing industrialisation

The other importance of the road network was that at Warrington it linked directly with the waterway system. Heavy bulk materials such as coal and salt, manufactured goods, cheese and other agricultural products, timber and bricks were brought by road to Warrington and then sent by water down the Mersey, while other commodities, such as copper ore, sugar and tobacco, were brought upriver to the town for inland distribution or processing. Many of Warrington's

Part of Donbavand's 1772 painting of the town of Warrington, showing the new industrial area which was developing alongside the river at Bank Quay. The view shows the glassworks and the copper smelter, as well as shipping tied up at the quay itself. Behind the cones of the glass furnaces can be seen the imposing classical mansion, Bank Hall, built by Thomas Patten and now Warrington Town Hall.

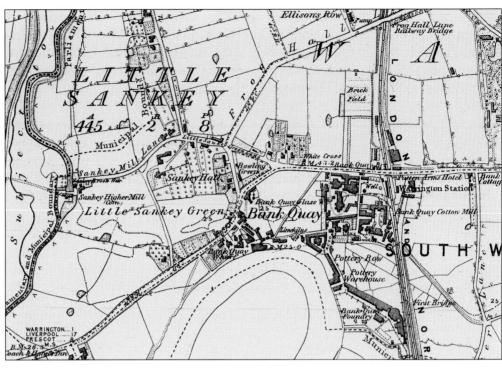

The Ordnance Survey 6-inch map of 1845, surveyed a few years after the main railway line had opened, shows the concentration of industries on the north side of the river at Bank Quay. Among the concerns named on the map are the glassworks, potteries, cotton mill, limekilns and foundry. The presence of the railway soon encouraged more extensive industrial development in the area.

Hamlet Winstanley's portrait of Thomas Patten junior, the wealthy Warrington industrialist who did so much to develop Bank Quay as an industrial area with wharves and port facilities. This picture was painted in the 1740s, shortly before Patten built his splendid new mansion at Bank Hall, on the edge of the old town.

developing industries were concentrated around the riverside at Bank Quay and Arpley, where the two elements in the transport network connected.

The pioneers in this crucial aspect of the 18th century town were Thomas Patten II (1662-1726) and his son, another Thomas (who died in 1772). The elder Thomas was responsible for improving the river up to Bank Quay, and he and his son were major investors in the Mersey & Irwell Navigation. After the works on the upper estuary were completed, Thomas senior began to import sugar and tobacco and to use Bank Quay as a warehousing and distribution centre for much of the North-West. But this site enjoyed another advantage: it was close to the coalfield, and this meant that industries which used coal as a fuel could locate there and make use of the water access to bring in other raw materials. In about 1695 a glasshouse was built by John Leafe, producing bottles, tableware and window-pane glass, and by 1717 a sugar-refinery had also been opened.

Between 1717 and 1719 the Bank Quay copper works was built by Thomas Patten senior. It used copper ore brought by sea from Cornwall (later from Parys Mountain on Anglesey) and zinc (using in making brass) from Derbyshire and Flintshire. Its smelting furnaces were fuelled by local coal and its output of copper and brass wire supplied manufacturing industries as far afield as Macclesfield and Wigan, though it also produced pots and pans, copper plate and rods. The first detailed description of copper-smelting in the area is given in Dr Richard Pococke's journal for 14 July 1750. He notes that the town 'has near it a smelting house for copper ore from Cornwall' and that copper was cast into pigs, some of which were sent to Holywell in Flintshire to be beaten into copper plates. Pococke also reports that Thomas Patten was using cast blocks, made by pouring molten copper slag into moulds, as a building material for the foundations of Bank Hall. Although this use of slag seems not to have been tried again, other uses were developed later in the

18th century. In 1776 it was being used for road-mending at Sankey and, although it was not easy to work with, John Holt recorded in 1795 that 'near Warrington, Mr. Kerfoot, who undertakes the management of the Prescot and Manchester turnpikes, has made admirable roads with copper slag ... [the] surveyor for one parish, made an attempt with copper slag, but it is difficult to get the slag sufficiently broken'.

In the early 1690s Matthew Page built a warehouse there as a rival to Patten's new premises, and established a saltworks which refined rock-salt, brought from the Northwich area, using coal from St Helens. Documents relating to this saltworks in the period 1695-1715, and to the shipments of rock salt and refined salt from Bank Quay, reveal something of the hazards of the river trade (though ultimately the saltworks itself came to an untimely end when in 1724 the entire stock of salt was destroyed by the flooding of the river):

> 66 James Gatecliffe keeper of the wharf at Bank Key near Warrington [testifies] that on 23 December [1698] he shipped on board the good ship *Hope Alice* of Liverpoole 147 bushels [4.59 tons] of rock salt ... the vessel sailed from Bank Key to a certain place called Sankey Bridge half a mile from the said Bank Key in order to load up with cheese [but it] happened to lie amongst some piles of wood which so crushed a plank in her side that she sprang a leak and sunk in the river 99
>
> *Lancashire RO QSP 823/58*

> 66 John Chaddock of Warrington [testifies] that John Taylor master of the good ship or Vessel called the *Unicorn* of Warrington loaded and took on board at Bank Key Salt Works on the 28 September [1701] 410 bushels [12.8 tons] of white salt bound for Fishguard in Wales ... from Mr Matthew Page and Mr John Kitchin, proprietors of the salt works ... but as he was sailing the said ship towards the said port of Fishguard near the coast of Holyhead in Wales [she was] by violent storm and weather sunk and then and there ... utterly perished 99
>
> *Lancashire RO QSP 888/25*

The Bank Quay copper works flourished until, in the late 1780s, it was closed as a result of the ruthless business dealings of Thomas Williams, the

Robert Booth's sketch of Litton's Mill and Patten's Quay in 1830 conveys the impression of industrial development as it gradually spread along the Mersey waterfront below Bank Quay in the early years of the 19th century.

owner of the Anglesey mines who cut off its supplies of ore to force it out of business. As we have seen, other entrepreneurs had been attracted to Bank Quay, but they always had to be aware that the Pattens ruled the roost. Their pre-eminence in the development of local industry is very apparent – with fingers in every pie, and with a developing network of power and influence, they were among the most important entrepreneurs in south Lancashire for over seventy years. The splendour of their ambition, and the wealth which flowed from their industrial ventures, was magnificently demonstrated by the construction of Bank Hall, just on the western edge of the town of Warrington, convenient for the riverside which was the source of their prosperity and – in the mid-1750s when it was built – with fine views across open country and over into Cheshire.

Within two generations the industrial success of the Pattens and those who emulated them meant that this attractive setting had been marred and spoiled by views of chimneys, smoke, railways and factories. In the mid-19th century, despite its grandeur, the house was hardly ever occupied by members of the family. By the late 1860s there was talk of the house being demolished, but in 1872, in a remarkably far-sighted and indeed visionary act, it was bought by Warrington Corporation for £22,000, much of the money being subscribed by local industrialists, and it became the new Town Hall. This preserved for posterity what is undoubtedly Warrington's finest building, one of the greatest of all the 18th-century country houses of the North-West – a decision which, given the Victorian dislike of the architecture of the Georgian period and their enthusiasm for building Gothic palaces as town halls, is in retrospect remarkable. The explanation is clear – the borough council in the 1870s hated spending money, and to buy a ready-made town hall at rock-bottom prices was a bargain they could not resist!

Thus, during the first half of the 18th century a range of new industries joined the existing craft-based trades which had been flourishing for two hundred years – spinning and weaving flax and hemp, and the domestic metal-working trades such as pinmaking (which is described in the next section) – to give Warrington an unusually diverse industrial and economic structure. Although industrial and manufacturing concerns frequently closed or contracted, the town was never in the position of relying on a single trade. This was a feature which observers from the late 18th century onwards often noted, contrasting it with the experience of places such as Blackburn and Oldham.

FURTHER READING: The industrial development of Warrington in the 18th century is discussed in S. Grealey (editor), *The Archaeology of Warrington's Past* (1976), O. Ashmore, *The industrial archaeology of north-west England* (1982), and I. Sellers, *Early Modern Warrington* (1998); see also W. Chaloner, 'Salt in Cheshire 1600-1870', in *Palatinate Studies* (Chetham Society 3rd series, vol.36, 1992)

The Growth of
Industrial Warrington

41. Looking back at the nineteenth century

During the 19th century Warrington changed almost beyond recognition

Industry, railways and workers' housing transformed the town

The older buildings gradually disappeared

Some people recorded their regrets as the old town they knew vanished

The 19th century saw those great changes which transformed not only Warrington but also every other town in south Lancashire and north Cheshire. Industrialisation brought a host of problems and opportunities. In 1800 the character of Warrington was altering as industrial development gathered pace, but it was still a busy country market town which retained its traditional crafts and domestic industries. Within thirty years, though, industry had brought unprecedented levels of pollution, squalor and poverty. People began to be nostalgic about the old days, fondly remembering a town which they thought had been a more attractive and more congenial place in which to live. Nostalgia often conceals the bad side of things – already in the later 18th century Warrington had its fair share of problems – but those negative aspects were easily forgotten.

In 1887 William Beamont, one of the great figures of Victorian Warrington, published a book taking readers on imaginary walks around the town in the early years of the century. He knew the faults of old Warrington (such as its lawlessness and reputation for drunkenness) but remembered the attractive buildings and streets of his youth:

> 66 an abundance of quaint, picturesque black and white structures … of wood and plaster, with patterns in black and white painted on their fronts, with carved weather boards on their eaves, narrow latticed windows, slightly projecting narrow gables, and roofs with dormers admitting light into their upper chambers … old white houses … of single storey, whose thatched roofs, bent and bowed like the shape of a hog's back, gave them an antique look … the picturesque old houses that formerly so bordered Church Street with architecture worth seeing are now nearly all gone, and the street is no longer what it was … its features have been altered for the worse and not improved 99

A friend of Beamont, Arthur Bennett, was more upset by the sorry state into which he felt the town had fallen by 1892, when he published *Warrington: as it was, as it is, and as it might be.* In the high days of late Victorian prosperity, he thought that a town 'more dreary or dismal, more dirty or damp, could not have been imagined, had not Widnes happily sprung into existence and revealed a still lower depth of ugliness'. He remembered, over-romantically, a time when

> 66 Warrington's streets were picturesque and her occupations cleanly, her flowing river a dream of clear loveliness, bearing on its flood the merry boaters, yielding sweetly to the embrace of strong swimmers, and affording

A relic of old Warrington vanishes: on 17 May 1904 Alderman Arthur Bennett [in bowler hat] inspects the remains of the Old Crow Inn just before its final demolition. Bennett, a pioneering conservationist and visionary, lamented the loss of such ancient landmarks while also seeking to improve the town's environment and social conditions.

to the angler a never-ending source of pleasure and profit; whilst overhead the air was clear and the sky was blue, and underfoot the soil was rich and generous to gardener and husbandman. **99**

Bridge Foot in the late 1890s, looking from Arpley towards the present-day Riverside Retail Park (then Bishop's Wharf). The smoking chimneys, and silting of the river after the building of the Ship Canal, create a somewhat desolate impression.

Bennett knew that industrialisation lay behind these changes, but he also blamed the people of the town and the borough council. He believed that Warringtonians did not care sufficiently about what happened to their town, and he campaigned for what would now be called conservation as well as for improved housing and a better environment. In truth, the effects of industrialisation here were certainly no worse than in most large industrial towns of Lancashire and Cheshire, but Bennett loved his town and had a vision of a Warrington which was clean, prosperous, well-governed, healthy and content.

42. *Warrington's railways 1825-1900*

Railways came early to Warrington and exerted a major impact upon its industrial and commercial development as well as upon its landscape. They became the framework around which the Victorian industrial town grew. The first line in the present borough was the Liverpool and Manchester, opened in September 1830 and slashing in a direct line across the grain of the countryside through Newton-le-Willows and north of Culcheth. Even before that line opened there were projects for branches to link it with nearby towns, among them the four-mile Warrington and Newton Railway from Earlestown through Winwick to a terminus at Dallam Lane in Warrington, with a freight branch to the river at Bank Quay. This was the town's first railway and gave much improved communication with Manchester and Liverpool.

Warrington's first railway was a branch from the Liverpool & Manchester line

By 1846 the town was on the main London-Glasgow trunk route

The railway network was always inconvenient for passengers

Rail development greatly enhanced Warrington's accessibility and boosted its industrial expansion

Given Warrington's geographical location, and its centuries of importance as a route centre and crossing point, it is not surprising that this branch should eventually have formed part of the main West Coast route from London to Glasgow, but that line came about in a piecemeal and awkward fashion. The Wigan Branch Railway, from Parkside, opened in 1832 and the route was extended north to Preston in 1838 and by 1848 to Glasgow. Yet until 1847 trains from the south reversed at Parkside, since the junction faced Manchester: only in 1864 was the direct line from Winwick to Golborne opened. This stretch of the route evolved 'accidentally' and the legacy of this is the double curve north of Bank Quay station and the bend south of Vulcan Village, where the 'new' main line diverges from the older route. Southwards, the Grand Junction line to Birmingham opened in 1837, crossing the Mersey by the 'Twelve Arches', one of the finest viaducts of its age. The line joined the Bank Quay branch of the Warrington & Newton Railway and the inadequate terminus at Dallam was closed. From 1837, therefore, Warrington was on a through main line, and from 1848 on one of the great national trunk routes.

The Grand Junction Railway line approaching Bank Quay station from the Mersey viaduct, c.1840. The tower of St Elphin's can be seen to the right, above the trees, while the town, after half a century of industrial growth, is now marked by an array of tall chimneys belching out smoke.

The later history of the town's Victorian railways is dominated by the theme of wasteful competition. The London & North Western Railway (formed 1846) exerted a powerful influence over the economic life of the region and was widely held to abuse its monopoly position. Other companies sought to gain access to coalfields, industrial areas and ports, and towns lobbied for new lines to break the monopoly and reduce freight rates. The first was from Warrington to Stockport (1853), part of a strategy by the Manchester, Sheffield and Lincolnshire Railway to reach Liverpool and its superabundant trade. In the same year the St Helens Railway, which had access to collieries around Widnes, opened a line along the bank of the canal via Fiddlers Ferry to Arpley. Two years later these lines were connected and linked with Bank Quay, forming a direct route from Liverpool to Stockport. The LNWR, anxious to protect its dominant position, tried to acquire any rivals and in 1864 absorbed both these small companies. In the 1870s a more powerful competitor arose. The Cheshire Lines Railway, jointly owned by the Manchester, Sheffield & Lincolnshire, the Midland, and the Great Northern, built a new line between Liverpool and Manchester, four miles south of the LMR route of 1830. The new line ran across the northern edge of Warrington and at first the CLR proposed a station at the Longford Street crossing, far from the town centre and inconvenient for potential passengers. The borough council was outraged and eventually the company built a loop line between Padgate and Bewsey via a better-placed station, Warrington Central. The last new line was the branch from Glazebrook via

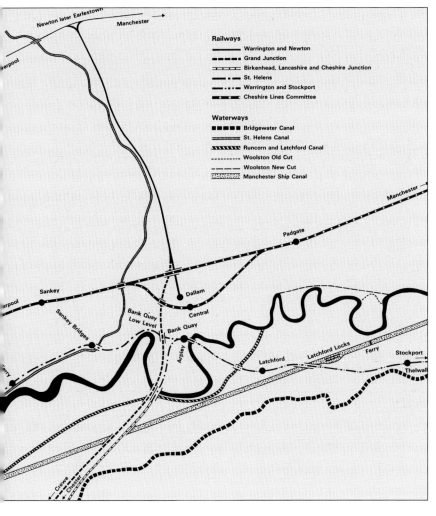

Railways
- Warrington and Newton
- Grand Junction
- Birkenhead, Lancashire and Cheshire Junction
- St. Helens
- Warrington and Stockport
- Cheshire Lines Committee

Waterways
- Bridgewater Canal
- St. Helens Canal
- Runcorn and Latchford Canal
- Woolston Old Cut
- Woolston New Cut
- Manchester Ship Canal

Opening dates of Warrington railways

1830	Liverpool and Manchester Railway
1831	Warrington and Newton Railway [branch from LMR]
1837	Warrington Bank Quay to Birmingham [Grand Junction Railway]
1850	Walton Junction to Chester via Frodsham
1853	Widnes [St Helens Railway] to White Cross
1853	Altrincham – Lymm – Wilderspool
1854	White Cross – Wilderspool
1873	Cheshire Lines Railway from Manchester to Liverpool via Padgate
1873	Loop line from Padgate to Sankey via Warrington Central
1893	Diversions associated with the Manchester Ship Canal

Culcheth to Wigan, opened in 1884, absorbed by the Great Central Railway in 1906, and intended to capture the coal traffic from Leigh and Abram. Finally, in 1893, the building of the Manchester Ship Canal meant that the lines to Crewe, Chester and Stockport had to be diverted on new alignments over impressive high-level girder bridges.

At the end of the 19th century the railway network of Warrington reached its maximum extent, with many sidings and branches serving factories and industrial complexes. The railway layout was awkward, a consequence of unrestrained competition between different companies. It would have been more efficient and convenient to have a single main station, but since 1873 Warrington has had two, unconnected and at opposite ends of the town centre. Nonetheless, the railway network greatly reinforced the town's role and it became one of the most important sources of traffic on the West Coast main line. Without the railways Warrington's later 19th-century expansion as an industrial centre would scarcely have been possible: they brought the coal to power those industries and they took away the finished goods.

FURTHER READING: G.O. Holt, *A Regional History of the Railways of Great Britain vol.10: The North-West* (David & Charles, 1986); P.A. Norton, *Railways and Waterways to Warrington* (Cheshire Libraries, 1984)

43. Brewing and Greenalls – supplying the nation

The town had a very important brewing industry from the mid-18th century

The Greenall family were intimately associated with the commercial and political life of Warrington for two centuries

The main focus of brewing was Wilderspool

Greenalls were innovative and pioneering, developing the 'tied house' system

The image of the early 19th-century brewery at the Saracen's Head *in Wilderspool was often used on Greenalls' trade advertisements [left]. The family's house can be seen next to the brewery on the right: it was later supplanted by the much more salubrious Walton Hall. The brewery was completely rebuilt in the late 1880s and the new and architecturally-impressive complex is illustrated [right] on a 1908 advert for Wilderspool Ales. This view was almost certainly drawn from a semi-aerial photograph, taken in 1901 during a visit by 'Hudson's War Balloon'.*

Brewing was one of the oldest trades in Warrington – every town had local breweries and in Warrington these went back many centuries, but the industry first assumed a more than local importance in the 1780s. Thomas Greenall went into partnership with William Orrett, the town's postmaster and also a merchant and trader, and Thomas Lyon of Appleton Hall who among other business activities owned the sugar refinery at Bank Quay. Greenall was from St Helens, where he had been involved in brewing since 1762, but was now expanding his business empire. The three men acquired the *Saracen's Head* at Wilderspool, a wholesale brewery dating from 1749 or earlier situated near the junction of Wilderspool Causeway and Greenalls Avenue. As business built up the premises quickly became inadequate and in 1791 an entirely new brewery was built on the site. The success of the venture is often attributed to the purity of water supplies from wells on the site, but there were wider factors: several local publicans, among them Peter Stubs, were already making substantial quantities of malt from Cheshire-grown barley, while – as is so often the case with Warrington industries – the excellence of transport played an important part.

Thomas Greenall and his business partner William Orrett both died in 1805. The business was bequeathed jointly to the three Greenall sons and the eldest, Edward, went into partnership in 1824 with a solicitor from Liverpool, John Whitley, who put a great deal of money into the firm and gave it the other half of its familiar name (officially adopted in 1880 but used informally many years before). A very large new brewery was built at Wilderspool in 1886, as the business moved from a local to a regional scale. This growth was helped by the other arm of the company's expanding commercial empire – the newly-rechristened organisation already had control of 195 tied houses, and this element in its development was to assume ever-greater significance as the years passed. By 1896 the number had grown to over one thousand and the

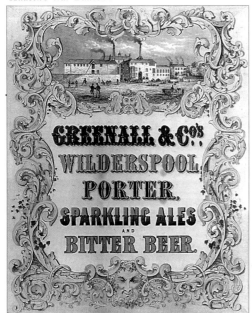

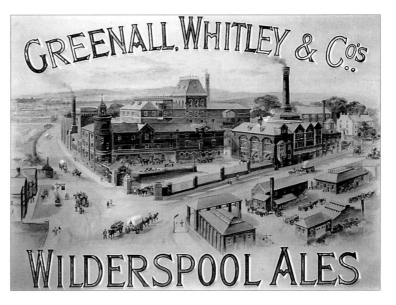

company was probably the largest owner of pubs in the country. Greenall Whitley prided itself on the efficiency and technical sophistication of its production, drawing a contrast with the often dubious methods employed by small 'backstreet' breweries and assuring customers in its promotional literature that

> ❝ only the best materials are used in the manufacture of the beer. The greatest possible care is exercised in their selection, neither time, trouble nor expense being spared with a view to turning out a really first-class article. The sanitary and other arrangements are absolutely perfect, every department being kept scrupulously clean, and the ventilating and lighting arrangements are quite up-to-date. ❞

(1908)

Although it was by far the most effective local brewery in terms of its publicity, and was by 1900 much the largest in the town, Greenall Whitley was not alone. In 1890 six other breweries were operating, the most prominent being the Dallam Brewery off Sankey Street, opened by Peter Walker in 1850 and tapping via a deep well 'an excellent natural spring of very good quality water'. Walker had taken over an existing small brewery in somewhat cramped premises in King Street four years earlier – in the early 19th century there had been several small private breweries operating in this part of the town, but that at King Street, with an output of 50 barrels a week, was the largest. Peter Walker & Son, whose products were later to be branded as 'Warrington Ales', was also innovative. In 1868 a particularly impressive engine house was built to accommodate the steam-engine which powered the plant, but the firm was also noted for the modern image of its tied houses, notably more comfortable and 'wholesome' than those of their competitors.

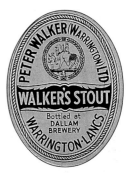

Walker's was Warrington's second most important brewery, and there was fierce local rivalry between the firm and the larger and more commercially-aggressive Greenalls.

FURTHER READING: 'Messrs Greenall, Whitley & Co. Ltd.,' in *Warrington of today* (Warrington Guardian, 1897); N.J. Slater, *A brewer's tale: the story of Greenall Whitley & Company through two centuries* (Greenall Whitley, 1980)

44. Tanneries and leather

Like brewing, the leather trades, including tanning, were a key industry in the town for over two centuries. They recalled the close links between Warrington and its agricultural hinterland – Cheshire and south Lancashire cattle were slaughtered here and their hides processed in the local tanneries as early as the 16th century. As the urban markets of the region expanded, and cattle trade increased, so the production of leather rose steadily and became an important element in the trade of Warrington market. By 1824 there were five tanneries in the town, including John Brint's in Tanners Lane, which of course acquired its name from the trade (there was a tannery here as early as 1772) and others in Friars Green, Bridge Street, Mersey Street and Latchford.

Tanning was a notoriously unpleasant trade. The stench from the decaying flesh on the hides and the rotting hair and fat, and the gross pollution of water supplies which it caused, meant that it was increasingly unacceptable in urban areas, and during the 1840s and 1850s some of the smaller town centre tanneries closed. The newer and larger concerns were located on what was

Tanning was one of the oldest industries in Warrington

By the late 18th century there were several tanneries near the town centre

In the mid-19th century large tanneries were built at Howley

The leather trade was also important: footwear and belts were produced

The industry disappeared in the early 1960s

LEFT *Dry hides arriving at the Central Tannery in Howley. The Warrington tanneries originally used locally-produced hides and skins, but by the early 20th century the industry had long outstripped local supplies, and imported them from all over the world.*

RIGHT *Fleming's Tannery in Fennel Street, illustrated in a publicity article in 1897. The rows of large rectangular tanpits can be seen behind the main buildings, while the terraced houses of the workers surround the works and sit cheek by jowl with the factory. This was typical of the tanneries in and around the town centre, but not of those at Howley which were on more spacious 'greenfield' sites by the river.*

then the edge of the town, in Tanners Lane and Orford (with seven major tanneries by 1870) and the riverside at Howley where the first tannery was opened in 1863. The development of the Winwick Street area after 1870 quickly meant that its tanneries were eventually surrounded by housing, deep within the built-up area, on sites which – unlike those at Howley, which survived until 1960 – offered no more room for expansion. Warrington in the early 20th century was the most important centre for leather production and tanning in northern England, specialising in thick leather soles for boots (the town was a major supplier of army and police footwear) and innumerable types of leather belt for driving machinery in mills and factories. For the workers the conditions in the trade were, by today's standards, appalling:

> 66 dry hides had to be got back to their natural condition ... by soaking them in water for seven days, then drawing them out of the pit and piling them flat overnight. Between sixty and eighty hides were then transferred to a pit ... called an 'old lime' [to be soaked in lime solution] ... the old lime liquor was drawn off – into the drain connected with the River Mersey, no less! A new lime liquor was made which consisted of one hundred weight of lime which was thoroughly slaked ... This was run into the pit with about 800 gallons of water. A two gallon bucket was then filled with sodium sulphide crystals and these were liquefied by blowing live steam into the bucket. This was then added to the pit [and the hides were similarly processed three more times] read for unhairing. Loosening the hair was partly achieved by the action of the lime and partly by the action of the sodium sulphide [which] was the cause of the awful smell in the lime yard of the tanneries, until you got used to it of course. The blood and dung on the hides also played a part ... the hides were then cleaned and ready for transfer to the fleshing machine. The blade of the fleshing machine was a ten-foot long steel-bladed cylinder travelling at 1500 revs per minute ... this resulted in a nice clean hide which was then given a further wash in clean water ... all were then ready for deliming and tanning 99

Jack Hamlett, who worked at Central Tanneries, Howley, from 1934 to 1960; from *Warrington Voices*

45. Peter Stubs and the file-making industry

One of the most important figures in Warrington history was Peter Stubs, born in the town in June 1756. He was found employment in the metal-working trade and by 1777 was a file-maker (tradition says that he started in 1773). In his mid-20s he became licensee of the *White Bear Inn* in Bridge Street, but continued file-making in a workshop in the inn yard. In 1802 he gave up the *White Bear* and opened a new fileworks in Scotland Road, the basis of the extensive complex of buildings occupied by the firm for almost two centuries. He was one of the people who brought the factory system to Warrington, organising his outworkers so that they no longer made tools in cottages and backyard sheds. By the time he died in 1806 he was one of the wealthiest businessmen in the town.

All sorts of specialised metal goods were produced in south Lancashire – clocks and watches at Prescot, nails and chains in the Atherton area – and there were already file-makers in Warrington and the villages on the Cheshire side.

Making files and other tools was a traditional south Lancashire industry

In the late 18th century Warrington began to specialise in this trade

The main firm, from the beginning, was Peter Stubs

Warrington files were sold all round the world and had the highest reputation

Most file-making was done by hand until the 1920s

Stockton Heath was particularly well-known for the trade and here, as elsewhere in the area, people made files in tiny workshops attached to cottages. The production of files and tools became a Warrington speciality, and the products of the town were supplied to a national market and even overseas, as well as more locally: the men who made watch parts at Prescot, for instance, used tiny files made in Warrington. It was a long, complex and difficult process and consisted of many separate stages.

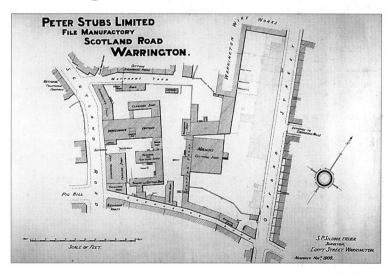

Plan of Peter Stubs' Scotland Road works in 1908. Although it had grown up piecemeal, the works was organised quite efficiently, with separate 'departments' for each stage of the file-making process.

Making a file in the 19th century

1. Cut rods of steel and shaped them to form blanks, using dies called swages
2. Smooth the blanks and make them red-hot, to soften or anneal the steel
3. Prepare to chisel the grooves on the face of the file
4. Hold the blank in a leather strap resting on a bed of pewter
5. The pewter is soft and it absorbs the impact of the hammer blows
6. Rest your elbow on your knee to steady your hand
7. Place the chisel almost vertically against the blank face of the file
8. Hit it with a hammer, making a groove in the file
9. Repeat the action hundreds of times along the length of the file
10. You won't be able to see the movements – the cutter is too fast
11. If the file is to be cross-cut it needs another set of intersecting grooves
12. Rub it down, relocate on the bench, and repeat the process
13. Rub the finished file vigorously with charcoal to remove particles of metal
14. This cleans out the grooves or teeth of the file where filings can accumulate
15. Cover it with a paste of malt dust and solids from the bottom of beer barrels
16. This helps to clean and polish the teeth and finishes off the surface
17. Heat it again to red heat
18. Plunge it into a salt and water solution to make it super-hard.

Art Deco style trade advertisement for Peter Stubs, dating from about 1930.

The variety of designs and sizes of file was almost infinite, and specialised products were made in small numbers for particular customers. By the early 20th century the firm also produced a huge range of other tools such as pliers, vices, nippers, shears, dividers and dentists' equipment. Peter Stubs' acquired a worldwide reputation for exceptional quality, continuous improvement of designs, and innovative marketing. As Lancashire and north-east Cheshire became heavily industrialised there was a constant demand for files designed for the cotton industry and machine-making trades, and it is no exaggeration to say that the Warrington file-makers provided an essential service to almost every industry in the region.

Some of the specialised files produced by Peter Stubs'

Round Bastard	Square Bastard
Shute File for Levelling	Half Round Bastard
Horse Rasp	Taper flat Bastard
Hand File Bastard	Smooth handfile
Handled Reaper 2nd Cut	Mill Saw Two Round Single Cut – 8"

Shoe Makers Rasp Punched Square Edge
Saw File 4½ Inch Double Cut
Slim Square Needle File 72 cuts/inch Safe Side
Slim Round Needle File

(part of a catalogue made by Fred Wright of Latchford, who worked for Stubs' from 1908 until 1953)

After Peter Stubs' death in 1806 two of his sons, William (1789-1854) and Joseph (1796-1861), ran the business and travelled widely in Europe and North America, selling the products. The firm became a private limited company in 1890 and in 1973 moved to new premises at Wilderspool Causeway, leaving the Scotland Road site after 170 years. By that time file-making had become a high technology business, far removed from the meticulous hand-crafting which was the rule for the first 150 years of the firm's existence.

FURTHER READING for sections 45 and 46: A background to metal-working in the district is given in O. Ashmore, *Industrial archaeology of north-west England* (1982); T. Ashton, *An eighteenth century industrialist: Peter Stubs of Warrington, 1756-1806* (Manchester University Press, 1939); E.S. Dane, *Peter Stubs and the Lancashire Hand Tool Industry* (1973)

46. Working in the file-making trade

File-making was a difficult and skilled job

The workers were badly-paid and working conditions were poor

In the Victorian period there were often strikes and labour disputes

The best way to appreciate the conditions under which people worked is to read their own testimony of times before modern employment laws, health and safety legislation, and a shorter working week. In 1943 a former Stubs' employee recalled life in the trade when he was interviewed by the *Warrington Guardian*: his memories give a flavour of life in the trade in what some people call the good old days.

❝ Apprenticeships were for a term of seven years, wages in the final year being 13s [65p] for a 66-hour week – the trade being referred to as poverty-knocking. Production was largely an affair of out-workers. The more skilled workers – the 'Wednesday men' – collected the rolled bar from the firm's warehouse every Wednesday. Forging and cutting was carried out in cottage workshops and the cut files were then brought in every two weeks. Payment was made to the worker for the file in the 'soft' or unhardened condition, and the finishing processes were then carried out on the firm's premises. The less skilled operatives – 'Saturday men' – collected their steel weekly on Saturday in the form of forged blanks. Their work consisted solely of preparing the blank and cutting it. A Stubs 'Wednesday man' rightly considered himself much superior to a 'Saturday man', and there are still men alive [1943] who are proud of having once been 'Stubs' Wednesday men'. The preparation of the file blank from the forged or rolled bar was done entirely by hand, as machine grinding had not been introduced. The bar, or blank as it is now called, was first cross-filed with a 'shoot' file – a file somewhat similar to a 16-inch hand file. It was then finished off with a plate file, both the 'shoot' and the plate file being purchased by the operative from the master. Gas, for lighting, was also charged up to the factory workers, with a different rate for summer and winter. Cutting was done entirely by hand with chisels which were also bought from the employer at 4d [2p] per dozen. The first cutting machine to be introduced was for cutting framesaw files. This was in 1896, the machine being operated by a wheel turned by hand. All finished work up to and including the cut stage was reckoned at fourteen to the dozen [i.e. the employee was paid for twelve files but had to produce fourteen]. **"**

A hand filecutter at work: this image of a craftsman working by hand in a typical small workshop dates from the early 1950s, but the scene would have been not dissimilar a century and a half earlier when Peter Stubs was starting out in the business.

Backyard workshops and cottage production remained the rule until the 1920s and earnings were always low though it was a highly-skilled trade. During a major strike at Stubs' in 1874 it was claimed that 'the men … are the worst paid skilled artizans in the Country'. A skilled filesmith who had served his long apprenticeship and worked for years might take home £1 for a 60-hour week, less than an ordinary labourer. Add to this the physical conditions in the industry, with the danger of burns and lacerations, and the constant breathing of fine metal dust during the grinding and polishing stages, and the harshness of life is clear. Women only participated in the last stage. Hardening files was undertaken by skilled employees who, as a special privilege, only worked a half-day on Saturdays. A hardener would deal with 48 dozen 4½-inch hand-files per day, during a five-and-a-half day week – 3,456 files each working week or approximately 170,000 per year. The hardened files were cleaned by women, who sat in the 'scratching shop' scouring them with coconut husks dipped in coke ashes, before rubbing them with oil, wiping off the surplus grease, and wrapping them in a 'rope paper' which had been specially seasoned to avoid any problems with spotting or rusting.

47. Pin-making

Pin-making was a specialised trade for which Warrington was famous

Pins were hand-made but, because they were so tiny, child labour was used

In the 1830s the child pinmakers were investigated by social reformers

Their reports give us detailed descriptions of the conditions in the trade

The ending of child labour forced the manufacturers to mechanise

Warrington was especially noted for the making of pins, a trade unmechanised before the 1870s. It originated in the 17th century and by the 1750s had become one of the town's most important crafts, carried out mainly in domestic premises. During the second half of the century it gradually concentrated in small workshops, most of them north of the centre around Winwick Street, Pinners Brow and Lythgoe Lane. By the 1820s the majority of the trade had been cornered by three firms, each owned by a member of the Edleston family. When the two most detailed accounts of the industry appeared in the 1830s, much of the work was still done by nimble-fingered children, working in appalling conditions in sub-standard buildings. In 1835 Sir George Head travelled around northern England and recorded in vivid detail the industries and social conditions which he encountered. His description of pin-making in Warrington is especially valuable. Pins were made of brass wire brought from Staffordshire in great rolls. The first task was to straighten the wire by stretching it between rows of pegs fixed to a table. It was then cut into lengths of five or six inches, and each bundle of pieces was given to a workman sitting at a bench:

> 66 sitting behind two little wheels, like those of a scissor-grinder, excepting that, instead of stone, they are of steel … He no sooner receives the little bundle of wires, than in an instant they are assorted in his hand like a pack of cards in an even row; one touch on each wheel perfects the points of one end; and then, by a turn of the hand, the points of the

other end are made in like manner; and the bundle handed to another operator who, by the eye alone, snips off a pin's length from each end. The cutting is performed by a large pair of scissors fixed to the table, the blade of which is as big as a shoulder of mutton. The wires are now repointed as before, till the whole are divided into pins' shafts **99**

The pin shafts were then *headed*, and this was where children, with their much smaller fingers, were employed. Each pin was held separately, and two delicate manoeuvres performed: adults were too clumsy to do the job. The first stage was to cut tiny fragments from a very fine and tightly-coiled brass wire:

66 To make the heads, two little boys are employed [exhibiting] a degree of cunning workmanship hardly to be expected from an artist so young … from a piece of elastic wire … with an ordinary pair of scissors, he snips off, as quick as he can open and shut the scissors, just two threads of the spiral …Were he to cut one thread or three, the head of the pin [would be] too large or too small … the elastic wire is prepared by another little boy in the same apartment, who rolls it round a piece of straight brass wire about three yards long, by the assistance of a large spinning wheel. As the wheel hums round, the covering creeps along from one end to another at the rate of two or three inches a second; and when the straight piece is thus entirely covered … it is drawn out without any difficulty **99**

Little girls made the pinheads. Each pin shaft was picked up and a minute double curl of brass wire threaded onto it, taken from a basin of pinheads on the lap of the little girl – Sir George noted that these coils were so tiny that it looked like a basin of poppy seeds. The girl sat in front of a machine, consisting of two little iron slabs controlled by a treadle. One turn of the treadle moved the two slabs apart. Two pin-shafts, each with its tiny coil of wire, were placed in two tiny horizontal holes, and another turn of the wheel made the two slabs move sharply together, riveting the pinheads to the shafts. The slabs were opened, and two freshly-made pins tumbled into a basin below. The pins were dipped in a tinning solution and were then inserted into a double-fold of paper ready for sale (the contemporary phrase was 'a paper of pins' and the process was known as 'pin-sheeting'). This was done by a machine controlled by a small girl: boys were never employed in this stage, on the grounds that they were dirty creatures and would soil the whiteness of the pin-papers.

FURTHER READING for sections 46 and 47: Sir George Head, *A Home Tour through the Manufacturing Districts of Great Britain* (1836) [reprint, Frank Cass, 1968]; D.A. Gatley (editor), *Child workers in Victorian Warrington: the report of the Children's Employment Commission 1843* (Staffordshire University, 1996)

FAR LEFT The large-scale Ordnance Survey map of 1850 shows pin manufactories in St John Street and Buckley's Court: these were among the larger pin-making shops, since much of the output was produced in small backyard workshops in the area of Pinners Brow, which leads off Winwick Street at Town End, though it is not named on the map.

LEFT The nearer building is the former Edleston's pinworks on Knutsford Road, photographed in about 1905 when it had become a part of the Mersey Works which produced pins, files and other tools.

48. Working in the pin-making trade

Sir George Head, so impressed with the extraordinary dexterity of the children, made no comment upon the employment of child labour. Others were more aware of that dark side of the trade. In 1841 approximately 560 children in Warrington between the ages of five and 14 were listed as workers. Of these 424, or 76 per cent, were in pin-making. It is common to think of Lancashire's coal and cotton industries as the employers of children, but many other trades

The 1843 report on pin-making highlighted the role of child labour

The working conditions in the industry were extremely bad

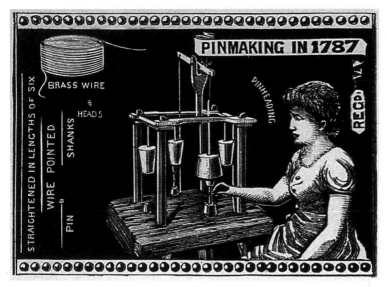

PINMAKING IN 1787

BRASS WIRE
HEADS
SHANKS
PIN
WIRE POINTED
STRAIGHTENED IN LENGTHS OF SIX
PINHEADING
REG'D. V.Y.

Illustration of a young child using pin-making machinery in the late 18th century, from an undated Edleston trade catalogue probably of the 1890s. The costume of the girl, and her casual nonchalance with which she is operating the equipment, are both far from truthful. The workers had to use intense concentration in working the machinery and in handling the minute scraps of wire from which pins were made.

did so and the Warrington pin-makers were one of the most important. Of the child pin-makers, 190 were aged 10 or less – the youngest, two six-year-old boys.

In 1843 the Child Employment Commission made a detailed investigation of the trade. Its report gives a wealth of information about early Victorian working-class life in Warrington. The Commission was especially concerned by the lack of schooling, and the possibility of immorality when children of both sexes worked in close proximity – the language of the girls was noted as being deplorable. The children earned pitifully little: for small pins a shilling [5p] per pound weight produced, for larger pins (which were easier to make) a mere penny [roughly ½p] per pound. A very skilled pinmaker could produce seven or eight pounds of pins each week. It is almost impossible to grasp the mind-numbing repetitive and painstaking labour involved and the smallness of the sums earned. One observer noted that 'it's a poor business, pin-making'. Another claimed that

> 66 at pin-making a person … can, if he or she has 'handled a pin' in earlier life, earn just enough to keep from starving 99

There were also dangers. Pin-making was less hazardous that the heavier industries, but the machines pinched the fingers, and bruising and torn skin were common. Pin-makers spent long hours hunched over their work, leading to eyestrain and crooked limbs. The children worked crowded on long benches in badly-ventilated rooms: smoky peat fires were kept burning even in summer months to soften the brass wire (peat gave a gentler heat than coal which might have burned the wire).

> 66 the children coming from that occupation have looked unusually ill, delicate and feeble; thin, no muscle … consumption [tuberculosis] has been the prevailing disease … [from] leaning over the bench on which they head their pins and to the confinement … they were subject to 99
> John Sharp, surgeon

Dr James Kendrick, who each week gave many hours of his time providing free advice and medical care to the town's poor, felt that the pin-makers were particularly unhealthy – much more so than those in the cotton mills or glass works, though he wisely notes that the main cause of ill-health everywhere was simply that people worked excessively long hours. Of the child pin-makers he says, 'they are poor and weakly, from being badly-fed and placed many together in rooms not sufficiently airy'. By the 1870s pin-making was declining. The mechanisation of the industry was in progress, hastened by the increasingly tight laws which prevented the employment of small children.

Adults could not make pins by hand as efficiently as children, so the development of machinery was essential. Today there is little trace, and little recollection, of this industry, but the reports of 1835 and 1843 mean that we know more about it in detail, and more about its workers, than any other industry in Victorian Warrington.

49. Fustian-cutting and velvet-making

The specialised textile trade known as fustian-cutting flourished in Warrington, Culcheth and Lymm for 150 years. Fustian is a general name for various fabrics, such as corduroy, velvet and velveteen, in which a high pile is created by cutting a raised loop of the weft which is woven into the cloth. It is the cutting of the loop, giving a long pile, which identifies fustians – in other cloths, such as denim, the pile is shorn by horizontal cutting across the cloth. The Lancashire fustian industry usually made cloth with a linen warp and a cotton weft. Cutting was a highly-specialised craft, because the cutters had to walk up and down lengths of cloth, passing an exceptionally sharp fine-bladed knife through the loops in one continuous motion. The loops were later known, from their form, as 'tunnels' but when the industry was unmechanised they were called 'races'. In each inch-width of cloth there would be 40-42 such races, and over the breadth of the cloth as a whole there would be 600 for the coarsest to 1,000 for the finest. By the 1880s the average length of a piece of cloth was 120-150 yards and it is easy to imagine the immense distances which could be travelled in moving up and down the long tables, all the time passing the razor-sharp blade along the race and through the loops. It has been estimated that the skilled cutters would walk about twenty miles each day.

Fustian-cutting was a highly skilled and specialised craft

It created the distinctive pile of corduroy and other cloths

There was a long tradition of the craft in the Warrington area

It was often done by women and older children

Fustian-cutting was primarily a domestic industry. The long garret along the second floor of this row of cottages in Manchester Road was a fustian-cutting workshop, illuminated by the distinctive large windows.

Warrington, although not one of the main textile towns, was an important centre for cutting: indeed, this finishing trade was particularly concentrated in towns and villages just beyond the main textile districts. Most cutting was done in workshops, often running in long attics above the workers' housing. There the master-cutters employed up to forty people. Lymm was another important local centre of the trade, which in the late 19th century employed about 200 people in the village, with cutting shops in Clay Terrace, Cherry Lane and Arley View. The first detailed trade directory of Warrington, published in 1834, lists 60 fustian-cutters, most of whom lived north and east of the town centre, around Church Street, Oliver Street, and Buttermarket Street. In 1869 there were 61 listed fustian-cutters, but their addresses show that the trade had become less concentrated and they were to be found in most parts of the town.

In 1840 there were about fifty such cutting shops in the town, as well as many smaller backroom shops.

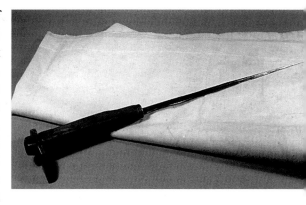

The fustian-cutter's knife typically had a very long, narrow and exceptionally sharp blade, which could be slid through the tiny loops in the pile of the cloth. The knife here rests on a folded piece of fustian, which has been partly-cut.

This was one of the last parts of the textile industry to be mechanised – in 1900 it had been almost unchanged for two hundred years. Payment was by piecework, at a rate of 8s. to 15s. per week (40p-75p) for a working day from 7 a.m. to 7 p.m. including two hours for meals. Special jobs were continued into the small hours, so as not to leave cloth unfinished, a particularly difficult task only feasible for skilled workers because poor lighting and exhaustion could produce errors – a cut even fractionally misplaced would ruin the appearance and value of the entire piece. Much of the work was done by women and older children – in Lymm women returned to work soon after giving birth, keeping their babies in cradles under the cutting-tables where they breathed the dust-laden atmosphere. This was probably responsible for the exceptionally high incidence of respiratory diseases among the fustian-cutters and their families. Workers might take less valuable cloth home to cut, but since all damage had to be paid for by the cutter there was no incentive to do this once larger cutting-shops had been set up in the 1840s and 1850s.

In 1899 the United Velvet Cutters Association Limited amalgamated the principal firms in the industry and absorbed many of the local cutting-shops. Mechanisation finally came in 1911 with the commercial production of a velvet-cutting machine, invented by the Netherwood brothers of Huddersfield. In 1912 the United Velvet Cutters Association opened its factory in Warrington, using the new machines, and in its heyday in the 1930s this employed over 450 people, becoming one of the town's largest industries. A new cutting-shed was built in stages between 1920 and 1932, and when finished was said to be the largest in the world, but in the 1950s the world market changed, competition from other countries became intense, and the demand for velvets and similar textiles was declining. In March 1959 the Warrington works closed.

FURTHER READING: D. Winterbotham, 'Sackclothes and fustyans and such like com'odyties', in E. Roberts (editor), *A History of Linen in the North West* (CNWRS Lancaster University, 1998)

50. The Warrington cotton industry

Cotton-spinning and weaving was an important Warrington industry

The town was not one of the main cotton towns but was a pioneer of steam power

The industry declined in the early 20th century

There are many oral history reminiscences of working at Armitage and Rigby

Warrington was not one of the leading Lancashire cotton towns and here the industry never occupied the dominant role that it enjoyed in places such as Bolton, Preston or Oldham. Nevertheless, cotton came early to Warrington and the one main factory, Cockhedge Mill, was comparatively large by Lancashire standards. The early cotton industry of south-east Lancashire was based on the availability of water power, for which Warrington had little potential, but when steam power provided an alternative the town was conveniently placed near the south Lancashire coalfield and able to benefit from its almost unsurpassed transport links.

In 1787 Peel's Cotton Works at Latchford was opened, the first cotton mill in the area and said by some to be first steam-powered mill in Lancashire. It was followed by a considerable number of small enterprises and a few of greater significance: in 1808 Thomas Ainsworth's Latchford spinning mill had 38,000 spindles and Naylor & Co. at Cockhedge mill had 12,000. These were medium-sized businesses by regional standards. Power-weaving was gradually introduced from 1810 and in 1825 there were eight steam-powered mills in Warrington, six spinning cotton and two weaving cloths including velveteen, calicoes and muslins. Warrington had close connections with the Bolton cotton industry – local cloth was sent to Bolton for bleaching and finishing, and several of the leading entrepreneurs, such as John Cockshott and Thomas Naylor, were Bolton men. In 1830, 23 different cotton factories were listed in the rate returns for Warrington, although most were of little wider significance.

The uncertainty of the local industry was demonstrated by the catastrophic failure of Cockshott & Green's Cockhedge Mills in 1829, when much local distress was caused. This collapse followed a long period of difficulty in the Warrington cotton industry. In the summer of 1826 there was a widespread fear of civil unrest in the cotton districts and the Wharf Mill on Mersey Street, one of the Cockshott factories, was guarded with a cannon at the entrance and paving stones stacked on the roof to use as missiles against possible rioters. A year later the mill was fired by arsonists, and shortly afterwards a flood swamped the buildings. The industry survived these setbacks and expanded rapidly during the 1830s: in 1841, with over 1,600 people employed either in mills or in handloom weaving, cotton and fustian were together the largest industry in the town, though that position was not sustained and textiles became relatively less important in the later 19th century. In 1902 the *Warrington Guardian* printed some recollections by Robert Davies, then in his 90s. He recalled life in the Warrington mills in the late 1820s. His father had been a partner in the Waterloo Mill at Latchford:

Robert Booth's 1830 sketch of the industrial areas north-east of the town centre shows the conical glass furnace (centre) and in the background to the right the newly-built Cockhedge cotton mill. It is topped with a tower from which the bell tolled each morning to summon the workers from their homes for a long day in the factory.

66 The workers earned low wages and were poorly clad, few of the men and boys wearing a jacket on working days, and the girls going about bare-headed, except in cold weather, when a shawl was drawn about their heads. All wore clogs, and their clothes were oily and flecked with cotton-down. They were called 'cotton dollies' and the hours of work were unlimited. I shall never forget hearing a cotton operative address a public meeting in later days. 'When I were a lad', he said, 'we geet to work by 6 o'clock, had ½ an hour for breakfast, an hour for dinner, ½ an hour for ??, and geet hoam sometimes at 8 and even 9 o'clock, weshed us and tumble into bed, and geet up agean when th'owd bell rung at half past five. You dunnot know you live nowadays. 99

More recently, Mrs. E. Hatton, who began work at Armitage and Rigby's mill before the First World War, wrote down her recollections:

The weaving shed at Cockhedge in the early 1950s. The concentration of the weaver, watching for broken threads and other flaws, contrasts with what the picture cannot reveal – the deafening noise and clatter of the machinery, the dust and lint in the atmosphere, and the smell of the oil used to lubricate the great looms.

" I was 13 years old ... a helper for a four loom weaver. I had to carry the finished cuts (cloth) to the warehouse and brought weft from the warehouse whenever it was required. My wages were 3s 6d [17½p per week] that was paid me by the four loom weaver who I worked for, if she had no change I had to wait for it till Saturday. After two years I was put on two looms when my wages were between £1 and £1 10s [£1.50]. Work began at 6 every morning and finished at 5.30 pm Monday to Friday and 12 noon Saturday we had ½ hour for breakfast and 1 hour for dinner ... the gates were closed at 6 o'clock, everybody who was late their name was taken ... No tea breaks and if you was seen talking we were sent home. We cleaned the looms during meal times so we could keep the looms running. No rest room and if anyone was hurt they went to the joiners shop where they received first aid if the joiner was in. We carried the finished cuts on our shoulder to the warehouse where they were weighed and examined, any spots of oil we had to go to the warehouse to clean them off, any faults and we were fined various amounts between 2d and 1s [1p and 5p]. Any breakdown of the engine all looms stopped and so did our money "

Warrington Voices, p.74

Ethel Whitfield went to work at Cockhedge in 1915, when she was 13, with a wage of 3s. 0d. [15p] a week. She remembered that, soon afterwards, many of the men went to the war and the girls could graduate to machines and earn better wages. Later she was chosen to be a guide, helping to show visitors around the mill, and in her recollections she described the different processes which were displayed on the tour:

" The raw cotton came as bales to the cotton shed and these were broken open by a man with an axe. Then the big pieces of cotton were taken away in a wheelbarrow or skip to the carding room which was on the bottom floor. Next you went up to the ring rooms where the mules spun long bobbins of cotton and later the smaller bobbins which went on the shuttles in the weaving shed. As it went from machine to machine the thread got narrower. The spinners were all on piece work so if they had a broken end they'd take the bobbin out, take the thread and twist it and make it one piece again, without stopping the machine. Next you went to the weaving shed and that was all on one floor. When I first went there you learned on two looms and if you were quick on your job you went to four looms ... After the weaver had finished a piece of cloth it went to the picking room where they looked it over to pick out the flaws and then it went on a big machine to be folded. From there it went to the warehouse for the buyers to see and then it went to other mills. If there were any pieces with flaws in that was cut off and the workers could buy it. "

Warrington Voices, p.75

FURTHER READING: For the general history of cotton, see G. Timmins, *Four centuries of Lancashire cotton* (Lancashire County Books, 1996) and M. Williams and D.A. Farnie, *Cotton Mills of Greater Manchester* (Royal Commission on the Historical Monuments of England, 1992) chapter 1; J. Hayes, *Warrington Voices* (2000); Warrington local studies collection holds manuscript material relating to the cotton industry, including Cockhedge Mills.

51. Wire-working

During the 19th century Warrington became the world's most important centre for the production of wire, with two firms, Nathaniel Greening & Sons and Ryland Brothers Ltd., dominating the industry. Rylands, in particular, was an important influence in the economy of the town, and of its appearance, while the Rylands family exerted a powerful political and social role. Their forebears were weavers from Culcheth, who in the early 18th century moved to Warrington and became leading figures in the sailcloth-manufacturing trade. In about 1805 John Rylands began to draw wire in a small mill in Bridge Street, though there was already wireworking in the town – William Houghton had established a business in Tanners Lane about a quarter of a century earlier. Rylands recognised the great potential for wire in agriculture, industry, mining and shipping. He took as a partner Nathaniel Greening, who had been in Warrington since 1799 in the copper wire trade. Greening had the know-how, Rylands the capital: a perfect combination. In 1817, following rapid expansion, they moved to Church Street and carried on the joint business until 1843, when they parted and set up separate rival concerns. Rylands stayed in Church Street and Greenings moved to Bewsey Street. There were several other wire-working firms in the town in the early 19th century, most of which were soon absorbed by the two giants.

The growth in the industry can be seen from census figures: in 1841, 51 people in Warrington were working in the wire-drawing trades, and ten years later the number had more than doubled to 119. In 1901, though, Rylands alone employed 1,100 men and produced over 60 tons of wire each week. Church Street works seemed to grow almost continuously and in the late 1820s was already notorious as one of the town's worst polluters. By 1905, when Rylands was the largest British manufacturer of wire, it occupied a great swathe of land at the eastern end of the town centre, extending for a third of a mile from the railway to Church Street (with the Boteler Grammar School tucked rather uncomfortably between the two main works).

> 66 While mentioning these pioneers of the wire trade in Warrington it is only right to add that the first man to weave wire by power … in England was Mr. Locker, who was a valued factor in the progress of the trade in Warrington when in its infancy 99
> *Liverpool Mercury*, 29 April 1901

The technological innovation of this period was crucial in assisting the expansion of the two large firms. In 1811 James Locker had managed to weave wire on a loom, and in the 1840s the use of steam to power the wire-looms was

Wire-drawing and wire-working became Warrington's greatest industry

It expanded rapidly in the 1840s and 1850s and continues today

The industry was dominated by two firms - Rylands and Greenings

The wire was exported across the world

The 1908 Warrington trade directory includes this advertisement for Rylands. The range of products, and the proud claim of a worldwide market, reinforces the message that this was Warrington's most important industry.

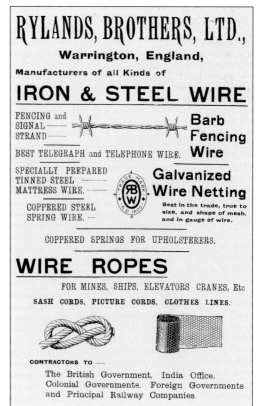

RYLANDS, BROTHERS, LTD.,
Warrington, England,
Manufacturers of all Kinds of
IRON & STEEL WIRE
FENCING and SIGNAL STRAND ——   **Barb Fencing Wire**
BEST TELEGRAPH and TELEPHONE WIRE.
SPECIALLY PREPARED TINNED STEEL MATTRESS WIRE. ——   **Galvanized Wire Netting**
COPPERED STEEL SPRING WIRE. ——   Best in the trade, true to size, and shape of mesh, and in gauge of wire.

COPPERED SPRINGS FOR UPHOLSTERERS.

WIRE ROPES
FOR MINES, SHIPS, ELEVATORS CRANES, Etc
SASH CORDS, PICTURE CORDS, CLOTHES LINES.

CONTRACTORS TO ——
The British Government, India Office, Colonial Governments, Foreign Governments, and Principal Railway Companies.

made possible. This meant that huge quantities of cheap wire meshes, screens and cloths could be woven, giving Warrington an internationally-important trade central to the development not only of the town but of many industries themselves – thus, the weaving of extremely fine wire gauze, pioneered in Warrington, was essential to the production of effective safety lamps for miners. In 1879 Thomas Locker, the son of James Locker, set up a small wire-weaving business in a workshop in Market Street. Within five years the growth of trade meant he had to move into a weaving shed 90 feet long, between Ellesmere Street and Church Street, and by 1890 this had itself been doubled in size. The company innovated in the development of perforated metal products, crucial to many newly-expanding food industries – sieves and perforated screens for grading flour, rice, and coffee for example – as well as to other processing trades such as cement-manufacturing.

The interior of part of Rylands' Church Street wireworks in about 1900. Although this was one of the world's largest wireworks, much of the manufacturing process was still, in essence, a craft process with manual labour being the main motive power. 'Health and Safety' was scarcely thought of, in the cluttered and crowded workshop. The site is now occupied by Sainsbury's.

Firth's Florence wire mill, shown in a 1908 advertisement. Although idealised (not least, because the surroundings are not shown at all), the view does reveal the orderly and planned design and – by the standards of the time – spacious layout of the works, which had been built on a greenfield site behind Howley Lane in the 1880s.

In 1864 the great Whitecross Wireworks at Bank Quay was opened by Frederick Monks, who had started his working life as an apprentice at Rylands. This was the most modern and largest works in the town and the first designed 'from scratch', with its own foundries and direct rail access. By 1905 it employed over 1,000 people and specialised in a range of new products, designed to capture the latest markets: galvanised, coppered and tinned wires, fencing wire, roofing nails (the endless rows of terraced houses being built across south Lancashire created a major demand), and wire ropes for tramways, colliery winding gear, and battleship hawsers.

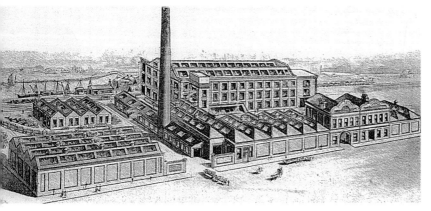

The expansion of these firms, and the construction of new works in the later 19th century, meant that by 1910 wire-working was, by a considerable margin, the most important element in the economy of Warrington, employing more people than any other industry. Wire-drawing, the most specialised element in the production, was a highly-skilled trade and the wire-drawers were the elite of the town's workforce:

❝ Wire drawers used to walk around with their best serge suits on, a gold
    guard across their chest and a gold watch on. They had Best Rooms in the

pubs. They put a penny extra on the drinks over the bar price to keep the rank and file out ... Labourers would no more dream of going in a Best Room than they would of flying. This applied all over Warrington because of all the wire works ... The wire drawers had this status that went with the lolly ... They'd got that extra quid, which was the difference between their standards of living and yours. **"**

Harry Hardman, in *Warrington Voices pp.82-83*

FURTHER READING: Despite its importance, there is no general history of wire in Warrington: see G.A. Carter, *The Whitecross Company Limited 1864-1964* (1964); [H. Janes], *Rylands of Warrington 1805-1955* (1956); *A History of Greenings, 1799-1949* (privately published, 1949); useful information is given in business and trade directories from the 19th and 20th centuries; the archives of Greenings are in Warrington local studies collection, ref. ms 2827.

52. Foundries and ironworks

There was a very long tradition of metal-working in the Warrington area, including pin-making, wire-drawing and the production of files and hand tools. However, it was not until the 1840s that iron and steel itself became an element in the town's economy, when the first important ironworks was opened at the Dallam Forge by William Neild, Henry Bleckly and Thomas Fell. Warrington was in important ways a difficult location for an iron industry – it was not on the coalfield, though close to it, and it had no local supplies of iron ore. It was, however, a major iron *using* area, and this was a prime consideration in the development of the Dallam works. The continued expansion of the metalworking trades created a demand for steel bars and rods – it was said in 1908 that

> Metalworking was a long-established local speciality
>
> In the mid-19th century foundries and ironworks were started in the town
>
> The wire industry created a large demand for iron rods
>
> Warrington became a major centre for the production of metal goods

66 Great difficulties had to be surmounted in the establishment and extension of the iron trade in competition with older iron districts of Yorkshire, Staffordshire and South Wales, which had for years enjoyed a well-deserved reputation ... all the world over ... in Lancashire there was no supply of trained labour connected with the trade, and this, as well as material, had to be imported from a distance **"**

Warrington Guardian Yearbook, 1908

In 1865 the Dallam Forge Company was established, coinciding with the opening of the Warrington Wire Iron Company, which produced wire rods, iron sheetings, hoops and bars. The two firms amalgamated in 1874, together with one of Wigan's largest colliery companies, under the title of Pearson & Knowles Coal and Iron Company. By 1908, when the company employed 4,500 people in the Warrington area, it was turning out about 2,800 tons of iron and steel products each week, together with 3,000 pairs of railway engine wheels and axles (Thomas Knowles, one of the partners, was a director of the LNWR), bridge girders, industrial plant fittings, tanking and valves, steel tubing and castings. On the eve of the First World War the complex of foundries and furnaces, wireworks, sidings and warehousing occupied a large

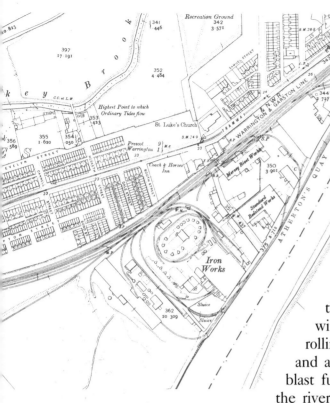

The 1905 Ordnance Survey map shows the great Monks Hall iron and steelworks along the banks of the Mersey. The works was integrated with steel-using factories including the bedstead, tube and rivet works. Over a mile of railway sidings threaded through the site linking with the LNWR line to Widnes, while Atherton's Quay on the river remained in regular use for waterborne deliveries (compare with the view opposite).

triangle of land north of Bewsey Road alongside the main railway line to Wigan.

In 1874 Warrington's second great ironworks opened on the north bank of the river at Atherton's Quay, just downstream from Bank Quay in an area which had started to acquire small industries and warehouses back in the early 18th century. The business was founded by Frederick Monks, the wire-drawer once apprenticed to Rylands Brothers who ten years earlier had started the new Whitecross Works. He was joined by his brother-in-law, William Hall, and as Monks, Hall & Co. the firm eventually became one of the largest ironworking companies in the world. By 1900 there were three forges on the site, with 25 iron-puddling furnaces, three forge mills, five re-rolling mills, a bedstead works, a welding and tube works, and a rivet works. The company brought in pig iron from blast furnaces which it owned at Scunthorpe, and although the riverside location was originally a key to its success (two ships owned by the firm exported metal goods to the Continent and brought in scrap iron for re-smelting) it came to depend on its excellent railway connections.

> 66 I will never forget that magical place – or so it seemed to me at the time – where huge, hot slabs of metal were rolled into sheets. At night in the dimly-lit mills the sparks would shoot off like fireworks from the glow of the metal. It was very hard work and grandad was literally wet through with sweat and this was all through his working life. 99
>
> Ernie Day, in *Warrington Voices*

There was also a multitude of smaller industrial concerns which used sheet metal and wire produced locally, or exploited the technical expertise of the Warrington workforce. Wire from the town's works was not only sent overseas and across the UK but also formed the basis of other manufacturing concerns in the town itself. Thus, the important bedstead and mattress industry developed in the second half of the 19th century, including (apart from the Atherton's Quay works operated by Monks) the Firth Company, which began operations in Firth Place, Froghall Lane in 1883 and in 1895 acquired the Florence Mills at Howley. The company produced a wide range of wire cloths and screens, but it began to specialise and its products were sold worldwide:

> 66 no matter where one goes it is impossible to find mattresses of better quality and finish than those turned out at the Florence Mills … the mattresses are fitted up in frames of the best American polished pitch pine, and are firmly braced together, perfectly adjustable and packed in small compass when required for shipment 99
>
> *Warrington Guardian Yearbook*, 1908

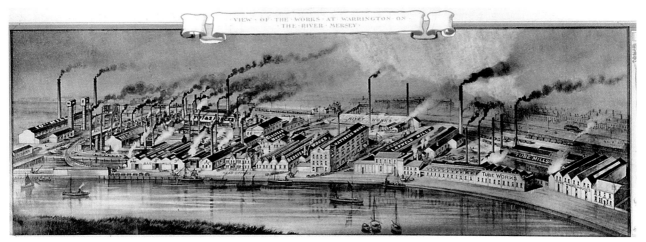

An unsung but very important late Victorian industry, which made a tremendous difference to the domestic lives of millions, was the production of gas cookers, stoves and other equipment. Richmonds, the pioneer, began to produce cookers in Scotland Road but in 1906 moved to the Latchford site on the north bank of the Ship Canal, while its great local rival, Fletcher Russell, opened its works at Wilderspool Causeway.

> 66 the Harris family used to pick up pig iron from Latchford railway station and take it to Richmonds by horse and cart. Then it was placed on the pig bank there for moulding and casting. There was the core shop where they made cores for things like gas burners. The mill room was where … you used to mix the enamel. Another part was the shot-room where they used to clean all the castings. The shot was very fine pellets fired under great pressure through a fine nozzle … The men went in a diver's suit and air was pumped into them. I worked on the air vents which used to extract the fumes. You also had the spray department and the mottling department 99
>
> Walter Norris, describing the 1930s, in *Warrington Voices*

Such industries reflected the town's metal-working skills and capitalised on its excellent location. They also indicate that Warrington's economy was quick to adapt to demand in the years before 1900 as the 'consumer age' dawned. When in 1884 Britain's first aluminium plant opened at Bank Quay, a new era in the metal-working industry began, for this was destined to become one of the most fundamental materials of 20th-century building and industry.

FURTHER READING: D.C. Johnson, *Industry and employment in Warrington 1800-1982* (University of Manchester MA thesis 1982); P. Croft, *The evolution of Warrington's townscape* (University of Hull BA dissertation, 1969) has useful material on industrial development; see also *Warrington of Today* (Warrington Guardian, 1897) for its sections on individual firms.

Artist's impression of the Monks Hall and related works, from an advertisement of about 1910. Note how almost forty large chimneys, and many smaller ones, belch out dark smoke: today no company would ever contemplate advertising itself as a polluter in this way, but in the early 20th century the message was stark and simple: smoking chimneys equal jobs in the factory equal prosperity for the town and its people.

53. Soap town: Crosfield's

Soap was another important element in Warrington's industrial growth and its products became a household name, while the soapworks at Bank Quay is still a landmark for all travellers on the main West Coast railway line. Joseph Crosfield, the founder of the business, was born here in 1792, though his

Soap-making was started in the town in 1815 by Joseph Crosfield at Bank Quay

By the late 19th century Warrington was a main centre of soap-making

The Bank Quay works expanded piecemeal and the site was cramped

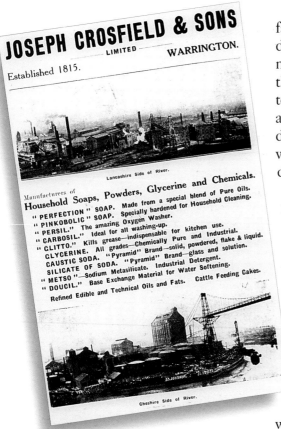

ABOVE *This advertisement for Crosfield's, from the 1935 Warrington trade directory, speaks for itself. PERSIL, 'The amazing Oxygen Washer', had transformed the firm's fortunes, though by this time it had been under the ownership of Levers for 16 years.*

BELOW *The large soap pans at Crosfield's, 1904. Although the pans were on a much larger scale* *than before, the technology of soapmaking had hardly changed in 200 years: the large paddles which stirred the contents can be seen at the left of each pan. However, the building, with its light and airy character, is in the forefront of technological progress: note the steel-girder construction of the roof, hardly different from the type of design which might be used today, a century later.*

family originated in Kendal. In 1815 Joseph bought a disused factory at Bank Quay and adapted it for soap-making. It was an ideal location, close to the coalfield and the Cheshire saltfield, and with its own wharf where 100-ton vessels could unload imported raw materials. It was also an ideal time: demand for soap was growing fast, for domestic use and also for the Lancashire textile industries, where huge quantities were used in the bleaching and dyeing processes.

Soap was made from tallow [beef fat], rendered down in large 'melting coppers' and mixed with imported palm oil. Liquid alkali or *lye* was produced from the ash of seaweed, brought from Scotland and Ireland, made caustic with the addition of lime. A boiling solution of caustic lye was pumped into the molten fat and stirred constantly. The soap separated and a strong brine solution (hence the Cheshire salt) was added to float it to the surface. The lye was pumped off and the process repeated with an even stronger solution, before the semi-liquid soap was ladled into vats, mixed with colours and perfumes, and carried in buckets to the 'frame room', where it was poured into wooden moulds to solidify. Finally, it was cut with wires into bars and blocks. High-quality toilet soaps were separately produced by remelting the soap, refining it, and mixing it with superior scents and dyes. Soft soap, made from whale oil, seal oil or linseed oil, retained most of its lye content and was stored in barrels. Candles were also made from the tallow and palm oil.

Business grew steadily. In 1837 there were five boiling coppers, and about 900 tons of soap were produced annually: the firm was at that time about 25th in size of the 296 soap manufacturers in England. Joseph Crosfield (who died in 1844) diversified into chemicals and related trades, buying a share in Robert Gamble's alkali works at St Helens and losing a good deal of money on other speculative business ventures. His son George, 24 when his father died, was more prudent. By the early 1860s the Bank Quay works was one of the five largest in Britain. More space was always needed, though the site was constricted by other industries and the river, while the railway line, so valuable for transport, was a barrier to eastward growth. In 1856-1872 Crosfield's bought up most of the remaining open land south of Liverpool Road, but for many years the unplanned piecemeal layout presented major problems. Indeed, in the mid-1880s William Lever, who opened his own rival soap factory next door in a former chemical works and there produced the first

Sunlight soap in 1885, decided that the problem of inadequate land was insoluble. With his interest in planning, modern methods and better conditions for the workers, he founded Port Sunlight as an alternative, but retained the Warrington plant and before long had gobbled up his older rival.

In the late 1870s Crosfield's developed close links with the fast-growing Brunner Mond & Co, to exploit cheaply-produced caustic soda from the Winnington works, and in 1883 the Warrington factory became one of the first industrial plants in the world to have electric lighting. The company was a pioneer of modern advertising, developing new ways of packaging and wrapping soap, and promoting attractive brand names such as La Belle, Duchess, and Countess. Yet there were problems. Nationally, about 260,000 tons of soap were produced in 1891, about five per cent manufactured by Crosfield's. In that year the company had about 750 employees, compared with about 300 in 1885, but though output grew continuously, the company could not increase its *overall* share of a fast-expanding market. Other firms (notably, of course, Lever Brothers) were growing more rapidly. But as early as 1896 the company was also producing what was known as 'dry soap' – in other words, soap powder – and it was this which would transform its prospects during the 20th century … but not under the ownership of the Crosfield's.

FURTHER READING for sections 53 and 54: A.E. Musson, *Enterprise in soap and chemicals: Joseph Crosfield and Sons Limited 1815-1965* (Manchester University Press, 1965)

54. Crosfield's: employers and employees

Although their reputation was overshadowed by the philanthropy of William Lever, Crosfield's were progressive employers. They had a workers' sick club as early as the 1860s, long before most large companies, and after 1903 had a fully-fledged staff welfare scheme. The company enjoyed good labour relations, partly because of such gestures but also because the soap industry was less affected by trade depressions, short-time working and wage cuts than many traditional trades. The staff were taken on excursions – in 1869, for example, 250 went to Llangollen and in 1883 over a thousand on a special train to Blackpool – and teas and fetes events were held. This may seem modest by today's standards, but it was unusually enlightened for the late Victorian period. The explanation lies in the Crosfield family themselves, with their firm belief in the work ethic, sobriety, education, self-improvement and respectability. They were generous donors to worthy causes and to the town, donating to many churches and schools, contributing £100 to the building of the Museum and Library in 1854, helping to found the School of Art, and holding 'drink-free evenings for working men'. In 1872 they gave

The Crosfield's Mixed Choir, 1904: the sober and socially-committed Crosfield family encouraged and supported the provision of leisure facilities and wholesome out-of-hours activities for their workforce, regarding this as an alternative to the public house and other undesirable pastimes.

Crosfield's were progressive employers

They believed that some element of workers' welfare was important

The family were major benefactors to the town, supporting philanthropic causes

most of the money with which the Corporation purchased Bank Hall and Park for the town. They were old-fashioned Liberals, strongly in favour of free enterprise and yet also reformers and champions of social responsibility.

> 66 When I started at Crosfield's [in 1866] it was a very small place, in fact the Works were in a field. There were very few hands employed; we knew everyone by name … my first job was running lurries from the cutters to the cutting machines. All soap was cut by the hand box – we had no patent cutting machines … We had to carry all the runnings to the frames and mix them in by hand crutch – we had no mixers in those days, I can assure you … We did not make many varieties, only three – pale, brown, and blue mottle. The soap was pumped down spouts, some we carried in pails on our heads … all the soap was boiled by fire, no steam then … 99
>
> quoted in Musson, *Enterprise in soap and chemicals*

55. Glass-making

Glass-making was a small-scale Warrington industry in the 1690s

It was re-established in the late 1750s at Bank Quay

By 1825 there were half a dozen glasshouses in the town

Robinson's of Warrington produced glassware until 1933

There was a glasshouse at Bank Quay as early as 1695, but that venture did not last: the founder, John Leafe, went to St Helens and opened the first works in what would be the world's greatest glass-making town. However, in 1757 a small flint-glass works was opened by Peter Seaman in Orford Lane. After he died in 1788 the works was run by a partnership whose names suggest connections with the flourishing glass-making industry at Stourbridge near Birmingham. Another glasshouse was opened at Bank Quay in the mid-1760s by the Perrin family – in 1767 they were advertising blue, green, white and painted glassware – and in the 1790s John Unsworth, cousin of Peter Stubs the file-maker, established a national reputation for his cut and engraved glassware (he

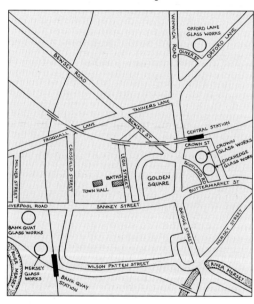

The location of the major glassworks in Warrington 1800-1930s.

claimed to produce engraved glass for the King and Prince of Wales). By 1828 Warrington glasshouses included Alderson, Perrin & Robinson (flint glass and watchglass) at Cockhedge; the Bank Quay Glass Company; Clare, Haddocks & Brown, crown glass, in Scotland Road; and Glazebrook, Kirkland & Co. in Orford Lane.

However, Warrington's glass-makers faced fierce competition from the larger, better-organised and highly-capitalised producers of St Helens. They fought hard to keep the business, sometimes using curious marketing techniques: in 1830 they wore glass hats during a procession celebrating the coronation of William IV. As late as 1851 there were still 162 people employed in the Warrington glass industry, but this was only a tenth of the figure for St Helens. Glass-making continued on a modest scale throughout the 19th century, and Warrington's last producers, Robinson's, did not close until 1933.

LEFT *The interior of Robinson's cutting shop in about 1890: the width and height of the workshop is characteristic of glassworks architecture in the second half of the 19th century. The firm survived until the 1930s.*

BELOW *The Bank Quay glassworks and other industrial sites, 1850.*

It never developed into a major industry because the vital raw materials – sand and coal – were not found on the spot, whereas the glass industry at St Helens stood on top of these key ingredients.

FURTHER READING: Trade and business directories provide useful information about the makers of glass; see also D.C. Johnson, *Industry and employment in Warrington 1800-1982* (University of Manchester MA thesis 1982): Warrington Museum has a comprehensive and extensive display of Warrington-made glassware.

56. *Shipbuilding*

In the first half of the 19th century small shipyards were established on the Mersey at Bank Quay, as an adjunct to the existing iron-making industry in the area. The Bridge Foundry Company built four iron paddle-steamers in the early 1840s, intended for use on the Mersey, and shortly after this the firm of Tayleur Sanderson & Co. began building at Bank Quay. Their iron ships were schooners for the Atlantic trade, as well as small steamers intended for passenger use. In 1853 the ill-fated iron clipper, *Tayleur*, claimed to be the largest iron vessel yet built on the Mersey, was launched at Warrington. She had accommodation for 680 passengers and was chartered by the White Star Line for the Australian run, but on her maiden voyage in January 1854 was wrecked in fog off the Irish coast and sank with the loss of 378 lives. Shipbuilding continued, with several large iron ships of over 1,000 tons being launched in 1855-6. The largest Warrington vessel, the *Sarah Palmer* of 1,325 tons, was completed in 1855 but there was no more potential for expansion. By 1862 the industry was declining and although river vessels and barges were built by Clare & Ridgway's at Sankey Bridges until just before the First World

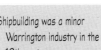

Shipbuilding was a minor Warrington industry in the 19th century

It failed to develop because the town was too far from the sea on a narrow river

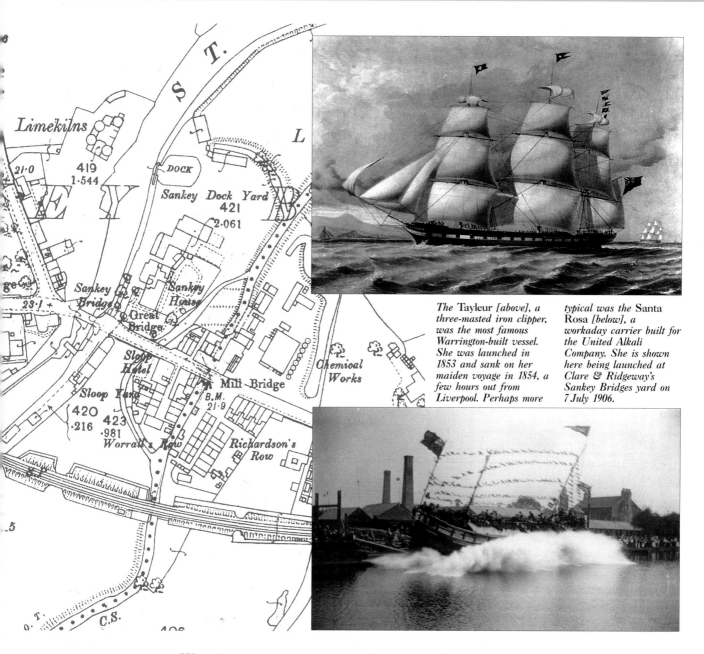

The Tayleur [above], a three-masted iron clipper, was the most famous Warrington-built vessel. She was launched in 1853 and sank on her maiden voyage in 1854, a few hours out from Liverpool. Perhaps more typical was the Santa Rosa [below], a workaday carrier built for the United Alkali Company. She is shown here being launched at Clare & Ridgeway's Sankey Bridges yard on 7 July 1906.

The extract from the 1895 OS map shows the 'sloop yard' below the bridge, together with limekilns, a small dock, and the chemical works. The Mersey Leadworks and the Sankey Wiremills are just off the map.

War, the narrowness of the shallow river, distant from the sea and deeper water, meant that the town could not develop as a shipbuilding centre.

57. The Manchester Ship Canal

Even though an intricate web of waterways and railways had been spun across south Lancashire and north Cheshire in the 150 years after 1720, the late Victorian merchants of Manchester were not content with the transport network. They were convinced that the city was being 'held to ransom' by railway companies and Liverpool shipping interests, and sought to break that alleged stranglehold by promoting new transport links. Schemes for electric monorails and competing railways came to nothing, but the extraordinary ambition of making Manchester a great inland port, with direct access to the sea, was fulfilled by the construction of the Ship Canal between 1885 and 1894. One of the engineering wonders of the 19th century, the canal had a profound effect upon Warrington and the surrounding area, though the aspirations of Warrington Corporation to have a complex of docks built at Latchford and so turn their town into another great port were stillborn. The canal company, which originally promised such a scheme, backtracked and by 1905 had abandoned any plans (if, indeed, it ever took them seriously in the first place).

The Ship Canal used the approximate alignment of the Mersey and the Irwell, widening, straightening and deepening the two rivers from Manchester down to Latchford, and then building a separate channel hugging the south shore along from Wilderspool to Eastham on Wirral. In building this remarkable waterway the city's engineers drastically altered the rivers – which had already experienced almost two centuries of gradual change because of navigation works – so that for long stretches all trace of the natural course has vanished. This is particularly so around Warrington. Below Woolston the original river survives with its long bends as far as Howley Quay (though bypassed on the north side by the Woolston New Cut) but at Latchford the old and very sharp loop of the river known as the 'Hell Hole' was cut through in the early 18th century by a short channel and reclaimed: Victoria Park lies across its site. Below Warrington Bridge the river now runs in a long straight artificial channel built parallel with Chester Road in 1884. The earlier course, which looped through Wilderspool, was filled in, though it is recalled by the name River Road which ran alongside the old channel. Under the abortive scheme to provide docks at Warrington the southern end of the old riverbed, south of Gainsborough Road, was destined to be excavated as the main dock.

The Ship Canal, slicing straight across the higher ground between Grappenhall and Moore and running in a rock cutting, was inevitably a major barrier to communications. The main railway lines were diverted to cross it; the old Runcorn and Latchford Canal was truncated by the new waterway and

The Canal was among the greatest engineering works of the 19th century

It slashed across the existing landscape and caused immense physical disruption

The docks planned for Warrington never materialised

The local economic impact of the Canal was therefore limited

Building the Ship Canal at Latchford, 1891. The old railway station is on the left next to the new canal cutting: it was closed in 1893 when the new high-level crossing of the canal was opened (the embankment and the great iron girder bridge are seen in the background). Behind the temporary, and alarmingly unstable-looking, trestle bridge is the new Knutsford Road swing bridge. The huge disruption caused by the Ship Canal, and its traumatic effect on the landscape, are abundantly demonstrated by this view.

Navvies playing cards during the dinner break, September 1893. In the background is the church of St Thomas, Stockton Heath.

eventually filled in – it is now the Black Bear Linear Park; and, most notoriously, the swing bridges on the canal greatly impeded the flow of road traffic. The swing bridges themselves are engineering marvels (as were the massive hydraulically-operated locks built at Latchford, the larger of which is 183 metres long and 20 metres across) but even in the 1880s when the canal was proposed there were concerns about the problem they might create for road traffic. Nobody, though, envisaged the tremendous growth of road usage over the next century, and during the canal's last really busy period, from the end of the Second World War until the early 1970s, the congestion which resulted meant that Warrington's already notorious position as a traffic bottleneck grew steadily worse. For through traffic at least, the opening of Thelwall Viaduct came as a real godsend.

FURTHER READING: P.A. Norton, *Railways and Waterways to Warrington* (Cheshire Libraries, 1984); D.A. Farnie, *The Manchester Ship Canal and the rise of the port of Manchester* (Manchester University Press, 1980); C. Hadfield, *The Canals of North West England* (2 vols) (David and Charles, 1970); J. Corbridge, *A Pictorial History of the Mersey and Irwell Navigation* (E.J. Morten, 1979)

Victorian Warrington: Town and People

58. The population of nineteenth-century Warrington

The population of the town increased sixfold during the 19th century

Much higher densities of population meant acute overcrowding of poor housing

This played a major role in the town's bad public health record

From 1801 a census was held every ten years, giving us reliable statistics. The original manuscript returns for each household were kept from 1841 onwards so we can investigate in detail the townspeople, their birthplaces and occupations, ages and family relationships. In 1801 the population of Warrington was 10,567; in 1901, 65,000, a sixfold increase over the century. Within that period the rate of growth was uneven: by far the largest increase was during the 1870s, when the population rose by 37 per cent, coinciding with major expansion of the town's key industries.

The figures shown on the graph are significant in another way. They relate to the same geographical area, the township of Warrington (that is, without the surrounding places such as Poulton with Fearnhead). This means that in 1901 there were six times as many people living in the same space, and the density of population per acre had risen from 3.66 in 1801 to 22.52 in 1901. That, in turn, emphasises the way in which overcrowding in the 'inner city' became a major problem in the Victorian town. Congested and insanitary housing in courts and rows crammed into small yards behind the main streets became typical. It was here that the worst public health problems, the highest death rates, and the severe outbreaks of epidemic disease were to be found.

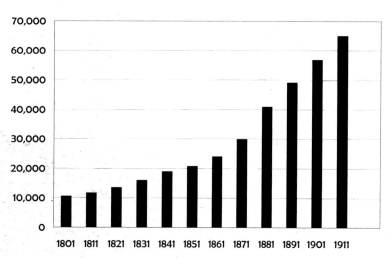

The population of Warrington 1801-1911

FURTHER READING: For Warrington, 19th-century population statistics will be found in the *Lancashire county volumes* of the national census, 1801-1901; for parishes south of the river the Cheshire volumes can be consulted. Statistics are summarised in P. Chadwick, *The sanitary state of Warrington from the early nineteenth century to the beginning of the twentieth century* (MA dissertation, University of Manchester, 1996): copy in Warrington Library local studies collection, ref. ms 2782; statistics for towns in Lancashire and Cheshire are given in C. Phillips and J.H. Smith, *Lancashire and Cheshire since 1540* (1994)

59. The townscape of Warrington in the nineteenth century

Population growth encouraged the development of slum housing

The railway north from Bank Quay was edged by industrial areas

Middle-class housing was laid out around Palmyra Square

By the late 19th century prosperous people were moving to the suburbs

In the early 19th century the town grew steadily but its built-up area remained small. The rapid population increase of the Victorian period was largely accommodated by ever-higher densities in the centre. Nonetheless, by 1900 Warrington was beginning to spread across the adjacent fields, foreshadowing the massive expansion of the urban area during the 20th century. North of the old town there developed an area of small workshops, haphazardly intermingled with cottages and rows of houses. This was the centre for the pin-making trade, a domestic-scale industry which created a very confused townscape characterised by an extremely irregular pattern of lanes and yards. Part of this tangle was swept away in the early 1870s when the railway through

Warrington Central Station slashed across its heart, and virtually all the rest has since disappeared as a result of slum clearance, town centre redevelopment and, most recently, the construction of Midland Way.

Already in the early 1830s the building of the railway from Tanners Lane to Newton le Willows, closely followed by the line through Bank Quay, had imposed its own straitjacket upon the town. The main West Coast line became a barrier to east-west movement, but of greater importance was the way in which the railways reinforced the existing concentration of industry around Bank Quay, encouraging the development of a broad strip of factories, warehousing, yards and sidings parallel with Winwick Road through Dallam to the river.

Terraced housing in the classic regional style, with regular rows and grid-iron patterns of streets, was relatively late to reach Warrington, and never

New rows of terraced housing in Latchford, 1905 [left]: the piecemeal character of the development, with short streets meeting at awkward angles and creating oddly-shaped plots, contrasts with the spacious elegance of Bold Street [below] at about the same date. Here the large houses of the 1850s, with their dark red brick and pale stone window and door surrounds, are set behind railings and look onto the private central gardens of what is now Palmyra Square. A 1902 description notes that 'Palmyra Square and Bold Street were ... very select. Nice people live there still' but it goes on to identify the ultimate fate of the whole of this part of the town: 'office and school and surgery are rapidly taking the neighbourhood for their own'.

achieved the dominance which it did in places such as Preston and Bolton. This is partly because Warrington's industries were diverse, partly because the town did not grow as dramatically as some during the 19th century, and partly because development around the town was limited when land-owners refused to sell. Another factor is that nearer to the centre the land was divided into many separate small estates, so that building schemes tended to be piecemeal and frag-mented. Even so, by the end of the century substantial areas of workers' housing had appeared. In the late 1870s and early 1880s, for example, the land on the east side of Winwick Road was developed with short terraced streets of very poor housing. From the mid-1880s the Corporation imposed building byelaws which raised the quality of new houses, and during this period the town began to extend more rapidly outwards.

Knutsford Road in about 1905, viewed from the railway bridge and looking towards town. The neat rows of housing dating from the 1880s and 1890s, with small front gardens and bay windows, typify the new suburbs of the late Victorian period, as white-collar workers, with gradually increasing wages, could afford to move out of the town centre to a more desirable location – helped, after 1902, by the new tramway route.

Warrington was particularly awkward in its shape because it was divided into almost self-contained sections by the railways, the river and (after 1894) the Ship Canal. Thus a series of physically distinct suburbs grew, where terraced housing and small villas were appearing in the late Victorian period – the terraced streets of Latchford, Little Sankey and Whitecross are typical. At Latchford, though, the impact of fragmented land ownership was emphasised by the odd angles of the streets and rows, where piecemeal development meant a lack of coherent planning.

One of the most distinctive areas of Warrington was the middle-class suburb which developed to a more orderly design south-west of the medieval town centre during the second half of the 19th century. Centred on the formality of Palmyra Square, this area was favoured by wealthier citizens, not least because of the social cachet of living near Bank Hall. In these substantial town houses, with small back gardens and gracious frontages, lived Warrington's professional classes. Palmyra Square is now a public park, Queen's Gardens, but it was originally an exclusive private garden available only to residents of the square. However, the attractions of the district were soon diminished by the creeping influence of the central area (eventually leading to the present ubiquity of solicitors' offices and other business uses), the nearby railways and the proximity to the industries of Bank Quay. In the earlier 19th century Church Street and Bewsey Street had both had a similar status, with their large (in the case of the former, half-timbered) houses, but industrialisa-tion (such as the filthily-polluting Rylands wireworks) meant that both went very rapidly down the social scale after the 1830s. By the late 19th century prosperous Warrington people were starting to move away from the town and over to the Cheshire side. The opening of the tramway along Knutsford Road to Grappenhall, for example, was an encouragement to lower-middle class commuting from that increasingly fashionable area.

FURTHER READING: P. Croft, *The evolution of Warrington's townscape* (BA dissertation, 1969: Warrington Library local studies collection ms 1622); file on *Public Health and Housing in Warrington 1840s to 1960s* [Warrington Museum]; also essential to any understanding of the town's development are Ordnance Survey maps. These begin with the six-inch to one-mile sheets of the mid-1840s and continue with very large scale and extremely detailed town maps of 1851. In the mid-1890s the OS produced its 25-inch to one-mile series, and another set of detailed town plans. Warrington Library local studies collection has a comprehensive range of OS maps from the 19th and 20th centuries.

60. The resort of society

As in other industrial towns, the middle classes became more influential in the early 19th century. Warrington's factories were manned by workers but managed by a fast-expanding white-collar sector, while the increasing population required the services of more professionals. The numbers of lawyers, teachers and doctors grew accordingly, while the expansion of the commercial sector meant more shopkeepers and traders. These elements of society aspired to good taste and elegance and demanded social and cultural facilities which befitted their status. Before the 1840s Warrington was a place to which people from neighbouring areas would go for evening entertainments and 'genteel' events. Thus, in its heyday between 1790 and 1835, the Assembly Rooms, behind the Old Coffee House in Horsemarket Street, drew the gentry and leaders of local society. In January 1797, for example, Catherine Gerard of Garswood, daughter of one of Lancashire's leading families, wrote to her sister:

> last night we went to an Assembly at Warrington we are Eight Miles Distance the Ladies got a pleasant dance & a Supper was given by a party of our Acquaintance. It was very near 5 o'Clock this Morning when we got Home

There were other signs of superior society. The Warrington Union Coffee Room, a select 'gentlemen's club', opened in Dolmans Lane in January 1813. Subscriptions were sought from suitable people – the gentry, professional classes and 'better' merchants and industrialists. The 1813 list shows 86 subscribers, headed by John Blackburne MP and J.J. Blackburne M.P., and including members of the Lyon and Rylands families. The annual subscription was two guineas (£2.10), but 'Gentlemen residing at a greater distance than one Mile from Market Gate and not having an Establishment in Town' were admitted at a reduced rate. The gentlemen enjoyed a quiet and exclusive town centre club where, of course, coffee was provided, as well as a selection of quality newspapers – five daily and weekly London ones and others from Liverpool, Manchester, Hull, Lancaster, Chester, Bristol, Dublin and Glasgow.

The Coffee Room minute book gives an intriguing glimpse of a period when the town was the resort of polite society and shows that in this busy place the newly-made men, people rising up the social scale on the strength of professional skills or entrepreneurial activity, used money to open doors into the upper levels of society. The town had its sophisticated and cultivated class. These men had another advantage. Communications were better than ever

Nineteenth-century Warrington had an increasingly large middle class

These people needed social and cultural facilities in the town

Warrington was a centre for fashionable people from the rural areas around

The Coffee Room was an exclusive club for the town's gentlemen before: people in Warrington might read a London daily paper, or enjoy the news from Dublin almost as soon as it was published. The town was part of a fast-growing national economy. Its businessmen and politicians were more conscious than ever before of the world and its challenges.

FURTHER READING: The minute book of the Union Coffee Room is in Warrington Library, ref. ms 1183

61. New local government: the Police Commissioners

Warrington, a growing town, needed better local government

The existing control, by the lord of the manor, was inadequate

There were many pressing problems to be tackled

A new body, the Warrington Police Commissioners, was created in 1813

It was not democratic, but worked hard to improve conditions in the town

Some of the town's more affluent citizens were increasingly discontented with the dirty and unsavoury appearance of the town, and ever more aware of its deficiencies. Warrington was certainly no worse, and maybe indeed rather better, than just about every other newly-industrialising town in the north-west, but its environment was deteriorating and its administration becoming more difficult year by year. The town was unpaved, with filthy congested streets; the market place was old-fashioned; there were almost no sewers or proper sanitation, no refuse collection or street-lighting; and the water supply was polluted. Crime, poverty and bad housing were everywhere apparent. People who observed this state of affairs did not blame individuals, or the industrialists whose actions were certainly responsible for some problems. Instead, they pointed to the failure of town government. The old manorial system, in which the lord of the manor and his steward ran Warrington as a personal possession, was incapable of dealing with the pressing problems of the new age.

The answer (as in other towns in a similar situation, such as Rochdale) was to establish a new body to take over the powers of the lord, and to make the improvements essential to a better future. In June 1813 *An Act for Paving and Improving the Town of Warrington, in the County of Lancaster and for building a New Bridewell in the said Town* was passed by Parliament. It set up a body known as the Police Commissioners, although the creation of a police force was only one of their many responsibilities. Any man owning property in Warrington worth £40 or more, or renting property worth £50 or more, could be a commissioner. Their powers were wide-ranging, including streets and paving, street-lighting, sewerage and drainage, refuse collection, traffic control, slaughterhouses and butchers' shops, law and order and the police force, markets and fairs, the bridewell or prison, and fire services. Although unelected, they were the forerunners of the town council. The scale of their work, and the amount of money they controlled, made them central to the life of the town. A small group of commissioners with particular talents and energies took most business into their own hands, governing the town with confidence. They were often divided among themselves: one faction preferred to keep the rates low, another wanted more public action and expenditure. Because they were unelected they did not put forward political agendas or set out policies, and there were no manifestos, but their activities were increasingly politicised and when the town became a borough in 1847 the party divide was firmly established. We must acknowledge the great contribution which, during their 34 years' existence, they made to Warrington life. They tried to deal with unprecedented problems, bringing modern urban ways to a town beset with difficulties, providing essential services, and laying the ground for the achievements of the council which followed. For many years their contribution was unsung: today they have a long overdue recognition.

FURTHER READING: The archives of the Police Commissioners are in Warrington Library local studies collection, and include minutes books and other formal records of proceedings. These [especially the minute books, references ms 1354/1 and 1354/2] have been used for most of the following sections, including those on police, the bridewell, roads, the market, fire, street-lighting and pollution. An excellent account of the Police Commissioners is given by I. Sellers in *Early Modern Warrington* (1998).

The bridewell and sessions house in Irlam Street, off Buttermarket Street, photographed in about 1900 just before its closure. The entrance was at first-floor level and the building was designed to withstand a siege, because it was constructed in the 1820s at a time when working-class agitation (and the possibility of insurrection) was a major preoccupation of the authorities.

62. The Poor Law Union

Other aspects of local administration were changed by national reforms. In 1834 the Poor Law Amendment Act restructured the system of poor law authorities and the management of the poor which had operated since the late 16th century. The multitude of individual authorities were replaced by a more logical and efficient structure of Poor Law Unions, covering whole districts and centred on market towns. Each union had to build a new workhouse, where the most desperate cases would be accommodated, but the basic premise was that, to keep down the costs, help would only be given as a last resort. The poor should be encouraged to 'stand on their own two feet', and the

In 1834 the government passed legislation to reform the Poor Law

The Warrington Poor Law Union was created, covering many local townships

A large new workhouse was built at Whitecross

workhouse was to be as unappealing and spartan as possible, with a strict regime and few concessions to comfort. The new Warrington Poor Law Union of 1834 included the whole of Warrington parish, with Great Sankey, Newton le Willows, Penketh, Cuerdley and Hulme. Its population was 28,000. The main existing workhouse was in the town, with another – notoriously badly-managed – at Newton. Population growth and industrialisation meant that problems of poverty were becoming acute, exacerbated after 1845 by large-scale migration from Ireland into south Lancashire.

Plans for a new central workhouse were prepared in 1844 (under pressure from the government) but it was not until 1851 that the new buildings at Whitecross were opened. The new workhouse was massive, with 'day rooms' for 314 men and the same number of women, strictly segregated to avoid any form of fraternising – even married couples were forcibly parted. There was a school for up to 50 pauper girls, and night-dormitories for a total of 160 men and 160 women. The workhouse had a separate infirmary building, with room for 26 men and 40 women, and isolation wards for a total of 24 people. It was managed by the Board of Guardians (hence the name Guardian Street) and functioned as a workhouse, though with a gradually less uncompromising regime, until the early 20th century. It was slowly recognised that incarcerating the poor in prison-like workhouses was not only unacceptable, but also self-defeating, doing nothing to solve the problems of poverty. The workhouse therefore became evolved into a hospital, catering for the long-term sick, the elderly, the disabled and other groups such as orphaned children. In 1900, in recognition of this changed strategy, a new Union Infirmary was opened, with two large wards catering primarily for the chronically sick poor and for maternity cases, and this formed the nucleus of what was, after 1929 (when the Poor Law was reformed again and the Unions and Boards of Guardians abolished), Warrington General Hospital.

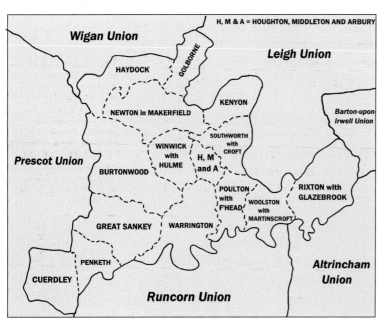

The Warrington Poor Law Union, 1834-1929.

FURTHER READING: information about Poor Law reforms in the two counties is summarised in C. Phillips and J.H. Smith, *Lancashire and Cheshire since 1540* (1994). See also G. Carter, *Warrington Hundred* (1947) for an overview of the social services and medical work of the borough and other authorities.

63. *Politics and elections in the nineteenth century*

During the early 19th century there was pressure for a reform of the parliamentary franchise and a redistribution of seats. Most large industrial towns were unrepresented in parliament and numerous very insignificant places, in contrast, sent two MPs to Westminster. The agitation towards reform culminated in the Reform Act of 1832, by which Warrington became a parliamentary borough electing one MP. The first member for the new constituency, the Whig candidate Edmund Hornby, was chosen at the general election of December 1832. Although the reforms produced a system in some ways more democratic, since the franchise was now based on a uniform national principle, the right to vote was still restricted to a small minority. In the 1832 election only 379 people in Warrington could vote, out of an adult male population of about 7,000. Furthermore, the election did not change the aristocratic domination of local affairs: Hornby was the grandson of the 12th Earl of Derby, while his Tory opponent, John Ireland Blackburne, was lord of the manor of Warrington. The Whigs claimed that the Blackburnes were trying to make Warrington a pocket borough, the Tories that the Whigs represented the outdated aristocratic interest. However, the inclusion of Latchford in the parliamentary constituency probably tipped the balance in favour of the Whigs, because it had a more 'ordinary' population.

The Whig triumph was short-lived. In 1834 Blackburne won for the Tories by a majority of 18 votes. Amid much bitterness and recrimination, and plentiful evidence of doubtful electoral practices, the next general election, in 1837, saw a shock Tory victory. The morale of local Whigs (increasingly known as Liberals) collapsed, and in 1841 Blackburne was returned unopposed. There

Warrington was given a parliamentary seat by the 1832 Reform Act

The Tories and Liberals were fiercely competitive in the later 19th century

The Greenall family were the leading Conservatives

The Crosfields were their political rivals, leaders of the local Liberal party

The boundaries of the new parliamentary borough of Warrington, 1832: at that date the built-up area was still quite small, and the township included extensive rural areas, but by 1880 almost all the land within these boundaries had been swallowed up by bricks and mortar.

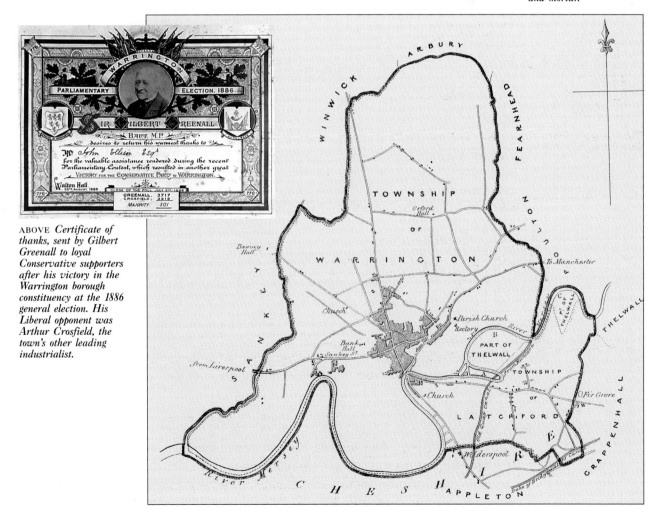

ABOVE *Certificate of thanks, sent by Gilbert Greenall to loyal Conservative supporters after his victory in the Warrington borough constituency at the 1886 general election. His Liberal opponent was Arthur Crosfield, the town's other leading industrialist.*

was now vicious rivalry not only between the two parties but also among the Liberals, against the background of the question of incorporation as a borough and the policy to be followed on key issues of local government. When the first elections to the new borough council were held in June 1847 the Liberals were resurgent: the first council had 16 Liberals and only four Tories. Six weeks later the town was the scene of dramatic events during the general election campaign – on 24 July, for example, a meeting of 5,000 people was held in the market place – when, to the amazement of all, the Tories won the seat by 29 votes. The reason was clear to some: the Tory candidate was Gilbert Greenall, not only one of the most respected men in Warrington but also one on whom many of the townspeople depended for their livelihood. There was no secret ballot. The Liberals, while championing the cause of reforms, could not readily defeat a man whose personal influence was so great. Greenall was elected unopposed at the next four general elections.

In 1868, however, the last election in Warrington before the introduction of the secret ballot caused a sensation. Gilbert Greenall, MP for 21 years, was opposed by Peter Rylands for the Liberals. The prospect of the two leading industrialists in the town locked in combat was exciting: the result even more so. Greenall was returned by a majority of 78 votes. The Liberals, who had campaigned with formidable skill, refused to accept the result and demanded a scrutiny of the ballot papers. This produced a dramatic change – Rylands, for the Liberals, was declared to have won by 27 votes, and accusations of bribery, corruption and fraud flew like mud, slung from both sides. The High Court eventually decided in favour of Rylands. The Tories had their revenge: Greenall won the seat back at the next election and served as MP for Warrington in 1874-1880 and 1885-1892, eventually totalling 34 years in the job.

FURTHER READING: O.E. Colling, *Gilbert Greenall and the 1868 parliamentary election in Warrington* (1968 dissertation; Warrington Central Library); file on *MPs for Warrington since 1832*, Warrington Library local studies collection ref. P8603.

64. *Incorporation as a borough*

Becoming a borough gave the town a new status

For many people it represented civic pride and local independence

It also gave new powers and responsibilities to local government

The new borough council was democratically elected

Warrington received its borough charter on 3 April 1847

The idea of the town becoming a borough provoked acrimonious debate in the mid-1840s. There were strong arguments in favour: civic pride would be conferred, more efficient local government would allegedly result, a democratic town council would replace the unelected Police Commissioners, and it was claimed that it would impose a 'greater degree of responsibility ... upon the parties who undertake the task of governing the Community'. Opponents feared increasing costs and hinted darkly that those promoting the idea were motivated not by the common good of the town but by personal gain. Meetings held to discuss the issue had record attendances, and were packed by both sides, but in January 1846 the Commissioners agreed by 58 votes to 34 to go ahead with the application. A month later, having drummed up all their supporters, the opposition reversed the decision, by 142 votes to 83, claiming that 'a Municipal form of Government is altogether inexpedient and objectionable in a Community like Warrington'.

This was not an academic argument. Great financial issues were involved, including the possible purchase of the gas company, building a new market

William Beamont, the first mayor of Warrington (1847-1848) and the driving force behind the incorporation as a borough. He was also the most important 19th-century historian of Warrington and a prominent figure in the intellectual and cultural life of north-west England as a whole. His offices were in the market place, next to the Barley Mow, where the building now has a commemorative plaque.

hall, providing a public water supply, and beginning work on a sewerage scheme. These projects would cost a lot of money and extend the powers of local government. Some people opposed this, and others feared a loss of their own influence, long enjoyed in the 'gentleman's club' atmosphere of the Police Commissioners. But the argument gradually moved in favour of borough status – not least because other towns in the region were doing the same – and on 3 April 1847 Warrington, by royal charter, became a municipal borough, with a mayor, aldermen and elected town council. On 15 July 1847 the Police Commissioners dissolved themselves, handed over their assets and responsibilities to the new council, and watched as the new era dawned.

The charter of Queen Victoria by which Warrington was created a borough, in July 1847, with the great royal seal attached.

FURTHER READING: The debates about incorporation are well covered by I. Sellers in *Early Modern Warrington* (1998); see also the minutes of the Police Commissioners, held at Warrington Library local studies collection ref. ms 1354/2

65. *Tidying up the market*

For centuries the market was at the heart of Warrington life, but by 1800 many local people viewed it with disapproval because it was chaotic and unruly. It was still owned by the lord of the manor but after 1813 the Police Commissioners intervened in its management, trying to compel people to sell particular goods in specified places. The market had long outgrown the old market place and spread along adjacent streets, where it got in the way of traffic and was more difficult to control. Sankey Street, lined with ancient half-timbered buildings and newer brick-fronted properties, its roadway not patterned with pedestrianised paving but made of mud, setts, running water and refuse. Stretched along the street on market days was a motley collection of stalls, baskets of produce spilling onto the road, hens, ducks and chickens scratching and pecking, or struggling and squawking in sacks and cages, and fish-sellers rinsing their sometimes pungent wares with water from the town pump – all full of life, noise, smells and colour.

All that was to end. In future, butter, eggs and fowls could be sold only on the south and west sides of the Great Cornmarket; greens, vegetables, garden seeds and fruit along the east side; potatoes and fish in a designated area of Bank Street; and mugs and earthenware on the east side of Three Crowns Yard. The traders affected by this resisted tenaciously, and it was years before the butchers grudgingly moved to their new place and the haberdashers and

Watercolour of part of Cornmarket painted by Gaskell in 1803. Most of the buildings shown are pubs and beerhouses – contemporaries noted that the density of drinking places in Warrington market was almost unequalled anywhere, and this was held to contribute to the raucous and rowdy character of market days.

toy-sellers shifted their pitches – and as soon as the attention of the authorities was elsewhere, they slipped back to their old places. In 1829 the Commissioners tried again, ordering that all traders should obey regulations about market hours and standards:

66 all butter shall be real and genuine, not adulterated or deceitfully made up … no unwholesome or bad fish, meat, fowl or other food is to be sold 99

It still did not work. In 1834 it was reported that

66 the greater part of the space of the Cornmarket is taken up by petty Tradesmen and persons exposing drapery goods for sale … many of them of inferior quality, suspected to be stolen or dishonestly come by, and to the great inconvenience or annoyance of the regular shopkeepers 99

In the mid-1840s the take-over of the market by the Commissioners became a major issue. John Ireland Blackburne, the lord of the manor, agreed in 1841 to lease the market rights and the market place to the town for 21 years at a rent of £257 per annum: ten years later he finally sold out to the Corporation, which in 1856 erected the new market hall. That was undoubtedly cleaner and more 'wholesome' than its predecessor, but less exciting and lively. William Beamont remembered how 'the floor of the Great Cornmarket [was] strewn with an abundance of all kinds of pottery and earthenware … laid out with narrow walks between for customers to walk in'. He also noted that the market had an unusually large number of public houses 'to show our ancestors to have been a thirsty race and that something stronger than water was required to quench their thirst'. That, too, contributed to the liveliness of the market of which the Commissioners heartily disapproved.

66. *Mean streets, middens and muck*

So, the Police Commissioners set about their task of modernising Warrington and updating not only its image but also its reality. It was not just a case of cosmetic improvements. Real practical policies had to be implemented to make a genuine difference to the town, but progress was slow and often hesitant, frustrated by financial limitations and vested interests. For example, irregular street frontages and narrow highways were seen as old-fashioned and highly inconvenient, but it was almost a century before the Corporation was able to tackle the problem in a systematic way. Progress with street-cleaning was rather more rapid – Warrington was once full of splendid black-and-white architecture, but walking through its streets 200 years ago we would have had little opportunity to appreciate the buildings since we would be watching our feet, to avoid treading in something unpleasant, and sweeping up was a priority for the Police Commissioners.

In 1814 a contract was let for refuse-collection and street-cleaning – Horsemarket Street, Buttermarket Street, Bridge Street and Sankey Street would be cleaned twice-weekly in winter and weekly in summer and the sweepings (dirt and manure) taken for sale to farmers. In 1816 the Commissioners decided to use pauper labour, and the town provided a cart, brushes and shovels. The inhabitants were required to sweep the pavements and streets in front of their houses every week, though despite constant reminders they usually neglected to do so. In 1833 it was ordered that the streets were to be swept on Saturday night or Sunday morning

> 66 so that the Town may on those days present a more decent and cleanly appearance & particularly in the Streets leading to places of worship 99

Widening the streets was a slow process. The Commissioners had no powers of compulsory purchase, but whenever a property was demolished they tried to buy a strip of land and push back the road a few yards. By the middle of the 19th century some streets – notably Bridge Street – were extremely irregular, with alternating wide and narrow stretches. Not until the end of the century was the Council able to tackle the problem systematically, creating the present width throughout.

Footpaths were obstructed by a multitude of cellar entrances with trapdoors or raised covers, railings and stone steps, and bow-fronted shop windows which presented hazards to passers-by. In 1815 it was reported

In 1813 the streets were largely unpaved: mud in winter, dust in summer

The old streets were crooked and narrow, making traffic movement difficult

The streets were unswept and all sorts of obstacles blocked the footpaths

A priority for the Commissioners after 1813 was to sort out these problems

By doing so they helped to create a cleaner and more orderly town centre

Cheapside, Golden Square, viewed from Horsemarket Street in a remarkable early photograph of 1855. This area of derelict or deteriorating property, dating from the 16th to early 18th centuries, was about to be cleared for redevelopment: the right-hand side made way for the new market hall.

that cellar door of Mr. Wilson, druggist, was 'almost constantly open so as to render it dangerous to persons passing along the footway there'. Such hazards were remedied at the expense of the property-owners. A different sort of public nuisance was created by drinkers who wanted to relieve themselves. They could use the 'stones adjoining the doors of different Public Houses … placed there for persons to make water'. In September 1838 it was ordered that these unsavoury features of the Warrington street scene, rudimentary open-air urinals, should be removed. They were not decent in a self-respecting town.

FURTHER READING: The Warrington local studies collection includes extensive material relating to the sanitary and environmental conditions in the town, including the reports of the Inspector of Nuisances which highlight individual cases, often in all-too-vivid detail!

67. Cart-parking and traffic problems

Warrington was on a busy main road: its narrow streets were congested

Traffic problems were an issue in the town two centuries ago

Bridge Street from Bridge Foot in 1887. The narrow main street was barely wide enough for two carriages to pass (a contemporary recorded that 'at its lower end boys used to leap in a hop jump from kerb to kerb'). During the next twenty years the west side [left] was demolished, the road widened, and new shops and public buildings constructed. This gave a new up-to-date image to the town's main approach though many ancient timber-framed buildings were lost in the process.

Traffic and car-parking are not only a headache of our time. They caused major difficulties in Warrington in the early 19th century, when a great volume of through-traffic crowded the narrow streets and, especially on market days, the centre was congested with people and carts. The Police Commissioners took steps to control parking and introduced waiting restrictions, passed byelaws forbidding such activities as sawing-up timber in the roadway, repairing vehicles in the street, or riding on the shafts of carts (a widespread dangerous custom), or feeding animals, and tried to punish any person who allowed

66 any Horse or Cattle drawing any such Cart, Waggon, Dray, Sledge or other Carriage, to go any pace faster than a walk' or to 'drive … so furiously as to thereby cause personal danger to any Person. 99

As with traffic regulations today, many people took no notice. In 1814 the numerous innkeepers of the town were sent a circular, warning against leaving chaises (light carriages) standing in the streets. Customers would call in for a drink and leave their chaise outside, impeding the traffic. Bad driving was also a problem, as fast vehicles sped along Bridge Street and Horsemarket Street. The surveyor of the highways was asked in 1822 to take steps to deal with reckless driving by 'the drivers of Coaches passing through the Town'. It all added to the excitement of the walk to market!

68. Street-lighting and gas supplies

At night the dark streets of Warrington were hazardous for pedestrians and vehicles, and it was thought that criminal activity was rife in the gloom. There were a few private lamps but nothing was done to provide public lighting until after 1813: the Improvement Act of that year stated that the 'Streets, Squares, Ways, Lanes and other public Passages and Places … are not properly paved, cleansed, lighted and watered'. In August 1813 the Commissioners appointed surveyors to decide on places for lamps, paying particular attention to lower Bridge Street, 'the passage of which by night is very inconvenient and dangerous' and Market Gate. Light – though not a lot of it – came to the streets at the beginning of November 1813, with 150 oil-lamps. Opinion was divided. Some people favoured more lighting, others thought it an expensive luxury. To economise on costs the lamps were not lit for six nights at full moon, and there was no lighting at all between late April and early September.

In 1816 Preston became the first provincial town with gas-lighting and other places quickly followed suit. The Warrington Gas Light & Coke Company was formed in December 1820, a gasworks was built in Mersey Street, and gas-lighting began in 1821. The company had a shaky start, constantly bickering with the Commissioners over the cost of street-lighting, and not until 1829 was the financial position was more secure. Initially there were few domestic purchasers of gas, but in that year prices were reduced by 10 per cent, demand increased, and production became more efficient. The price fell from 15 shillings (75p) per 1000 ft^3 in 1821 to 2s. 6d. (12½p) in 1884. Even modest levels of lighting transformed the night-time streets of the town, making them safer for pedestrians and for traffic – coverage was slowly extended, though as late as 1856 there were just 256 lamps in Warrington and a further 16 in Latchford.

For the first time a cheap, clean and efficient domestic fuel was available for lighting, cooking and heating. To keep pace with the fast growth in demand, the Mersey Street works was rebuilt in 1847 and again in 1862, by which time it also supplied nearby townships such as Latchford, Appleton, Winwick, and Burtonwood. In 1847 the undertaking produced 16 million ft^3 of gas, but by 1870 this had risen to 86 million. It was decided to build a completely new works, with direct rail access to bring in the huge quantities of coal needed. Warrington Corporation stepped in and made a bid to take over the company and, although this was a hard-fought battle, agreement was eventually reached. In June 1877 the shareholders were bought out for £174,000 (about £20 million in modern terms), which sweetened the pill. The new owners built a modern gasworks next to the railway at Longford in 1878-1880. Output then grew extremely quickly: in 1890, 183 million ft^3 was supplied to 4,000 households, together with industrial premises and the municipal departments, but in 1910 the figures were 447 million ft^3 and 17,000 consumers.

The Corporation Gas Department followed a very advanced policy of advertising, encouraging people to switch to gas for cooking and heating. In 1880, for example, councillors and officials attended the Gas Apparatus Exhibition in Glasgow and returned enthusing about the heaters, stoves, and

Until 1813 Warrington had no proper street-lighting

After that date the Police Commissioners provided some oil lamps

In 1821 gas-lighting was introduced

In the 1840s gas supplies to domestic premises became more common

The supply of gas began to transform the lives of ordinary people

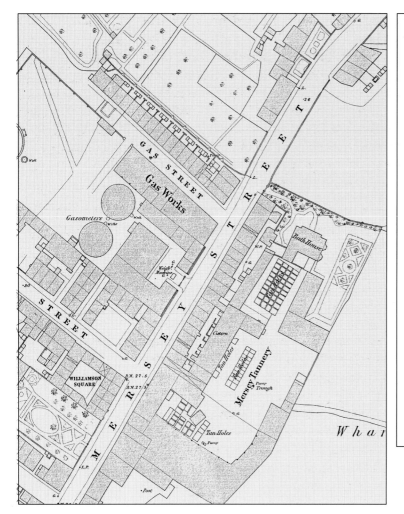

TO CONSUMERS OF GAS.

The Warrington Corporation Gas Committee, being desirous of further encouraging amongst their consumers the use of Gas, for cooking, and other purposes, are now prepared to sell, let out on hire, or purchase lease, Gas Cooking Stoves, at a small half-yearly rent-charge.

All stoves will be selected from the best makers, and constructed on the best scientific principles for economy in consumption of gas and perfection in cooking.

The Gas Committee, in order to make cooking by gas a success, will lay all extra services and connect the stoves ready for use, free of all expense to the consumer, whether supplied by the Corporation or any one else.

REASONS FOR COOKING BY GAS INSTEAD OF
COAL FIRES.

There is no lighting or making up of fires and subsequent removal of ashes and cinders.

A stove is portable, easily fixed, and more easily worked than a grate or range.

The demand of attention is greatly lessened, and it can be relied on to do its work in a given time.

A greater variety can be cooked at one time, and with much greater precision.

It is economical and convenient, and at your service instantly, day and night.

Gas cooking is less wasteful through loss of weight; the juices, instead of being separated as in the case of the ordinary process, remain thoroughly incorporated with the meat, a point of great importance in a nutritive as well as an economical sense.

In Summer, no fire need ever be lighted, thus ensuring a cool house in hot weather, with an entire absence of soot and smoke.

Half-yearly Rent-Charge for first-class Apparatus   2s.   6d.
On Purchase Lease for 7 years   -   -   -   6d.
Purchase Price to Consumers   -   -   -   50s.

By order,

JAMES PATERSON, Manager.

Gas Works, Warrington, 26th June, 1882.

LEFT *Warrington Gasworks in Mersey Street, from the large-scale Ordnance Survey plan of the early 1880s. The interior details of the Mersey Tannery are also very clearly shown. Part of the gasworks site was later used for the new tramways depot, opened in 1902.*

RIGHT *Warrington Corporation Gas Committee advertisement to encourage the use of gas for cooking, 1882. The Committee was a pioneer in this field, and also made strenuous efforts to promote gas lighting and gas heating for domestic premises.*

geysers. Not only did domestic supply offer more business, and give major improvements to people's lifestyles, but it also produced greater efficiency since water-heating and cooking required gas throughout the year – street-lighting and even domestic lighting showed inefficient seasonal variations. The same members of the Gas Committee were more sceptical of another novelty: 'we came away with the conviction that gas has very little to fear from electricity'. But when in 1900 the Corporation began generating electricity itself there was no argument at all about using it.

FURTHER READING: J. Paterson, *Brief sketch of the history of gas-lighting in Warrington* (1887), Warrington Library local studies collection P1995; *History of the Warrington Gas Department* (1947), ref. P824291 (reproduced in G. Carter, *Warrington Hundred*, 1947)

69. *Fire services*

Closely packed buildings of timber and thatch easily caught light, and fires could rage unchecked because extinguishing them was difficult without piped water. During the 18th century property owners began to take out fire insurance with companies which usually operated private fire services. In Warrington by 1815 six different firms maintained fire-engines, attending blazes only in properties insured by themselves. Cast-iron fire signs fixed to the buildings identified the insurer, but most buildings still had no cover and the fire-engines, though better than nothing, were small and inefficient. The need to improve this state of affairs was clear and in September 1828, after negotiations with the insurance companies, the Police Commissioners established a brigade and a fire station was provided at the old town hall in Market Street. During the next twenty years up-to-date equipment was purchased, including three manual pumps (*Duke* 1839, *Victoria* 1844 and *Water Witch* 1845), and the firemen, all volunteers on permanent stand-by, were given better training. In 1847 the town became a borough and a municipal brigade was formed. The new Fire Engine Committee of the town council recorded its aim:

Buildings of wood and plaster, with thatched roofs, easily caught fire

In the 18th century protection was provided by insurance firms

The town's first proper fire brigade was established in 1828

The fire brigade was taken over by the Corporation in 1847

66 to maintain in an efficient state the Fire Engine establishment, so that the same may always be ready for an emergency, and for that purpose to avail themselves of the services of any gentleman in the Borough, who may be willing to assist them, whether members of the Council or not 99

The minutes reveal the methods of fire-fighting in this period. Although there were now some reasonably effective manual engines, in 1850 operated by a brigade of 17 firemen, larger fires still required mass-mobilisation of the able-bodied men of the town. Thus in October 1850, when a blaze destroyed the premises of Allen Houghton & Co. in Buttermarket Street, the firemen were assisted by no fewer than 961 hastily-gathered volunteers ('all hands to the pump') and as late as 1872 the fire at Cockhedge Mill was fought by 366 'assistants' as well as the 18 uniformed men. At that fire the town's pride, the new manual engine *Nile* which was said to be the largest in England, was employed – it required 44 men working continuously to operate its nine-inch cylinders. It is not surprising that most large fires resulted in total destruction – in October 1874 the Manor Tannery in Latchford burned out of control for six days and five nights.

A new station was opened in Queen Street in 1879, housing six manual engines, a reel cart and a ladder cart, and the town's first horse-drawn

The Warrington Fire Brigade in about 1897, photographed in full splendour of brass helmets and polished buttons at the old Queen Street fire station. The two horse-drawn steam engines, Major (1880) and Captain (1894), continued in everyday service until 1928 and 1930 respectively.

Merryweather steam engine, *Major*, was delivered in 1880. A second, *Captain*, arrived in 1893, and their vastly greater efficiency, together with the availability of piped water at last made it possible to tackle fires effectively. By arrangement the Warrington brigade served places as far afield as Frodsham, Runcorn, Prescot and Golborne, in return for payment of fees and expenses. Such forays were made easier after 1913 when *Thomas Burton*, the first motor engine, was delivered, to be followed by *Victory* just after the First World War.

In August 1941 the Warrington Brigade became part of the National Fire Service, created to deal with the devastating bombing of cities. This section of the NFS had 16 permanent officers, 15 reservists, and about 600 volunteers, with three motor engines, two ambulances, 60 pumps, and 40 towing vehicles. The Warrington Brigade dealt with the results of the small number of air raids on the town itself, and performed valiantly in helping to tackle the massive fires which followed the blitz in Liverpool and Bootle, Wallasey and Birkenhead, Manchester, and even Coventry and Birmingham. It was a far cry from the few volunteers working the tiny manual pumps a hundred years before.

Mayoral inspection of the vehicles and equipment of the Warrington Auxiliary Fire Service, 1939. The photograph was taken from the top of the 60-foot escape ladder. It shows a miscellaneous variety of requisitioned and converted vehicles, each carefully picked out in white paint to be more visible during the blackout.

FURTHER READING: As well as the records of the Police Commissioners (reference ms 1354) and the fire brigade (ms 254-255, 279, 1550-1586) see also *County Borough of Warrington Fire Services Handbook* (1968) local studies collection ref. P2741, and G. Carter (ed.) *Warrington Hundred* (1947), which reproduces the material in *Warrington Fire Brigade: a history* (ref. P82429).

70. *Lock 'em up: the town bridewell before 1847*

The town had its own prison, the bridewell, in the 18th century

This was inadequate and in 1820 a new prison opened in Irlam Street

In 1837 there was a major scandal when a prisoner escaped

An investigation revealed that the prison was badly-run and sub-standard

John Howard, the greatest prison reformer of the 18th century, designed model jails and advocated more enlightened regimes for the management of prisons. He was closely connected with Warrington, where he had friends with whom he stayed for long periods, and he did a lot of his influential writing here. He recorded – without enthusiasm – the conditions in the town's tiny lock-up or bridewell in Church Street:

66 This place consisted of two rooms, one of which was about nine feet square, with bedsteads and straw, but no window. The other room was about nine feet long and four feet wide. There was no employment [that is, prisoners were not given tasks] and the food which was sent from the house was the same as the paupers, who judging from their looks, seemed to be humanly treated. 99

The replacement of this lock-up was a main aim of the Police Commissioners after 1813. Warrington had a poor reputation for lawlessness among the 'lower orders', a problem which was thought to be growing. The new prison was opened in Irlam Street in 1820, its first master being the ex-surveyor of highways, Paul Caldwell, who received an annual salary of £25, from which he had to

John Howard, the 18th-century prison reformer who had close connections with Warrington.

provide coal and candles for the building – though he did have the benefit of a rent-free house. Most prisoners stayed only a few days before either being released or sent on to Kirkdale jail in Liverpool or New Bailey prison in Salford.

The next keeper of the bridewell was the deputy constable James Jones, over the years the subject of many complaints. In December 1837 a prisoner, Henry Appleton, escaped and the resulting enquiry revealed administrative chaos. There was space for 12 male prisoners, but the bridewell was grossly overcrowded at the time of the escape, with 17 inmates. The extra five male prisoners had been put in an empty female cell, which had inadequate locks and opened on a yard with a lower wall (female prisoners were thought less capable of climbing over). Appleton had an accomplice, William Tilley, a youth unofficially employed by Jones to guard the bridewell. The evidence of irregular and lax practices came after a vocal campaign about the policing of the town, and was grist to the mill of those demanding reforms.

Not until 1844, though, did the Police Commissioners agree that prisoners should be sent to other jails as soon as possible, and that nobody should be imprisoned for drunkenness or illegal gambling (fines were levied instead). Figures were quoted which demonstrated that the overcrowding stemmed from the practice of locking-up all suspects, even for trivial offences. During 1834, 437 different prisoners spent time in the Warrington bridewell, in 1843, 563 offenders. Even more indicative of the sorry state of administration is that the governor of Kirkdale Prison complained about the filthiness of prisoners arriving from Warrington – the bridewell, subject to strict economies imposed by the Commissioners, had no soap!

The cell corridor of the old bridewell in Irlam Street, photographed in 1900 just before the building was closed and replaced by the present police station on the corner of Arpley Street and Wilson Patten Street.

FURTHER READING for sections 70 and 71: W. Beamont, *Walks about Warrington* (1887) includes useful descriptions of the old bridewell; see also G. Carter, *Warrington Hundred* (1947), and the records of the Police Commissioners ms 1354/1 and 1354/2. For post-1847 records see particularly the minutes of the Borough Watch Committee (Warrington local studies collection)

71. The police force

In 18th-century Warrington there were a few men, elderly and, according to contemporary belief, the worse for drink, who patrolled the streets as a night-watch. In addition, the manor court appointed, from among the ratepayers, four constables who delegated their powers to a paid deputy constable and his assistant. These two, with the motley collection of watchmen, were the only security force in the town. The provision of more effective policing was high on the agenda after 1813, but the Police Commissioners continued with this unsatisfactory arrangement because the cost of anything better was a major deterrent. In September 1816 policing on the cheap was suggested but rejected:

66 owing to the want of Employment it was probable that several persons might be found who would be willing to engage as Watchmen during the ensuing winter at a very low Rate of Wages **99**

In 1820 the formation of a watch to operate only in the darker winter months was approved but seven years later, during an economy drive, the Commissioners voted to disband it. There was constant battle between 'economisers' and 'spenders', according to who could muster the most votes. The deputy constable, Thomas Joynson (on a salary of £60 per year) and the governor of the bridewell, James Jones, were the only proper officers for the whole town – though the note in November 1833 that Jones was 'to be provided with pistols' suggests that he at least might be taken rather more seriously. In autumn 1836 Joynson was accused of a long list of offences involving dereliction of duty, partiality and incompetence. Most were dropped, but this episode (and the escape of Henry Appleton from the bridewell) forced the town to accept that it was virtually unprotected and its policing 'wholly inadequate as respects detection of offenders, the suppression of disturbances, and especially the prevention of disorder and crime'.

A proper force was at last set up, comprising four assistants and the deputy constable, with a police station at Market Gate (soon relocated to Golden Square), uniforms, and a generous weekly wage for an ordinary constable of 21 shillings (£1.05). This was intended to ensure that good men applied, although they also fell from grace: in March 1838 James Holt was discharged for being 'more than once in a state of intoxication, absence from duty, and making false entries in the report book'. In January 1839 the Commissioners proudly reported that transgressions among the officers had been dealt with swiftly and that

66 the town is no longer the resort of so many depredators, who expelled from neighbouring Towns where a vigilant police force exists [i.e. Liverpool and Manchester],

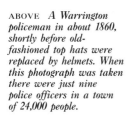

ABOVE *A Warrington policeman in about 1860, shortly before old-fashioned top hats were replaced by helmets. When this photograph was taken there were just nine police officers in a town of 24,000 people.*

RIGHT *The interior of the Irlam Street bridewell and police station, photographed in 1900, and showing the police accommodation. There are pegs for uniforms and helmets, and a bicycle leans against the back wall.*

practice their Evil Courses in places where they can pursue them unmolested. The Security of Person and Property is increased and the series of riot and disorder consequent upon Drunkenness which used so frequently to disgrace our Streets especially on the Sabbath are in great measure prevented **"**

Lancashire County Constabulary was created in 1839 and the town fought successfully to avoid giving up its police to the county force. The Commissioners knew that a *borough* was entitled to keep its own independent police force and this became a main theme in the campaign to apply for a municipal charter. Meanwhile, the police were still subject to debate and dispute. In 1845 it was recorded that there had been problems with money – the chequebook and the financial records were 'very loose and irregular and [have] been a great source of temptation to the Police Officers'. New procedures and new bureaucracy were introduced: James Jones, in a modern-sounding complaint, said that 'various Books and Accounts having to be kept on a much improved plan requires more of my time and consequently I am confined to the Office when my services would be of greater value in the streets'.

The uniform of the Warrington Police, November 1844
blue uniform with collars marked P1, P2, P3, P4
a great-coat; an oil-cloth cape; an under-coat;
a pair of trowsers; a leather stock [truncheon];
a hat similar to those worn by the Liverpool Police

In July 1847 the force came under the control of the newly created borough council and thereafter was slowly expanded. When Charles Stewart, the first chief constable, left in 1852 the manpower comprised one sergeant, three constables, three assistant constables and a clerk, and the police force budget was just over £270 a year. By 1880 there were 37 men and by 1895 this had risen to 54, an increase which, according to the contemporary explanation, was required because of the lawlessness of the navvies building the Ship Canal. The completion of that project did not, however, lead to improvements: in 1907 there were 73 men, so perhaps lawlessness among resident Warringtonians was an equally valid explanation? The Warrington Borough Police force survived until the national reform of police forces in the late 1960s. In 1968, together with those of 12 other boroughs such as Wigan and St Helens, it was absorbed by the Lancashire Constabulary, 129 years after such a union had first been proposed.

72. *Dirty air and effluent*

Unpleasant for all the citizens, rich and poor, was the growing pollution of the town's air and water. The Commissioners' scope for action was limited because they had no powers of enforcement, but there was also an obvious conflict of interest – many were the owners or managers of the industrial plants which belched forth smoke or disgorged effluent. In 1821 attention was drawn 'to the nuisances existing from the smoke issuing from furnaces employed in the

Industry meant air pollution: Warrington skies became smoky and dirty

There were few sewers and noxious effluent ran in the gutters and streets

Attempts to provide proper sanitation were slow and uncertain

The polluted water supplies were a major threat to public health

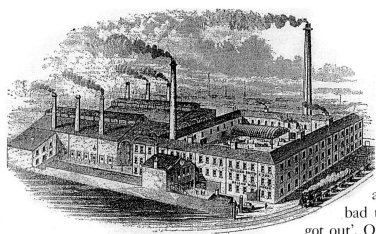

Dallam Wireworks, 1908: pollution was a very serious problem in all the industrial towns of the region. A description of Warrington in 1890 said that 'there were ... 147 factory chimneys emitting black smoke daily, Sundays only excepted. A perpetual smoke hangs over the city like a pall, through which the sunlight only occasionally penetrates'.

working of Engines by Steam' and the most persistent problem emerged as Rylands wireworks in Church Street, where the chimneys produced an 'intolerable smoke'. In 1846 the pollution was such that Mrs John Taylor was hindered in the time-honoured pastime of watching what was going on in the street: 'she had seen carriages stop at Mr. Bostock's and Mr. Dale's when the smoke was so bad that she could not see the Ladies who got out'. Other neighbours were less critical of the problem: perhaps they did not want Mrs Taylor to see what they were up to!

The absence of sanitation was even more serious. There was almost no provision for drainage, the unpaved streets often flooded after rain, and effluent from the top of the town trickled away as best it could. In 1814 there were complaints about 'the water lying in the Channels in Stanley Street and at the Top of Friars Green for want of a Drain or Gutter' and in 1822 some of the more affluent neighbours protested about the sewer (a partly-open channel) through the area, filled to the brim with 'noxious and stagnated matter'. The few short lengths of drain, none flushed by regular running water, emptied into stagnant ditches notorious for their stench. In 1831 a survey found that the ditches along Mill Lane in Howley were blocked and formed pools of raw sewage. In Horsemarket Street privy waste flowed down the road and at the ironically-named Dutton's Honeypot a drain from the town ended in a festering swamp near the river. In the late 1830s some short sewers were constructed in developing middle-class areas and in 1836 it was agreed in principle to provide an effective system, draining to the river. But nothing was done: the Police Commission was dissolved before work was undertaken and, though the introduction of proper sanitation was high on the agenda of the new borough council, it, too, was dilatory and casual about action.

73. *The 1832 cholera epidemic*

In 1832 cholera epidemics raged in many English towns

The disease, from the Far East, was spread by polluted drinking water

Warrington was the scene of one of the worst outbreaks

Over a hundred people died in the town

The authorities were helpless and had few means of tackling the crisis

Cholera, a devastating disease spread by bacteria in polluted drinking water, became a scourge in 19th-century European cities. The disease provoked the first major health scare of the industrial age, bringing to the attention of government and public the need to improve standards of housing, sanitation and medical administration. In the autumn of 1831, before the cholera epidemic reached England, the government passed emergency legislation allowing Boards of Health to be established in places at risk, with unprecedented powers of direct action. A Board of Health was formed in Warrington in February 1832, though there was no certainty that cholera would come to the town. The Board discussed the provision of a hospital, appointed doctors to inspect lodging houses, and tried to deal with insanitary middens and broken drains. Work was hampered by bureaucratic inefficiency, shortage of funds, and complete uncertainty about what action would be effective.

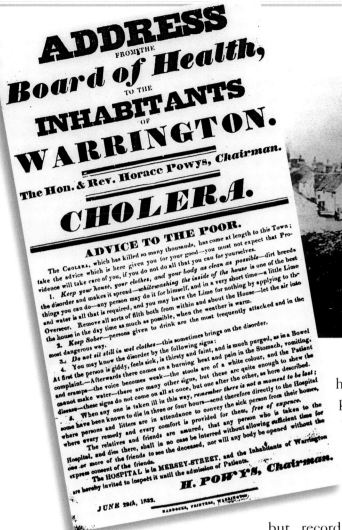

ADDRESS
FROM THE
Board of Health,
TO THE
INHABITANTS
OF
WARRINGTON.
The Hon. & Rev. Horace Powys, Chairman.

CHOLERA.

ADVICE TO THE POOR.

The CHOLERA, which has killed so many thousands, has come at length to this Town; take the advice which is here given you for your good—you must not expect that Providence will take care of you, if you do not do all that you can for yourselves.

1. *Keep your house, your clothes, and your body as clean as possible*—dirt breeds the disorder and makes it spread—whitewashing the inside of the house is one of the best things you can do—any person may do it for himself, and in a very short time—a little Lime and water is all that is required, and you may have the Lime for nothing by applying to the Overseer. Remove all sorts of filth both from within and about the House—let the air into the house in the day time as much as possible, when the weather is warm.

2. *Keep Sober*—persons given to drink are the most frequently attacked and in the most dangerous way.

3. *Do not sit still in wet clothes*—this sometimes brings on the disorder, as in a Bowel complaint.

4. You may know the disorder by the following signs:

At first the person is giddy, feels sick, is thirsty and faint, and is much purged, as in the Stomach, vomiting, and cramps—the voice becomes weak—the stools are of a white colour, and the Patient cannot make water—there are many other signs, but these are quite enough to shew the disease—these signs do not come on all at once, but one after the other, as here described.

5. When any one is taken ill in this way, *remember there is not a moment to be lost*; some have been known to die in three or four hours—send therefore directly to the Hospital where persons and litters are in attendance to convey the sick person from their homes, that any person who is taken to the Hospital, and dies there, shall in no case be interred without allowing sufficient time for one or more of the friends to see the deceased, nor will any body be opened without the express consent of the friends.

The relatives and friends are assured, free of expence, and every comfort is provided for them,

The HOSPITAL is in MERSEY-STREET, and the Inhabitants of Warrington are hereby invited to inspect it until the admission of Patients.

H. POWYS, Chairman.

JUNE 29th, 1832.

MADDOCKS, PRINTER, WARRINGTON.

LEFT *Poster advertising precautions to be taken against cholera infection, 1832. It assumed, probably in most cases wrongly, that the poor were sufficiently literate to be able to read the densely-printed text.*

ABOVE *The Warrington township workhouse in Church Street [right] was particularly badly affected by the cholera outbreak. Many inmates died and the building had to be evacuated.*

The town waited anxiously, hoping that nothing would happen, but on 28 May a suspected case was reported and on 6 June there was a confirmed fatality in Oliver Street. Two weeks later it was clear that the much-feared epidemic had started. The authorities could do little but record the number of cases, burn bedding and clothing in infected houses, and isolate victims as soon as possible. On 27 June cholera broke out among the occupants of the workhouse and by 5 July a total of 115 cases had been notified, with about twenty new ones each day. In the closely-packed courts and yards, especially on the north side of the town, the panic-stricken people could not escape the infection. During mid-August patients were being removed to the isolation hospital set up in the hastily-evacuated asylum in Church Street, but what could the poor do? They could not move elsewhere, and they had no money to take other action, while the hospital, though useful, could not accommodate all the victims. Between late June and mid-August at least 300 people were infected, while the total number of fatalities listed by the Board of Health is 117, so well over one in three victims died.

The epidemic reached its peak in late July and on 24 September the Board held its last regular meeting, but this traumatic event was etched on people's memories. Not only was the disease was so destructive but – like bubonic plague in previous centuries – nobody seemed able to stop it. Fifteen years later, when cholera again began to spread, the government conceded that public health could not be left to chance but required public action. Legislation was passed which, for the first time, obliged local authorities to take serious steps to deal with it.

Dr James Kendrick senior, the leading medical man of Warrington in the first half of the 19th century. He was one of those who struggled to prevent the arrival of cholera in 1832, and who encountered major problems of bureaucratic inertia and shortage of money. When the disease arrived, he sought to tackle it, but with little success as medical knowledge at the time was rudimentary.

FURTHER READING: The original records of the 1832 Board of Health are in Warrington Library, including the *Memorandum Book* which gives detailed records of the progress of the epidemic: ref. ms 50; I. Sellers, *Early modern Warrington*, deals with the epidemic in detail, as does P. Chadwick, *The sanitary state of Warrington from the early nineteenth century to the beginning of the twentieth century* (MA dissertation, University of Manchester, 1996) – copy in local studies collection, ref. ms 2782; a contemporary account is T.K. Glazebrook, *A record of events during the prevalence of cholera in Warrington* (1833).

74. Public health in the nineteenth century

Public health improvements were desperately needed but action was slow

Epidemics were frequent, the death rate high, and sanitation minimal

Reports highlighted deplorable housing conditions and the lack of basic facilities

After the late 1850s work on sewerage schemes and piped water was undertaken

The Reverend Philip Carpenter (1819-77), minister at Cairo Street chapel, was a leading campaigner on many health, sanitation and social issues in Warrington in the late 1840s and early 1850s. He recorded his dismay and shock at the squalid conditions in lodging houses and slum housing areas and urged the new borough council to take action to alleviate these problems.

Dealing with public health was a responsibility of the borough council after 1847 and the first mayor, William Beamont, took the task seriously: one of his first acts was to write to the acknowledged national expert on the subject, Edwin Chadwick, to seek advice. The poor record of the town, the conspicuously bad housing and sanitation, and the recurrence of epidemics meant that there was pressure for action, spearheaded by a vociferous campaign waged by the Warrington Working Men's Health of Towns Association (led by the Reverend Philip Carpenter of Cairo Street Chapel) between 1847 and 1850. It publicised disturbing statistics. A survey of 616 houses in the town centre showed that 132 had no privy of any sort, 423 had no water supply, and 533 had no drains. In the 484 houses with access to a privy, there was an average of almost 12 people per privy, while those with water supplies had an average of 24 people per water pump (the town had no piped water at all). Only 44 per cent of the streets were paved, and scavenging, the removal of refuse and 'night soil' or human excreta, was grossly inadequate – as late as 1867, privies were emptied on average only twice a year.

From 1857 a sewerage system, a project first seriously considered twenty years before, was finally built. The town centre was sewered by 1862, Bank Quay from 1866, Howley in 1869-1872, Bewsey and Winwick Road in 1874-1877, and Latchford in the early 1880s, but until 1886, when the first treatment works was opened at Longford, all effluent still flowed untreated straight into the Mersey. From 1857 the Corporation tried to tackle the problem of smoke pollution in and around the town centre. It was hindered not only by the unwillingness of factory owners to take action, but also by the attitude of the townspeople, for whom – not surprisingly – smoking chimneys represented work: one contemporary spoke of the 'sadness at finding chimneys smokeless'.

FURTHER READING: P. Chadwick, *The sanitary state of Warrington from the early nineteenth century to the beginning of the twentieth century* (MA dissertation, University of Manchester, 1996) – local studies collection ref. ms 2782

75. The sanitary condition of Warrington, 1872

As more statistical data became available, and medical research gave explanations of the causes of epidemic disease, the link between poor sanitation and unsatisfactory public health was brought into focus. Local authorities were compelled to take basic action on health and housing matters: slowly, death rates started to fall and the standard of public health to rise, assisted by measures such as the provision of clean piped water. The prelude to action was frequently a detailed report into the sanitary condition of a town, undertaken by a doctor commissioned by the government – an outsider less likely to be influenced by a desire to conceal the bad points. In the case of Warrington, a series of fever outbreaks prompted the government to send in Dr Robert Ballard in the autumn of 1871.

He noted that epidemic disease was rife – in 1870 there had been 30 deaths from smallpox, 56 from measles, 20 from scarlet fever, 36 from whooping cough, 56 from typhoid and typhus, and 94 from diarrhoea. An average of fifty children a year died from diarrhoea (gastro-enteritis), and typhoid and typhus accounted for 12 per cent of all deaths in the town The death rate, at 30 per 1000, was one of the highest in the country, and Ballard noted with concern that 'typhoid fever has gradually become more prevalent

Dr Ballard's report on the public health of the town was published in 1872

It highlighted the poor record in all aspects of health, hygiene and sanitation

Numerous detailed examples of disgraceful housing conditions were quoted

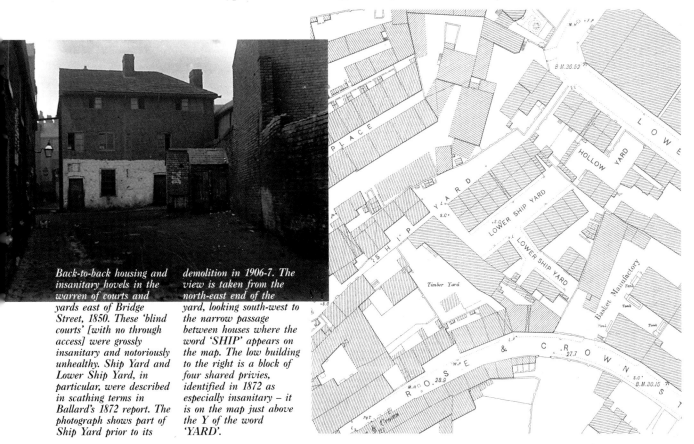

Back-to-back housing and insanitary hovels in the warren of courts and yards east of Bridge Street, 1850. These 'blind courts' [with no through access] were grossly insanitary and notoriously unhealthy. Ship Yard and Lower Ship Yard, in particular, were described in scathing terms in Ballard's 1872 report. The photograph shows part of Ship Yard prior to its demolition in 1906-7. The view is taken from the north-east end of the yard, looking south-west to the narrow passage between houses where the word 'SHIP' appears on the map. The low building to the right is a block of four shared privies, identified in 1872 as especially insanitary – it is on the map just above the Y of the word 'YARD'.

of late years, not among the poor alone … but among the class of persons who when they are ill apply to a private medical practitioner' – in other words, the lower middle classes were beginning to be affected. The town was becoming unhealthier year after year.

He commented particularly on how epidemics raged through the tightly-packed courts of the town centre, occupied by the very poorest classes: 'Many of the houses of the poor which I visited were very old, dilapidated, and very dirty, quite unfit for human habitation'. In Silver Street he found an upper floor room used for a family *and* its pigeons, with at the rear of the houses a large open space dotted with pools of liquid effluent and a row of sheds in which pigs and a donkey were housed 'in a state of extreme filth'. A midden closet used by all the inhabitants of the row was 'nearly full of excrement to the seat, and very offensive'. In a dead-end passage only three feet wide, beside a lodging house in Scotland Road, was one privy shared between four houses: the effluent from the privy drained through cracks in a stone wall into one of the houses. All over the town centre similar examples of filth and squalor were found.

The poorer houses were reliant on wells for their water supplies, but as 'the contents of the numerous middens must necessarily soak more or less into [the soil] and when, in addition, other contaminations, as from grave-yards, imperfectly-drained stables, pigsties &c are taken into account' the well water was seriously polluted. Piped water, though, was not much better. It was 'sometimes turbid and abounding in animalculae' and in the dry seasons was sent from Appleton unfiltered and impure, carrying the drainage of 'manured tillage … farmyards, cottages discharging sewage into the river, and cesspools'.

Ballard made a series of practical recommendations to the council. First, they should appoint a medical officer of health (Liverpool had done so in 1847 but towns as such as Warrington were reluctant to add to the salary bill and resented the idea of expert 'interference'). They should tackle the most pressing sanitary problems: replace earth-closets and middens with flushing WCs; use recent legislation to demolish the worst slum housing (though they did not have to provide replacement housing, so clearance added to overcrowding as displaced residents moved in with other families); improve the water supply for domestic consumption; and introduce contingency plans for dealing with epidemics. These were modest but realistic aspirations, and over the next twenty years the Corporation implemented more active policies towards health, sanitation and medical provision. Most important of all, Winwick water became generally available, and no longer was a glass of Warrington's tapwater full of 'animalculae' – minuscule wriggling and swimming creatures. And yet … there were nine major scarlet fever epidemics between 1875 and 1892, accounting for the terrible total of 432 deaths, and a smallpox outbreak in 1892-1893 killed 63 people. There was plenty still to do.

FURTHER READING: Dr. Ballard's *Report on the Sanitary Condition of Warrington, and the prevalence of fever in the town* (1872) – local studies collection ref. P1787; P. Chadwick, *The sanitary state of Warrington from the early nineteenth century to the beginning of the twentieth century* (MA dissertation, University of Manchester, 1996) local studies collection ref. ms 2782

76. Water supplies

Piped water supplies were gradually introduced after 1847

The water came originally from Appleton, later from Winwick

The waterworks company was bought by the Corporation in 1890

The provision of piped water was the greatest single cause of improving public health

Until the mid-19th century Warrington was supplied with water only from wells and pumps within the town. By the 1840s all were becoming grossly polluted and unfit for drinking. Although contemporaries were unaware of it, this was the main cause of the town's increasingly bad public health record. There was another problem: industries were demanding ever-larger quantities of water, for processing and to supply steam engines, and the wells could not cope with this. In 1846 the Warrington Waterworks Company received parliamentary powers to provide a public supply of piped water, and in the following year the 540-acre reservoir at Appleton was completed, holding over

50 million gallons. Demand grew rapidly and, although the reservoir was extended in 1858 and additional culverts were laid to tap the Daresbury and Halton Brooks, the Cheshire sources were overstretched by the mid-1860s.

In 1868, on the advice of Thomas Duncan, Liverpool's water engineer, two new wells were sunk into the sandstone beneath Winwick, linked to a pumping station. Thereafter the domestic supply came from Winwick while the Appleton reservoir was given over to supplying industries because, as we have seen, that source supply was itself polluted by the run-off from farms and cottages. Warrington Corporation bought the waterworks company for £278,000 in 1890. The population had risen from 34,000 in 1861 to 80,000 in 1901 and industrial growth also created a large new demand for water. New wells were sunk in the Winwick area and in 1903 Appleton Reservoir was further increased in size.

By this time many towns in Lancashire and Cheshire were looking further afield for water: thus, Manchester turned to Thirlmere, and Stockport to the Peak District. Warrington was badly placed, since it was distant from any upland area and local streams could not be dammed to create sizeable lakes. After the First World War the Waterworks Department searched for a long-distance supply and in 1923 announced plans for two large reservoirs in the upper Ceiriog valley in Denbighshire. There was a vociferous campaign against the plan on environmental grounds and because this was one of the heartlands of traditional Welsh rural life and culture. The plan provoked an early flowering of Welsh nationalism and was defeated in parliament.

From 1928, therefore, Warrington had to take water from Liverpool's Vyrnwy Aqueduct, while in 1930 a new treatment works was constructed at Howley to make (relatively) clean the dirty waters of the Mersey, not for drinking but to supply the town's industries. This works was extended in 1939, while at the same time new domestic supplies were provided from underground sources on the ridge behind Frodsham. Demand grew extremely rapidly: in 1898 the Warrington Waterworks supplied a total of 680 million gallons, of which 32 per cent was used in industry. In 1947, by contrast, the supply was 4,380 million gallons, about 85 per cent of which went for industrial use.

A reliable water supply transformed the lives of Warringtonians. Not only was safe drinking water available by 1900 to almost everybody, but domestic supplies meant that houses, clothes and people were cleaner than had ever before been possible. Piped water was instrumental in improving public health: water-closets were installed even in ordinary houses, replacing ash-cans and earth-closets. Sewers were flushed regularly – a major problem had been that drains were choked with filth because the contents were not washed through. Water allowed basic domestic hygiene, especially when combined with another local product – cheap soap. Watering-carts, sent round to lay dust and wash the

Child at risk! The drinking fountain in Sankey Street, outside Holy Trinity church, was erected in 1860 using money donated by Benjamin Pierpoint, 'for the relief of travellers'. It was removed in the mid-1930s because the great improvement in medical knowledge had revealed that communal drinking cups represented a health hazard – while the ubiquity of piped water now made such a source largely superfluous.

paving, became a feature of the summer months in Warrington as in other industrial towns. The great expansion of manufacturing in the town would not have been possible without the ready availability of water. We simply turn on the tap, but going to the well for heavy pails of precious water was an almost universal feature of Warrington life only 150 years ago. The investment made from the late 1840s onwards was money well spent.

FURTHER READING: J. Deas, *The Warrington Corporation Waterworks* (1901) local studies collection ref. P2101; A.T. Davies, *Evicting a community: the case for the preservation of the historical and beautiful valley of the Ceiriog in North Wales* (Cymmrodorion, 1923); *History of the Warrington Water Department* (1947), local studies collection ref. P8242992, reprinted in G. Carter, *Warrington Hundred* (1947)

77. *Irish immigration in the nineteenth century*

Warrington experienced substantial Irish immigration in the years after 1845

The Irish crowded into insanitary housing in courts behind town centre streets

They were blamed for most social ills and evils, usually without cause

As in all other towns in the north-west, the years after 1845 saw the emergence of 'the Irish problem'. The Great Famine of 1845-6 forced massive emigration from Ireland, much of which was destined for Liverpool, but many migrants did not stay on Merseyside and moved on to other towns. Many of these Irish were pitifully poor vagrants and this attracted the attention of the authorities. In April 1849 the Watch Committee of the Corporation heard that

“ in consequence of the serious increase of the vagrancy in the Borough arising from the great influx of Irish paupers … Mr Alderman Beamont suggested that the opinion of Captain Stewart (Police) should be asked as to how far it would be practicable to require all vagrants to present themselves at the police office for a ticket, prior to admission into the vagrant office [which provided temporary shelter for these people] ”

An 1830 illustration of the typical housing of Irish peasants: it was from such conditions that, even before the 1840s, many migrants had come to north-west England. The terrible famine of 1845-6 swelled a steady stream to a flood, and many pitifully poor Irish migrants came to towns such as Warrington in the next twenty years.

That summer the Corporation petitioned the Privy Council, expressing alarm at the numbers of Irish landing at Liverpool and the fever which they allegedly brought to Warrington, but since Ireland was part of the United Kingdom the migration could not be stopped. A year later the Watch Committee heard of the 'numbers of Irishmen thronging the streets and courts of the town but especially Bridge and Buttermarket Streets' and in 1858 the *Warrington Guardian* reported that the cost simply of removing Irish paupers from the town was equivalent to a penny on the rates.

The newcomers were forced to live in the most insanitary courts off Bridge Street and Horsemarket Street. One of the most notorious was Ship Yard, a chaos of back-to-back houses and sheds behind Bridge Street and Lower Bank Street. The 1851 census shows that it was almost entirely occupied by recently arrived Irish, crammed into the little hovels. Here is the entry for just one household, living in a single tiny house in the yard:

Name	Status	Married?	Age	Occupation	Birthplace
Andrew Golighe	head	married	35	agricultural labourer	Ireland
Betty Golighe	wife	married	30	labourer	Ireland
Bridget Golighe	daughter	unmarried	8		Ireland
Elizabeth Golighe	daughter	unmarried	11mth		England
Michael McDenitt	lodger	unmarried	25	agricultural labourer	Ireland
John Egan	lodger	unmarried	26	agricultural labourer	Ireland
Patrick Beren	lodger	married	37	agricultural labourer	Ireland
Bridget Beren	lodger	married	38	labourer	Ireland
Libby Beren	lodger	unmarried	9		Ireland
Laurence Mars	lodger	married	46	labourer	Ireland
Mary Mars	lodger	married	36	labourer	Ireland
Patrick McDermott	lodger	unmarried	30	labourer	Ireland
Michael McDermott	lodger	unmarried	18	labourer	Ireland
Martin Burls	lodger	unmarried	26	labourer	Ireland
Michael McCook	lodger	unmarried	37	labourer	Ireland
John Egan	lodger	unmarried	25	labourer	Ireland
Bridget Joys	lodger	married	52	labourer	Ireland
Thomas Jurdan	lodger	married	21	labourer	Ireland
John Tunny	lodger	married	46	labourer	Ireland
Michael Ware	lodger	unmarried	21	labourer	Ireland

Inevitably, perhaps, relations between the Irish and the existing English population were often hostile, and Frederick Monks, writing in 1897 about life in Warrington in the 1840s, recalled the violent disturbances which regularly broke out:

66 The disturbances, or Irish rows as they were called, were a special feature at harvest time. Many have been the times on a Sunday afternoon when a few roughs from 'Town's End' (as Winwick Road was then called) have started one by wilfully and deliberately knocking a few Irishmen down in the neighbourhood of Town Hill or Buttermarket Street. The screams and shouts of the wounded very soon brought scores of their countrymen to the rescue. 99

The Irish became the universal scapegoats, blamed (usually wrongly, here as everywhere else) for all sorts of evils and problems – disease, insanitary housing, crime, drunkenness, prostitution and filth. When contemporaries really looked at the circumstances in which they lived, their often-pitiful plight became all too apparent – but many had fled from death by slow starvation, and even the worst housing in a Lancashire town seemed better than that fate.

66 I never knew such a winter and spring and summer [1847] ... inundated with many thousands of starving Irish of the worst class ... To go into the bed-room of an Irish lodging-house, with one or two ill of fever, and no windows open, walls and floor and everywhere recking of filth 99
Reverend Philip Carpenter, minister of Cairo Street Chapel

FURTHER READING: census returns for 1851; J.K. Walton, *Lancashire: a social history 1558-1939* (1987) gives useful background material on Irish migration.

78. The Warrington Infirmary

An important aspect of health improvement was the provision of medical care

Warrington's first dispensary for the poor was opened in 1810

In 1876 the town's first general hospital, the Infirmary, was opened

Until the early 19th century medical care of any sort was minimal. Warrington had apothecaries and unqualified doctors – for example, after a mining accident at Whiston in 1690 the injured were treated at cost by Mr Booth of Warrington, a public-spirited apothecary – but for most people no help was available. During the later 18th century larger towns and cities saw attempts to provide more effective medical services, and charitable dispensaries were opened to help the deserving poor. In Warrington such a project was suggested in 1809 and at a public meeting in January 1810, chaired by John Blackburne MP, it was agreed that

> 66 a dispensary for the relief of the sick poor in this town and neighbourhood should, if possible, be established, and in order to carry so desirable an object into effect, a committee be appointed [and] a building procured for the purpose of being converted into a Dispensary containing … one small room for the physicians, one small room for the surgeons, open waiting room for the patients, a shop for the more readily preparing and dispensing of medicines, and rooms for a residentiary apothecary 99

The dispensary opened in April 1810 in a building in Market Street, staffed part-time by two physicians in ordinary (i.e. general practitioners), one of whom was James Kendrick senior, perhaps the greatest doctor in 19th-century Warrington. Two surgeons were in attendance and there was a full-time apothecary who had 'a house, fire, candles, at the expense of the Institution, with a salary of not less than £70 per annum, including the maintenance and wages of a female servant'. During the first nine months 697 patients were seen, £531 was raised in subscriptions, and a profit of £277 carried forward. In later years other sources of funding were tried, such as benefit concerts (one at the New Theatre in 1819 raised £11 3s. 6d.). The sick poor had to apply to a subscriber for a recommendation to the dispensary, thus ensuring that only the more deserving cases (or the more 'respectable' patients) were seen. Afterwards they were expected to make public acknowledgement of the help received:

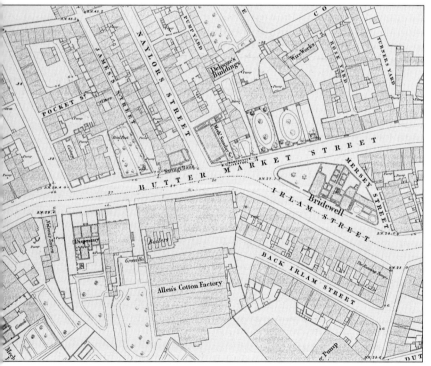

The original Warrington Dispensary was in Buttermarket Street [lower left of map] not far from the old bridewell in Irlam Street. Note the densely-packed working class housing in the Naylor Street and Cockhedge area, and the narrow courts and yards.

> 66 Accept my grateful acknowledgements for the recommendation to the physicians and medical officers of the Dispensary with which you favoured me, through whose kind attentions and the blessing of God, I am now recovered 99

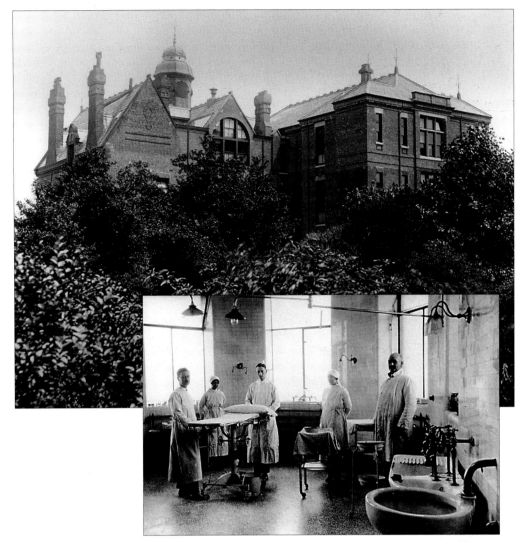

Warrington Infirmary photographed in 1897: its imposing architecture, with large gables, tall ornamental chimneys and a cupola, was typical of later Victorian public institutions, but its situation at the back of Bank Park also demanded an appropriately impressive appearance.

The new operating theatre in the infirmary, 1924: a contemporary humorist said of the operating table which is shown in this picture that 'it has not learnt to do operations yet, but I have no doubt that we shall teach it to do so'.

The dispensary moved in 1819 to purpose-built premises in Buttermarket Street, and in the same year a 'ladies' charity' was formed to give maternity help to poor women. In 1840 the House of Recovery, an isolation hospital for fever cases, opened in Orford Street. However, population growth, the shocking state of public health, and rising expectations of what should be done for the poor, meant that the accommodation became quite inadequate. The town needed a proper well-equipped hospital, but not until 1876 was the Warrington Infirmary and Dispensary built in Kendrick Street, paid for largely by private donations: Thomas Parr gave £1,000 and James Hatton £10,000, and the Corporation gave the land which had formed part of Bank Park. So rapidly did demand for medical care increase that in 1900 it was decided to demolish the hospital and rebuild it on the same site, a project completed in March 1908. Again the entire cost, £15,000, came from public and private subscription.

FURTHER READING: anon., *Warrington Infirmary and Dispensary: an epitome* (1921) local studies collection ref. P2322; P. Chadwick, *The sanitary state of Warrington from the early nineteenth century to the beginning of the twentieth century* (MA dissertation, University of Manchester, 1996) ref. ms 2782; R.G. Guest Gornall, *Warrington Infirmary 1877-1977* (Cheshire Area Health Authority, 1977)

During the 19th century many new churches and chapels were opened

The Roman Catholics were able to worship freely and their numbers grew fast

Warrington was more Anglican than most Lancashire towns

In 1851, 46 per cent of its population regularly attended worship

The rebuilding of the parish church, and the construction of its great spire, was carried out in 1859-67. All over England such 'restoration' work was in progress as churches were improved by the Victorians, but very few have such a priceless record of the work being undertaken. This photograph was almost certainly taken by the Reverend Quekett, whose diary records the purchase of a camera shortly before and who had spearheaded the campaign to raise funds for the rebuilding.

Religion played an important part in the lives of many citizens of Victorian Warrington, not only in the form of church-going but also in the education of the children, the work of charities, and the strong influence exercised by the clergy and the leading churchgoers over the moral lives of their fellow-citizens. Yet here, as in other towns in the north-west, religion was not universally popular, and the Christian faith was divided among itself.

The 250 years after the Reformation saw damaging neglect of the fabric of St Elphin's parish church, followed by piecemeal and inadequate patching. Despite the rebuilding of the tower and nave, and the insertion of wooden galleries in approved Georgian fashion, by 1850 the church was in a dangerous condition and major reconstruction work was approved. The architects Frederick and Horace Francis designed a new church which incorporated some of the existing fabric, and the work was carried out in 1859-67. They sought, very successfully, to use a medieval style in keeping with the retained parts of the old church, but swept away the intrusive 18th-century

Possibly the earliest Warrington photograph, showing the parish church in about 1854, prior to its reconstruction and before the clearance of the graveyard after the opening of the new cemetery. The extraordinary number of gravestones testifies to the fact that this was the only burial place in the whole parish until the mid-1850s.

features. The nave and south transept were completely reconstructed, the tower partly rebuilt with impressive new crossing piers, and crowning the work was the magnificent 281-foot spire, the third highest on an English parish church. The present building, very impressive though now somewhat stranded amid the development of the 20th century, is thus an outstanding example of Victorian architecture, masquerading as medieval.

Several new Anglican churches were built during the 19th century, including St Paul, Bewsey Road (1830), St Ann (1864), St Barnabas, Lovely Lane (1879), St Peter (1891) and St Luke (1893). These reflect the increasing sense of urgency within the Church of England about the need to provide churches in working-class areas. The percentage of the population regularly attending church was already in decline, and new churches were seen as one answer to the problem. The Anglicans faced strong competition from other denominations. After the 1820s, when the last of the laws restricting religious freedom had been abolished, the Roman Catholic Church enjoyed a remarkable new phase of growth. In Warrington, as

elsewhere in the north-west, the influx of Irish migrants from the mid-1840s greatly strengthened their numbers. St Alban (Bewsey Street), the first purpose-built Catholic church in the town, was opened in 1823 and was followed by others, such as St Mary, Buttermarket Street with its tall tower by Pugin (1877), and Sacred Heart, Bank Quay (1894). During the early 19th century the nonconformists in Warrington experienced a succession of splits and internal disputes, but by the 1840s their fortunes were reviving. The Wesleyan Methodists, in particular, were reinvigorated and their Bank Street (later Bold Street) chapel became a focus for evangelical and temperance activity, with a very large Sunday School and a prominent social role in charity work in the town.

The 1851 census of religious worship provided a national survey of church attendance and showed the strength of the different denominations. It also revealed the increasing failure of religion as a whole to inspire the mass of the people. In Lancashire only 35 per cent of the population attended church on census Sunday – Warrington, with 46 per cent attendance, was thus relatively devout. In the town 25 per cent of the population attended an Anglican church on that day, seven per cent a Methodist chapel, seven per cent a Catholic church, and four per cent a place of worship of another denomination. In relative terms, Warrington was one of the most Anglican places in the north-west (at Rochdale, Preston and Liverpool, for example, only 11 per cent of the people went to an Anglican church) and its proportion of Catholics was, not unexpectedly, a long way below that of Liverpool.

The completion of St Mary's Roman Catholic church, Buttermarket Street, showing the ceremony for the capping of the pinnacles, 10 September 1906. The main part of the church was finished in the early 1880s. The church catered for a mainly working-class congregation and was built on the site of the former Allen's cotton factory.

FURTHER READING: The statistics are from C. Phillips and J.H. Smith, *Lancashire and Cheshire since 1540* (1994); the *Victoria County History of Lancashire* (vol.3) gives useful accounts of the main churches in the town. Ian Sellers, *Early modern Warrington*, is especially informative about the religious history of the town in the first half of the 19th century.

80. *Education in the nineteenth century*

Traditionally, education and religion were closely related. Warrington's two older schools, the Boteler Grammar School and the Bluecoat School, were both Anglican foundations where religious instruction and attendance at the parish church were compulsory, while the Academy was a focus of nonconformist religious belief. In the early 19th century new attitudes to education emerged, as local and national government began to play an ever-greater role. From 1813 the state gave funds to the National Society for the Education of the Poor in the Principles of the Church of England, which ran 'National Schools': the first in Warrington was in Church Street (1833). The nonconformists, as the Warrington Education Society, also became involved in education provision, in 1841 opening Newton Street British school (which later became the admirable People's College – the Anglican rector vehemently opposed its establishment).

Educational provision was poor throughout the 19th century

The town council refused to play any part in education or schools until 1903

Total reliance was placed upon the religious denominations

Literacy levels in Warrington in the 1880s were among the worst in the region

Pupils of the Warrington or Boteler Grammar School stand outside the school buildings in School Brow off Manchester Road, 1905.

Elementary education was not compulsory until 1870, but Warrington was notably slow in the provision of schooling not only before that date but also after it. The town did not take advantage of the powers to establish School Boards which could build and manage elementary schools and instead relied very heavily upon the work of the churches. In 1853 the Heathside National School was built and this was followed by a succession of other Church of England schools (St Ann's 1864, St James 1868, Trinity 1868 and Hamilton Street 1877). The nonconformists opened the Wycliffe Schools in 1868 and Silver Street in 1887, and the Catholic schools included Our Lady in 1872 and St Benedict and St Mary in the 1880s. The effect of this was that the borough council played no part in educational provision until April 1903, when it was forced to do so under the terms of the 1902 Education Act.

The consequences of poor educational provision before the 1880s are clear. In 1851 only one Warrington child in eight received any education at day school, a figure about the national average, but the town had far fewer Sunday schools than most places of its size – probably because the nonconformists, strong advocates of these schools, were relatively weak here. This meant that the proportion of children who received *any* sort of education was well below the national average. And the education system failed to expand in the way that it did elsewhere. In 1864, when only 46 per cent of people marrying in Warrington were able to sign their names in the register, the town had the fourth-highest rate of illiteracy in north-west England, twice the national level. In

The National School in Church Street was opened in 1833: this photograph was taken in about 1900. In the Victorian school system, teaching took place in one huge central classroom (note its very large main windows) with the numerous children monitored by pupil teachers.

1883 the rate was still 26 per cent, still double the national average, and in the early 1890s a Royal Commission reported, rather delicately, that educational provision in the town was 'not above the average'.

Secondary education, moreover, was entirely inadequate. After a series of crises the Boteler Grammar School closed completely in 1858. Five years later it reopened in a new building and by 1867 had 62 day boys and eight boarders – in that year it was said that 'many of the people ... in Warrington declared that they had never remembered it so prosperous and popular' – but the school was an elitist institution: few sons of clerks or working people were educated there and hardly any scholarships for poor boys were available. There was, furthermore, no girls' grammar school, and other secondary education was minimal. It was not an impressive record for a town which in the 18th century had been 'the Athens of the North'.

FURTHER READING: anon., *History of the elementary schools of Warrington* (Warrington Guardian, 1933); H. Lievesley, *Boteler Grammar School, Warrington 1526-1976*; W.B. Stephens, *Adult education and society in an industrial town: Warrington 1800-1900* (University of Exeter Press, 1980)

81. *The Museum and Library*

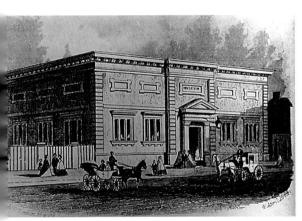

The Academy encouraged the development of cultural life in the town. A local printing business, Eyres' Press, specialised in the publishing of scholarly works, a field in which Warrington had few rivals among provincial towns. The Eyres family also ran a bookshop and started the *Warrington Advertiser* (1756). Private libraries flourished from the middle of the 18th century. The Circulating Library (founded 1760 and linked with the Academy) was one of the earliest in the north-west: it was a private subscription library, most of whose members were among the social elite. The same men also patronised the learned societies of early 19th-century Warrington. The Institution for the Cultivation of Sciences, Literature and The Arts was founded in 1811: its members established a museum of natural history, heard lectures, and discussed the scientific and philosophical issues of the day. By 1807 there was a Botanical Society and in 1838 the Natural History Society was formed. Numerous other, often shadowy, societies are noted in passing references during the next hundred years. The town's intellectual life was flourishing and Warrington probably saw a good deal more such activity than other comparable towns in the region. The inspiration of the Academy was crucial.

Several societies collected curiosities and scientific specimens, or built up libraries of books and papers, but there were problems in accommodating these. In 1838 the Circulating Library, in a poor state and with an uncertain future, amalgamated with the new Natural History Society, which also absorbed the museum of the Warrington Institution. Many members wanted

Engraving of the Museum and Library building, 1864. Economies necessitated the scaling-down of the original design, but nonetheless this view illustrates the elegance and simplicity of the building. Subsequent extensions have altered the symmetry. Note that at this stage Museum Street did not yet exist.

In the late 18th and early 19th centuries learned societies appeared

Warrington had a thriving cultural life among the wealthier citizens

The town had Britain's first municipal library (1845) and third municipal museum

Laying the foundation stone of the Museum and Library, 22 September 1855. The event was attended by over 2,000 people, and was presided over by William Beamont. The greenfield site is apparent from the photograph – in the background can be seen the enclosed gardens which occupied much of the site and were possibly those known to have been held by Warrington friary in the later Middle Ages.

the collections to be more widely available for the instruction and edification of the townspeople and in 1844 negotiations to give public access began. The granting of borough status in 1847 encouraged this idea and in 1848 the first Town Clerk, John Fitchett Marsh, negotiated for the property of the library and the institution to be vested in the council. He planned to make use of the 1845 Museums Act, which allowed towns to fund museums from the rates, and in the autumn 1848 Warrington Museum and Library was founded. The town was only the third in Britain to have a municipal museum and, almost by accident, it became the very first to have a municipal library. This was a proud achievement for enlightened civic enterprise, reinforced by the building in 1855-7 of the present Museum and Library on the corner of Bold Street. Warrington could claim to be a true centre of cultural excellence: in 1886, partly because its collections dated back to the 1760s, the library, with 20,000 volumes, was larger per head of population than that of almost any other English provincial town.

FURTHER READING: The *minute book of the Circulating Library* 1760-1841 is in the Warrington local studies collection, reference ms1; G. Carter, *Warrington Hundred* (1947), gives a useful summary of the history of the museum and library; W.B. Stephens, *Adult education and society in an industrial town: Warrington 1800-1900* (University of Exeter Press, 1980) is very informative on the development of the learned societies and institutions.

82. *Leisure, entertainment and sport in the nineteenth century*

At the beginning of the 19th century only the elite had leisure time. Everybody else worked exceptionally long hours and holidays were rare. By the end of the century working hours were substantially reduced, wage levels improved, paid holidays becoming commonplace, and Bank Holidays had been enforced since 1872. Most working people had some spare time for leisure, recreation and entertainment, and a bit of money to spend on it. This fundamental change is reflected in the much wider variety of leisure and entertainment on offer.

There are references to musical concerts in Warrington as early as the 1750s, and by the 1780s more detailed accounts of entertainments appear. In October 1784, for example, magic and illusionist shows were held at the *Red Lion* in Bridge Street; plays and entertainments were performed at the Old Coffee House in Horsemarket Street from at least 1788; there were theatrical performances for the members of local society at the Assembly Rooms; and Mr Munden, a well-known comedian, came to the town with his company in 1790 and 1793. The Warrington Gentlemen's Catch and Glee Club met regularly at the *Red Lion* in the years after 1809 and by the 1830s its concerts were a major attraction, with a resident six-piece band. The Warrington Musical Society was founded in about 1815, and was associated with the musical evenings and concerts held regularly at the *Red Lion* during the 1830s and 1840s.

The first theatre was in Scotland Road – it probably opened in about 1805 though the first definite reference is from 1818. It closed in 1838, when theatrical performances were transferred to the Music Hall in the Market Place, but reopened in 1846 as the Theatre Royal. From 1862 it had a rival in the new Public Hall in Rylands Street – the theatre was taken over in 1872 by the famous impresario Richard Brinsley Sheridan and renamed the Prince of Wales, with a revived reputation, and in 1884 was completely rebuilt to become, once again, the Theatre Royal. Other short-lived theatres came and went, while venues such as the Public Hall (which survived only until 1892, before being transformed into the Royal Court Theatre and then burned to the ground at Christmas 1906), relied heavily on melodramas, musical entertainments and variety acts such as jugglers and ventriloquists. It was also the setting for more elevated musical entertainments, such as Mr Oakden's popular annual subscription concerts, held during the 1860s and 1870s. The opening of the Parr Hall in Palmyra Square in September 1895 at last gave the town a full-scale public entertainment venue.

Working hours slowly reduced and wages slowly rose during the 19th century

For the workers, leisure activities, sport and entertainment became a possibility

Warrington had numerous clubs and societies for sports after the 1850s

Fairs, sideshows, circuses, theatre, concerts and music hall also developed

The Public Hall in Rylands Street, in 1864. Opened in 1862, this was the town's main venue for entertainment in the 1860s and 1870s. In 1872 Charles Dickens was there, reading extracts from Pickwick Papers. *The Hall was later renamed the Royal Court Theatre and was demolished in 1960.*

There were also attractions of a more traditional kind. The fair ground at the end of Queen Street was an irregular patch of waste ground which had, long ago, been on the edge of Warrington Heath (at the north-west corner of the Golden Square shopping centre). Warrington fair was still being held in the closing years of the 19th century, though it was a pale reflection of its old glory, and the ground was scruffy, overshadowed by buildings and the railway viaduct. Through the year, here and on vacant land around the town, fairs, circuses and sideshows would pitch for a couple of days at a time. The Corporation charged promoters for use of the land, and the notebook of an unknown council official from the years 1896-1904 records details of many:

Warrington Regatta in the mid-1840s. The highlight of the town's sporting and entertainment year, the regatta invariably attracted a large crowd: 'There was always a great gathering of ladies, the schools had a half holiday, and bands welcoming the winner with "See the Conquering Hero Comes" and "Rule Britannia!".'

April 15, 1897

Lord George Sanger on the ground by the Blue Coat School

one day including Water	£6-10-0
Charges for Fair	
Large set Horses 60 ft diam.	£5-10-0
Less in proportion	
Set large Swings	£1-10-0
- small -	£0-15-0
Emma[?]	£0-15-0
Double shooting Gallery	£1-0-0
Single	£0-10-0
Booths 20ft by 30	£1-10-0
Ice Cream} per day	£0-0-6
Other Stalls}	£0-1-0

Gentlemen bowlers at Arpley, in about 1900.

The official noted a great variety of attractions: Chipperfield's Small Menagerie on 'the old fair ground' for a Friday and Saturday in March 1898; Marcus the Strongman on 'Queen Street ground' in the following month, Bartlett's lion show in March 1903, and the celebrated Buffalo Bill at Wilderspool Meadow in May that year. And in October 1898 he lists, in a rough note, what was probably the first ever showing in Warrington of that soon-to-be universal entertainment, the motion picture:

66 Wallis on Ground behind Blue Coat School with Clarkes Living Pictures, Sedgwicks Menagerie, another living picture show, Various swings, sheets etc. £4/10/0 per week including water. A water tap was fixed at the Orford Lane end of the ground. 99

The development of sport can also be traced back to the early 19th century and the gradual increase in the time available to working men. In the early Victorian period, before the Mersey became so filthily polluted that it was almost impossible to go near the water, it was a recreational area for the people of Warrington. Swimming in the river was a popular pastime and in the 1840s the famous Warrington Regattas were still being held, with rowing races, sailing and entertainments. As late as the 1870s, when the Amateur Rowing Club was founded, the river could still be used, though its ever blacker waters were ever less appealing. A Public Bath Company was formed before 1836 and in 1851 a bathhouse was opened in the former infant schoolroom in Church Street. The Warrington Baths Company opened purpose-built baths in Legh Street in 1865 and, when in 1873 this went bankrupt, the Corporation took over the undertaking. The Swimming Club was founded in 1879.

Many societies, such as the Chess Club (1889) and Cricket Club (1852), were aimed mainly at a lower middle-class or superior working-class clientele, and it was not until the late 1870s that, in Warrington and other towns in the north-west, mass attendance at working-class sporting events became common. Only then was leisure time was available and ticket prices affordable. In Warrington's case the most important event was the founding in 1879 of the Rugby League club, which signified not only the modern era of sport, but also gave the town a new form of identity and led it into fierce, often vitriolic, rivalry with its neighbours.

FURTHER READING: G.S. Aspden, *Up in the gallery: a study of Warrington's music hall and theatre from its beginnings to the outbreak of the First World War* (1973): copy in local studies collection, ref. ms 1763. The notebook of the unknown borough official is also there: ref. ms 2302

Twentieth-Century Warrington

83. The royal visit of 1913

King George V and Queen Mary visited the north-west in 1913

Their first stop was at Warrington, the 'Gateway to Lancashire'

Symbolically, the king opened the new Warrington Bridge

The royal couple toured Crosfield's works at Bank Quay

In July 1913 King George V and Queen Mary went on a tour of Lancashire, which was at the height of its industrial and commercial might – and, though nobody yet appreciated this, in the last year of its smoky golden age. Warrington was an important industrial centre, and also a focus of the transport network (the 'Gateway to Lancashire') and it was therefore the appropriate place to start the royal tour:

> " The inhabitants of Warrington, supplemented by tens of thousands of people from surrounding districts both of Lancashire and Cheshire, thronged its narrow streets from an early hour viewing the final preparations for the Royal visit today. It was a grey morning with signs of rain later in the day, but everybody was hopeful of brighter things. The decorations were very lavish, showing ingenuity and keen competition for the most telling effects. But up to noon today they were by no means complete and everywhere crowds of workers were adding the final touches to scenes which in bright sunlight would have been brilliant in the extreme "
>
> *Lancashire Daily Post, 7 July 1913*

The king and queen arrived by train at Arpley Station at 3 p.m. and, after being greeted by the Earl and Countess of Derby, Lord Shuttleworth (the Lord Lieutenant) and the High Sheriff of Lancashire,

> " proceeded in open carriages along Arpley Road to Warrington Bridge and along Bridge Street and Sankey Street to the lawn before the Town Hall

King George V, watched by Queen Mary, stands on a dais outside the town hall on 7 July 1913, pressing an electric button which officially declared the new Warrington Bridge open.

> ... Throughout the route the streets, behind stout barricades, were packed with dense crowds of cheering people. As the Royal procession approached the east gate of the Municipal Gardens, 10,000 schoolchildren broke into song with the first verse of the National Anthem, followed by cheering and the waving of flags **"**
>
> *Lancashire Daily Post, 7 July 1913*

At the Town Hall they were introduced to a long line of the great and good of Warrington – Greenalls, Crosfields, aldermen and councillors – before the king stepped onto a special dais and pressed 'an electric button'. By the wonders of modern technology this fired a gun to signal 'the severing of a rope which had been stretched across the north end of the new bridge' as His Majesty declared the bridge open by remote control. The royal couple then inspected Crosfield's works at Bank Quay, where the process of soapmaking was explained and they were 'assured that the physical aspect of education was not overlooked, all boys and girls being taught to swim, the firm providing all the cost, and young women have to undergo courses of gymnastics, instructresses being provided'. The queen stopped to 'chat with workpeople', namely Miss Cotterill (who was working in the paper-bag department and, in answer to the inevitable royal question, said that she made 13,000 a day), and Peter Lythgoe and James Gleave who had been employees of Crosfield's for, respectively, 51 and 63 years – no early retirement in 1913! The visit was, of course, brief but it demonstrated the fever pitch of patriotic excitement generated by such events in a period when royal visits were rare, Britannia ruled the waves, and pride in Lancashire's industrial and commercial supremacy was at its height.

FURTHER READING: local newspaper reports for July 1913 give very detailed and comprehensive eyewitness accounts of the royal visit.

84. *Change in the twentieth century*

Thus, the year 1913 has been seen by many as the high water mark in the fortunes of north-west England. It was followed by four years of warfare, and then by protracted economic difficulties. Huge changes in employment and society were set in motion, changes which accelerated after the Second World War with revolutions in technology, manufacturing, the environment and the make-up of society itself. The history of the 20th century in Warrington is one of constant reshaping. Whole areas have altered beyond recognition with urban renewal and the construction of great areas of new housing; the town centre has been remodelled and new shopping precincts created; all the major industries have either gone or been comprehensively restructured; a network of major new roads has been constructed; and the environment, public health, and housing conditions are in general much improved. People will always have criticisms, but nobody should forget that in the past life was anything but easy, clean or healthy for the majority of the town's citizens.

The most far-reaching change was the decision in the early 1960s to create a new town based on the old borough. This had a profound impact upon the landscape, social structure and economic base of the district. It could not have happened without the other vital development – the growth of the motorway

Warrington experienced many changes during the 20th century

The town shared in the transformation of the region

Economic problems in the first half of the century were particularly severe

Early 20th-century rebuilding work in Warrington town centre. The old town began to disappear as familiar landmarks were demolished and gleaming modern buildings took their place. Here, at the junction of Buttermarket Street and Bridge Street, change is in progress in about 1912. Note that, despite the scale of the project, traditional horses and carts, wheelbarrows and manual labour are still unchallenged.

Warrington grew in population until the early 1930s

After that, people began to move out of the town to live in nearby villages

The population of the old borough then began to decline

network. The M6, M62 and M56 have been the framework within which new Warrington has arisen. Without them its fortunes would have been very different. The M6, now almost half a century old, has become as much a part of the town's history as railways or the medieval bridge. All have emphasised the key role which transport played in Warrington's fortunes down the centuries. Accessibility and excellent communications will continue to be the underlying theme in the town's history.

85. *Population in the early twentieth century*

In 1901 the census showed that the borough of Warrington had a population of just under 65,000, and that figure increased steadily as the industrial expansion of the Edwardian period attracted newcomers to the town. By 1921 the population was almost 77,000 and growth continued until 1931, when with 81,500 people the old county borough recorded its highest ever figure. After this a decline set in, as people moved voluntarily out of the town into the new suburbs beyond its boundaries (most notably into the Cheshire villages – Stockton Heath, Grappenhall and Thelwall – which were administratively not part of the borough though within the built-up area of 'greater Warrington'). During the 1930s, too, the increasing amount of slum clearance in the town centre and the early Victorian industrial areas meant that many people were moved out of the 'inner city' to the new council estates which were being built on the outskirts.

FURTHER READING: The Lancashire and Cheshire county volumes of the national censuses [held in 1901, 1911, 1921, 1931 and 1951] give statistics for Warrington, neighbouring villages and parishes, and individual wards within the borough.

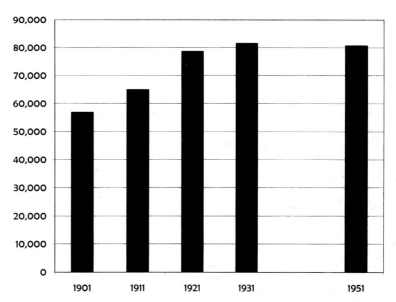

RIGHT *Population growth in Warrington 1901-51: the Second World War meant that there was no census in 1941.*

86. The pattern of local government

Local government has provided a framework for change. After 1847 Warrington was a municipal borough within Lancashire, enjoying local control over most aspects of administration including the police force (a main reason for seeking borough status in the first place). In 1889, however, a democratically elected County Council was created, with considerably greater powers over Warrington and other medium-sized towns. A dozen larger places were made county boroughs, administratively quite separate from Lancashire County Council, but Warrington (being deemed just too small) was not among them, though places such as Bury and Barrow-in-Furness were. This rankled with the leading citizens of Warrington and the town council campaigned to become a county borough, achieving its objective in 1900. Thenceforth the town, though within Lancashire for 'ceremonial' purposes, was completely self-governing. In 1902 it became an education authority and it also had quarter sessions courts separate from those of the county.

At the same time the southern boundary of the borough was altered. Previously it had followed the old channel of the Mersey, but it was now shifted to the line of the new Ship Canal, a more orderly arrangement which brought Latchford and Wilderspool within the borough (and out of Cheshire). Under the Warrington Extension Act of 1933, the borough was further extended to include parts of Burtonwood, Winwick, and Great Sankey – and, in particular, the area which the council planned to develop as the Orford and Hulme estates.

In 1974 the structure of English local government was controversially reformed. The creation of two new metropolitan counties, Merseyside and Greater Manchester, meant that Warrington no longer had a common border with Lancashire, so it was transferred to Cheshire (for want of any apparent alternative) and became one of eight district councils in the county. The borough thereby lost many of its powers – it was no longer, for example, an education authority. Its boundaries were, however, massively extended to include large areas of the rural and semi-rural land to the north and south,

The town became a county borough in 1900

In 1974 it was transferred from Lancashire to Cheshire as a district authority

In 1998 Warrington became a unitary authority

The post-1974 coat of arms of the borough of Warrington combines the lioncels of the de Vilars family, the early medieval lords of the manor, with Cheshire sheaves, red roses for Lancashire, the wolf of Hugh Lupus, 1st Earl of Chester, and the unicorn rampant of the Boteler family.

Warrington Rural District

from Golborne Urban District

Culcheth

Burtonwood

Winwick

Croft

Rixton with Glazebrook

Poulton with Fearnhead

WARRINGTON COUNTY BOROUGH

Woolston

Great Sankey

Lymm Urban District

LYMM

Penketh

Grappenhall

Cuerdley

Stockton Heath

Appleton

Walton

from Runcorn Rural District

Stretton

Hatton

The boundaries of the post-1974 borough, showing the territory of the earlier local authorities which had been combined to create the new and greatly-enlarged district.

bringing in places such as Culcheth, Burtonwood and Great Sankey from what had been Lancashire, and Walton, Hatton, Appleton, Grappenhall and Lymm. In 1973, before the reforms, Warrington County Borough covered 4,320 acres and had a population of about 67,000. After 1974 the new district had 43,500 acres and 164,000 people, a tenfold increase in size and near tripling in population. Then in 1998, in yet another reform of the structure of local government, the borough, like neighbouring Halton, became a unitary authority. Though, technically, Warrington is still in the county of Cheshire (to the chagrin of many Lancastrians!) in reality it is now proudly independent, controlling the entire range of local government services.

FURTHER READING: The reforms of 1974 and 1998 were preceded by a series of reports and government White Papers, which give some useful detail about the authorities involved; see also J.D. Marshall, *The history of Lancashire County Council 1889-1974* (Martin Robertson, 1977). The archives of the Warrington County Borough Council are held in the Warrington local studies collection.

87. *Politics in the twentieth century*

The traditional political rivalry was between Conservatives and Liberals

The rise of the Labour Party after 1918 challenged the old order

Warrington's first Labour MP was elected in 1923

Since 1945 Labour has dominated the town's parliamentary politics

The pattern of Warrington politics in the Victorian period involved a close rivalry between the Tories, symbolised by the Greenall family, and the Liberals represented by the Crosfields and Rylands. These commercial dynasties dominated the town's political life for decades. The Greenall family was most influential, though Peter Rylands was MP from 1868 to 1874 and Arthur Crosfield in 1906-1910 (at the second election of 1910 the constituency went against the national trend, electing a Tory during a Liberal landslide). In the early 20th century Lady Greenall, a formidable figure who in other circumstances would surely have been the candidate herself, regularly drew large audiences to her campaign speeches and used her extensive powers of patronage and influence to further the Conservative cause. The Liberals, try as they might, had nobody to match her.

At the first postwar election, in 1918, a new element disturbed the tradition. Harold Smith won for the Conservative and Unionist Party, but the Labour candidate polled over 5,000 votes. Less than a year later Labour won its first seat on the borough council and in May 1919 the municipal elections saw Labour councillors returned for Orford, Whitecross, Fairfield, and Latchford wards. Thereafter the story is of the rise of the Labour Party to a dominant position in parliamentary elections, but with a less certain hold upon

the borough council. The first Labour MP for Warrington was Charles Dukes (national organiser of the General and Municipal Workers Union and its general secretary 1934-1946), who was elected in December 1923, defeated in October 1924, elected again in May 1929, and defeated again in October 1931. Sir Noel Barré Goldie was then Conservative MP until July 1945 when Warrington contributed to Labour's post-war election victory. Since then the Labour Party has predominated in parliamentary politics, with only one Conservative MP (Christopher Butler, for Warrington South in 1983-1992). In local elections the Labour Party has also been the most successful, while the Conservative strength has dwindled very sharply. In the 1970s, for example, the Liberals began to make their presence felt, especially in wards on the Cheshire side of the river, while in the Warrington by-election of 1981 the Social Democrat leader, Roy Jenkins, almost took the seat. After the May 2002 elections the composition of the borough council was Labour 41, Liberal Democrat 15 and Conservative 4 members.

ABOVE LEFT *Charles Dukes, Warrington's first Labour MP.*
ABOVE RIGHT *standing on the left [not her usual political position] is the formidable Lady Greenall, a tireless campaigner for the Conservatives in Warrington in the years around the First World War.*
BELOW *Roy Jenkins, the SDP candidate, narrowly missed a sensational victory in the 1981 Warrington by-election.*

MPs for Warrington 1945-2002

1945-1950	Edward Porter (Lab)
1950-1955	Bernard Wenceslaus Morgan (Lab)
1955-1961	Edith Summerskill (Lab)
1961-1981	Thomas Williams (Lab)
1981-1983	Doug Hoyle (Lab)
1983-1997	Doug Hoyle [Warrington North] (Lab)
1983-1992	Christopher Butler [Warrington South] (Con)
1992-1997	Mike Hall [Warrington South] (Lab)
1997-	Helen Jones [Warrington North] (Lab)
1997-	Helen Southworth [Warrington South] (Lab)

FURTHER READING: Warrington local studies collection, file of photocopied material on *Warrington MPs 1832-1983* (reference P8603): since the 1980s a series of national parliamentary yearbooks and election guides, in the reference section of Warrington library, details MPs, their biographies and election results.

88. *Warrington in the First World War 1914-1918*

The First World War was traumatic, with massive loss of life

Many hundreds of young men from Warrington were killed

Orford Barracks became a major war hospital

Local people raised money and collected clothing and comforts for the troops

After the war, the cenotaph was unveiled to commemorate the dead

66 Warrington, renowned for its loyalty and patriotism, has responded to the call of duty nobly. In the early days of the war, the young manhood of the borough went forth willingly to fight the enemy. They have won renown in many a hard-fought battle, have earned fame and glory that will never fade; and as we think of all those who have passed the great barrier, and lie sleeping peacefully amid the din of conflict, we reverently salute their memory. Others have gone to fill up the gaps and still more will follow 99

Warrington Guardian Yearbook, 1917

Contemporary reports of Warrington in the First World War emphasise the stirring patriotism and selfless sacrifice of those who went to fight and the major contribution to the war effort of those left at home. Fundraising and morale-boosting campaigns were much publicised: in August 1916, for example, £2,150 was raised on Navy Day [about £250,000 in today's values]. The leading ladies of the community spearheaded voluntary efforts in other ways. Lady Greenall, backed by the Women's Conservative Association, knitted and collected 'warm clothing and other comforts to the men serving on land and sea' – the *Guardian* rather grudgingly noted that the Women's Liberal Association also did such work, but Lady Greenall was a much better publi-

cist! The War Office which was set up in Parr Hall looked after the interests of soldiers' and sailors' families, and sent parcels to POWs in Germany (by the end of 1916, 35 tons of food, 10 tons of clothing and numerous pairs of boots).

Such activities were at least as important psychologically as practically – they meant that people 'at home' felt they did their bit for the war effort. But truly heroic effort was that of the small number of nurses and doctors who manned the military hospital established in 1914 at Orford Barracks, headquarters of the South Lancashire Regiment. By the end of 1919 it had treated over 100,000 casualties, from the war itself and the two devastating influenza epidemics which raged in 1918. Through its wards passed the victims of gassing, frostbite, neurasthenia, shellshock, malaria, and tuberculosis.

None of this, of course, equated with the sacrifice of so many young men and the grief of their families. Warrington mourned the loss of half a generation: the war may not have come to its streets, but death was no less real. A total of 5,550 men from the South Lancashire Regiment, mostly from the Warrington and Leigh area, were killed during the war. As Austin Crowe, twice mayor of Warrington in the 1930s, put it:

> 66 The war casualty list was enormous and few Warrington families were unaffected … the scenes of jubilation enacted in the streets [on Armistice Day] will long be remembered, although the painful aftermath of such colossal sacrifice of life and treasure, with its dire consequences, cast a menacing shadow over all human joy … which could only be mitigated by the healing hand of time. 99
>
> A.M. Crowe, *Warrington Ancient and Modern: a history of the town and neighbourhood*, 1947

Territorials in training in Bank Park, 1915: St Paul's church, Bewsey Road, is in the background.

The cenotaph at Warrington Bridge, symbolic perhaps of arrival and departure, commemorated the dead. Among other memorials to the fallen, and to the efforts of those who returned, was the acquisition of Orford Hall and its 18 acres of grounds as a public park. Its purchase from Colonel Ireland Blackburn was secured in 1916, after a campaign headed by the indefatigable Alderman Arthur Bennett, to commemorate 'the valour of the lads of Warrington in the Great War'.

FURTHER READING: The *Warrington Guardian Yearbooks* for 1917 and 1918 include detailed and informative accounts of the war work (including voluntary charity, fund-raising and medical help) undertaken by the people of the town.

89. Housing in Warrington 1900–1939

Warrington's first council houses were built in the early 1920s

In the 1930s the council embarked upon slum clearance programmes

New council estates were built mainly on the edges of the town

Private house-building was especially important on the Cheshire side

Alderman Arthur Bennett was an energetic promoter of many good causes in Warrington until his death in 1933. He favoured environmental improvement, heritage conservation, and the development of socially-balanced housing estates built to the best standards, all issues which were not fashionable or prominent at the time. His campaigns were usually thwarted by financial problems, cost-cutting, and bureaucratic restrictions, but he was an influential figure in Warrington for many years.

The legacy of bad housing, poor sanitation and environmental damage which Warrington inherited from Victorian industrialisation was less serious than in towns such as St Helens, but much had to be done if the health and living conditions of Warringtonians were to be improved. One solution to the problem of poor housing, grudgingly accepted by central government, was that local authorities should play a part in slum clearance and the provision of replacement dwellings. In many towns such schemes began in the 1890s, when legislation for the first time allowed councils to intervene, but Warrington showed no enthusiasm. In 1918, though, the government ordered councils to implement such plans and Warrington had no choice but to start. During the following decade the council acquired, and began to develop, several sites on the outskirts, taking advantage of the compact nature of the town (which meant that plenty of suitable land was reasonably near the centre) and low land values.

At the same time, private housebuilders were developing suburban estates. Among the earliest and most intriguing were those planned by the Warrington Garden Suburbs Limited, a company promoted by the ubiquitous Arthur Bennett, pioneer of many environmental projects in the town between 1890 and 1930. The company, modelled on those building garden cities in southern England, began work on the 20-acre Great Sankey Garden Suburb in 1908. The original plan was never completed and its successor, a project for a 265-house garden suburb beside the Ship Canal at Grappenhall, was abortive (both were eventually developed with housing to more conventional designs), but the ideas behind them encouraged Arthur Bennett to push for high-quality building in the first council estates constructed after 1920. Between the wars 3,645 council houses were built in the borough, the main estates being at Bewsey, Westy, Loushers Lane, and Orford. The Bewsey estate, in which the first houses were occupied in July 1927, was designed on garden suburb lines on the insistence of Arthur Bennett, and had unusually high specifications as a result.

> 66 Nobody can convince me that it is necessary for an industrial town to be unhealthy. I don't think we can claim to be a really civilised community until we have made the dirtiest and sorriest towns in Lancashire better places. We have a long way to go in Warrington 99
>
> *Arthur Bennett, quoted in* Warrington Examiner, *30 July 1927*

Later estates followed the more usual pattern of inter-war council housing, because the government placed tight restrictions on expenditure: lower design standards were the inevitable consequence. Nonetheless, these semi-detached properties with relatively large gardens were far superior to the houses from which most of the tenants had come. The estates were landscaped with grass verges, areas of open ground, and avenues of trees, and in each case the council attempted to provide parks and recreation grounds. After 1930 the clearance of slum property in the town centre became a major element of housing policy and most of the remaining courts and yard houses disappeared before 1939. Much of the resultant vacant land was not built over until the redevelopment of the commercial area in the 1960s and 1970s.

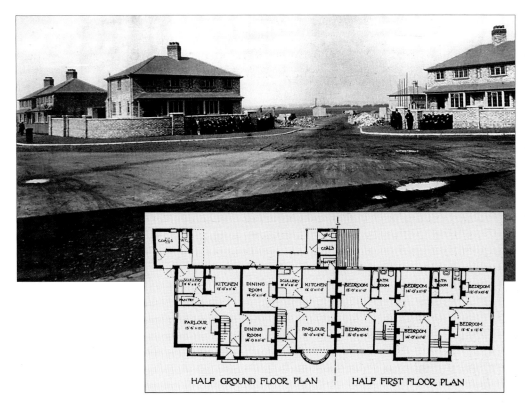

Ideal homes for heroes and workers? In July 1927 Arthur Bennett is seen formally opening the new Bewsey Garden Suburb, a council estate designed on enlightened 'garden city' principles. Bennett's influence had ensured that the new estate was of a high standard, though it was not the true garden city of which he had long dreamed. The plan shows the floor plan of houses which were built in the first stage of the ultimately abortive Sankey Garden Suburb (designed by local architects Wright, Garner and Wright, in 1908).

HALF GROUND FLOOR PLAN | HALF FIRST FLOOR PLAN

Between the wars private housebuilding continued, though here, as elsewhere in the north-west, the economic problems of the 1920s and 1930s put something of a damper on the private sector. Some districts were particularly favoured for private estates – notably, and not unexpectedly, the Cheshire side of the Ship Canal, where in the area south of the old village of Stockton Heath, and along the north side of Chester Road and Stockport Road in Grappenhall, considerable numbers of new houses were built. The advantages were not only a Cheshire address, but also a comfortable distance from the polluting factories and ugly industry of the areas on the north side of the river. Many of the private houses were advertised with enticing offers and special financial packages – in the late 1930s a deposit of £10 could secure a property, and a purchase price of £300-£450 could be repaid on long-term mortgage. With workers in many Warrington industries enjoying better rates of pay, moving to the suburbs became for the first time a practical proposition.

FURTHER READING: Street and trade directories can help to establish when individual roads were constructed, and they also include advertisements for new housing in the 1920s and 1930s; Ordnance Survey maps are also useful in plotting the expansion of the town and the layout of new housing areas. The Warrington local studies collection includes a great deal of material on housing, in the form of reports, brochures, sale plans, newspaper articles and publicity literature.

90. Winwick Hospital

In the later 19th century Lancashire County Council followed a very active policy in building what were then known as 'lunatic asylums', choosing large greenfield sites close to the main towns – ideally, places where an extensive

Winwick was one of
Lancashire's largest mental
hospitals

It was the size of a small town
in its own right

The hospital was handed over
to the military authorities in
both World Wars

It closed in the late 1990s as
policies towards mental
health changed

country estate was being sold off by its owners. In 1894 the Council purchased 207 acres of land from the Hornby family, part of the Winwick Rectory Estate and including Winwick Hall, and a new county asylum was built there in 1895-1902. Although 'exceeding the estimates' is thought of as a modern problem, the cost of the scheme (£385,000) was eventually 55 per cent over budget. The old house was demolished and the grounds redeveloped with a complex of wards, staff cottages and ancillary buildings. The hospital took patients of all ages and conditions (one early group was described in the politically incorrect parlance of the time as 'idiot boys') but in 1905 it began to admit people needing short-term treatment, the 'curables'. Nevertheless,

> 66 the function of the asylum was still mainly custodial. There was little recognition of the need for individual or intensive treatment, but there was a growing emphasis placed on the actual care of patients as compared with mere incarceration 99
>
> *Jubilee Souvenir, 1952*

During the First World War most of the 2,160 resident patients were transferred elsewhere. Winwick was renamed the Lord Derby War Hospital and between 1915 and 1920 treated some 56,000 wounded servicemen. Afterwards, the asylum was reopened and major expansion took place in the 1920s: another 67 acres of land were bought and several new wards built. The climate of opinion on how to treat patients in hospitals such as Winwick was changing fast. The terminology became less harsh: the 'asylum' became the 'mental hospital', 'attendants' became 'nurses', and 'lunatics' became 'persons of unsound mind'. Treatment, therapy and support were given instead of imprisonment and punishment, and recreational facilities were provided to stimulate the patients (a cinema was opened at Winwick in the early 1920s, wireless was installed in 1929, a bowling green in 1923, a shop in 1937 and a hairdressing salon in 1939). In such seemingly unremarkable ways the institution adapted to the new age.

The Second World War again saw the site pressed into military use, with an Emergency Medical Service Hospital opened with 80 beds. It specialised in neuro-surgery, orthopaedics and neurology and dealt with over 19,000 cases between 1940 and 1947. Winwick reopened as a mental hospital in 1947 and in 1951, with 450 acres of land, 2,200 patients, and a staff of over 800, it was the size of a small town. The hospital had its own farm, which until the late 1940s made it almost self-sufficient in food – in an average year it produced 17,000lb of tomatoes, 200,000lb of cabbages and sprouts, up to 400 tons of potatoes, and 77,000 gallons of milk.

By the 1980s, though, the philosophy of mental health care was changing again. Community-based treatment was regarded as more appropriate and the great hospitals such as Winwick were seen as outdated and anachronistic. In

A small army in itself – the staff of the Lord Derby War Hospital [Winwick Hospital] in 1917.

1999, after several years of gradual downsizing, it closed and the site, with some of the buildings, was turned over for large-scale residential development, a change helped by its excellent location close to the motorways.

FURTHER READING: A very useful introduction is given in *Winwick Hospital, Warrington: Jubilee Souvenir* (January 1952), copy in Warrington local studies collection ref. p2526

91. Education in twentieth-century Warrington

The town had a poor record in the field of school provision and much work had to be done after 1902 when it became an education authority. At that time the Technical Institute was housed in an old converted barracks in Arpley Street, and there was almost no secondary education for girls. The new Education Committee took its responsibilities seriously. In 1907 the first council school opened in Beamont Street, and a new mixed technical secondary school was built. Between the wars there was further major expansion in school provision, with the construction of the St Augustine's Roman Catholic schools, the Richard Fairclough Senior School at Latchford (opened 1934), the Bewsey schools, and the new buildings for the Boteler Grammar School, which moved from the congested industrialised surroundings of School Brow to the spacious new site at Latchford in 1937.

By 1972, on the eve of its demotion to the status of a district council in Cheshire without educational powers, Warrington could point to a good record in the field of education provision. It had 43 primary, two grammar and ten 'secondary modern' schools, as well as the newly completed technical college in Winwick Road. A total of 13,000 children attended its schools and the borough employed over 600 teachers and lecturers. In addition there were several private schools, for which no statistics were available. The education authority, in its final report, emphasised that since 1945 it had carried on a continuous programme of building and improvement, so that almost 60 per cent of its children were now educated in schools either newly built or extensively reconstructed in the previous quarter-century.

Standard IVA boys at Beamont Junior School, in about 1928. Although the school was only 20 years old it was already beginning to look a little old-fashioned, with a miscellany of pictures and diagrams on the walls. It had been the first school built by the county borough after it became an education authority in 1902.

The town made strenuous efforts after 1902 to improve education facilities

By the late 1960s most Warrington schools were new or recently improved

Higher education (Warrington Collegiate Institute) is now an important feature

Since that time educational opportunities and facilities have expanded very rapidly to cater for the major increase in population. Today, in the enlarged area of the borough, there are almost eighty primary schools, 12 secondary schools and the Priestley College in Loushers Lane, a sixth-form college which also serves as a community college of further education. Warrington Collegiate Institute is an innovative centre for further, higher, continuing and vocational education, with university courses validated by Manchester University. Almost 250 years after the opening of Warrington Academy, that would-be university of the 18th century, the town now has a university-sector college which is

A drawing of the new primary school on the Dallam Farm Estate, designed in 1952 by the borough surveyor, J.Y. Hughes. With its stark simple lines and large recreation areas and playgrounds the school was in the forefront of the post-Second World War education revolution.

developing an excellent reputation in such fields as management, entertainment and the performing arts, sport and leisure management, and media studies. The pioneers of the Academy would not have recognised, or perhaps even understood, any of these, but they would be gratified to know that such an institution flourishes in the 'Athens of the North'.

FURTHER READING: anon., *History of the Elementary Schools of Warrington* (Warrington Guardian, 1933), H. Lievesley, *Boteler Grammar School, Warrington 1526-1976*; Latchford History Group, *The Best Worst Days of Our Lives: Bolton Council Schools 1920s-1950s* (LHG and Warrington Borough Council, 1999); successive *Official Guides* to the borough give useful contemporary facts and figures on schools and education

92. WIRE Wolves

Warrington was a founder member of the Rugby League

The club has always had a prominent place in rugby league history

Fierce rivalry with other local clubs has been a feature since 1895

Now renamed Warrington Wolves, WIRE plays in the RL Super League

In the late 1860s and early 1870s in many Lancashire and Yorkshire towns, rugby union football clubs were being formed. The game had hitherto been a mainly upper class pursuit, played by gentlemen – in this region, the owners of mills and factories were often participants or supporters. But major conflict soon became apparent: the rapid growth in working-class interest in the game was viewed with displeasure by the gentlemen players, while they, being 'of private means', could play without needing wages or expenses and so remained 'amateur'. Working-class players could not afford the time or train fares to away games and so – if they were good at the game – sought to acquire 'professional' status and receive payment. These problems became especially clear after 1870, when county teams were created and longer distance fixtures arranged. Working-class players were, accidentally or deliberately, excluded. This helped

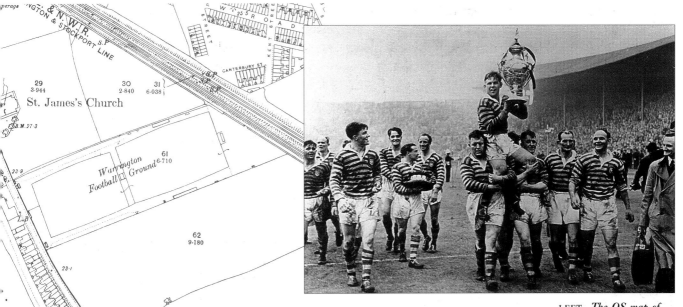

LEFT *The OS map of 1895 shows the Warrington Football Ground next to St James's church, Wilderspool Causeway, with no facilities at all apart from a couple of very primitive stands. By 1905 Fletcher Street and Priory Street had been built on the western half of the ground.*

RIGHT *Harry Bath proudly displays the Rugby League Challenge Cup which Warrington RFC won in 1950, having defeated local rivals Widnes in the final.*

to create a north-south divide, since most working-class players were in Lancashire and Yorkshire. In 1895, at Huddersfield, 22 clubs from the two counties broke away to create the Northern Union, and in a short time this was being called Rugby League to distinguish it from the old national body.

The first two formally constituted Warrington rugby union clubs, Padgate and Zingari, amalgamated in 1879 to form Warrington RUFC, and in 1895 this was one of the founder-members of the new league. It joined other local clubs, such as Widnes and St Helens, and in dong so firmly established not only the town's most important sport, but also its intense rivalry with the neighbours which has continued to the present day. The rise of Warrington, like that of clubs in other industrial towns, was in large measure the result of the shorter working week and increasing wages of working people – not only those who played, but also those who could afford the gate money and a Saturday afternoon off to go to Wilderspool (where the ground was opened in 1898) and see the WIRE. Like association football, rugby league gave a strong identity to the towns where it was played, and attracted a growing army of followers.

In 1901 and 1904 Warrington were defeated in the Challenge Cup Final, but when in 1905 they won for the first time (against Hull Kingston Rovers) their top position was confirmed. There were the inevitable ups and downs in fortunes. In many people's eyes the first really great period was the mid-1950s, especially the celebrated 1953-4 season when Warrington won the Challenge Cup, Championship Trophy and Lancashire League Cup, and the replay against Halifax at Odsal Stadium, Bradford, was watched by an official figure of 102,000 people and a lot of others who weren't counted. The other golden age was the early 1970s, including the 1973-4 season when a cluster of cups and trophies was paraded.

Today, rechristened Warrington Wolves and playing in the Super League, the club continues to represent Warrington nationally and internationally, though at the time of writing its fortunes are not altogether glittering. The probability of a completely new stadium, partly-funded by the development of a new Tesco superstore north of Central station, on the former Tetley Walker brewery site, offers a completely fresh start and – all being well – will help to secure the club's future in the Super League.

FURTHER READING: The club's website gives useful historical information; see also W. Gavin, *Warrington Rugby League Football Club Centenary 1879-1979* (Warrington Guardian, 1979); E. Fuller and G. Slater, *Warrington Rugby League Club 1970-2000* (Tempus Publishing, 2000); the *Warrington Borough Guide* for 1971 includes 'Warrington at Leisure', a useful summary of sports facilities and clubs in the town and their history

93. *Public transport*

There was no public transport in Warrington until 1902

In that year the tramway network was opened

It closed in 1935 and was replaced by bus services

Late 19th-century Warrington had no public transport system, though private horse-bus routes operated from Market Gate to, for example, Manchester Road cemetery and Sankey Bridges. By this time every self-respecting commercial town needed trams and in 1900 the Corporation obtained powers to build a short network of routes linking the town centre with the important suburbs. Some, such as the lines to Padgate and Bruche, were never built, but the remainder (to Latchford, Sankey, Wilderspool, the Cemetery, and Longford, a total of just under seven miles) opened in stages during 1902. Three years later the Wilderspool line was extended by a separate company, the Stockton Heath Light Railway, over the canal and along London Road. The tramways depot was built in Mersey Street on the old gasworks site.

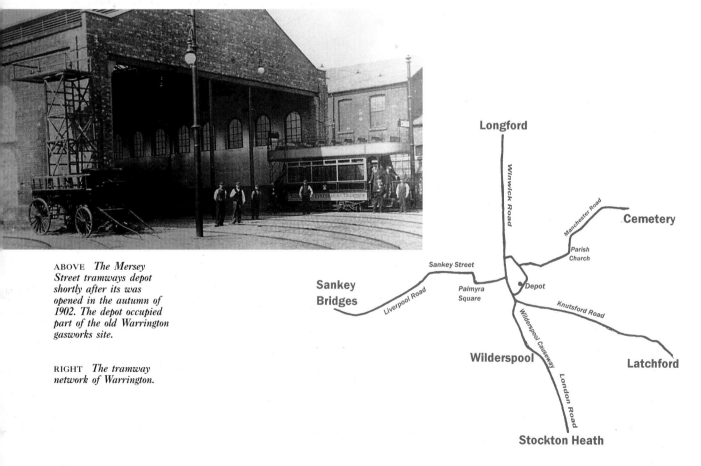

ABOVE *The Mersey Street tramways depot shortly after its was opened in the autumn of 1902. The depot occupied part of the old Warrington gasworks site.*

RIGHT *The tramway network of Warrington.*

The tramway system was successful for a couple of decades. It had been relatively cheap to build (£135,000, perhaps £15 million in modern terms) and was efficient, safe and clean. There were 27 tramcars and the fares were 1d. or 1½d. (about 2p today). But the threat of competition began as early as 1913, when the Corporation purchased three petrol-electric motorbuses to operate to Bewsey and Orford. In the 1920s the bus network was gradually extended, the Padgate route beginning in 1928, and in 1931 the Longford tram route (always the poor relation) and the Stockton Heath Light Railway were closed. In 1935 the tramway system was abandoned. During its 33 years it carried 225 million passengers with just one fatality; the chocolate-brown and yellow tramcars were estimated to have travelled 15 million miles in total; and, perhaps the most revealing statistic, it had made a profit in every year except one. In other words, the Corporation trams were abandoned when still viable, because fashion turned against them. After 1935 the bus transport network expanded rapidly, so that by 1947 there were 77 vehicles carrying an annual total of over 33 million passengers. Since then the undertaking has continued to develop, weathering the problems of deregulation in 1986 and providing an efficient and effective public transport service to the borough.

FURTHER READING: J.P. Robinson, *Warrington Trams and Buses* (Cheshire Libraries, 1987); Warrington Borough Transport Department, *75 Years of Municipal Transport in Warrington* (1977)

94. *Roads and bridges before 1939*

The growth in heavy industrial traffic and the expansion of commercial and residential areas south of the river placed increasing pressure upon Warrington bridge, at the beginning of the 20th century still the only road crossing. The three-arched Victoria Bridge (1835-7) had soon proved too narrow for the volume of traffic. It became a major bottleneck, but building a replacement presented major logistical difficulties since the bridge had to be kept open throughout. Finally, in 1911, work began on a reinforced concrete bridge, 80 feet wide, immediately beside the existing arches. The king opened the downstream half in July 1913 and the old bridge was then demolished, the other half being built on its foundations. By this ingenious solution traffic flow was maintained without interruption.

Proposals for other bridges had been put forward for over a century –

Warrington Corporation Tramways Tilling-Stevens 40hp petrol-electric omnibus, acquired in 1913 to operate the Bewsey Circular service (which was opened instead of a tramway route previously proposed). The bus carried 15,979 passengers in its first fortnight of operation.

The main road network of south Lancashire and north Cheshire, in 1939. The construction of the East Lancashire Road was a sign of the future, but the network was still essentially that of the turnpike era. The map demonstrates how road traffic was funnelled through Warrington because 12 major routes focused on the key bridge over the Mersey.

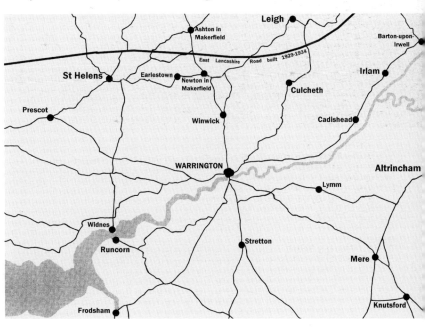

Warrington Bridge was rebuilt
in 1913-15 to cater for
heavy traffic

A second river crossing was
opened at Kingsway Bridge
in 1934

By 1939 planning of a new
motorway network had
started

in 1825, for example, the celebrated Thomas Telford had suggested a Warrington bypass and a new bridge at Latchford, 'in order that the narrow streets of Warrington may be avoided as well as any interference with the coaches between Liverpool and Manchester', but this scheme was not implemented. By the early 1920s continued congestion at Warrington Bridge, and the general growth of traffic, made a second Mersey crossing essential. The latest idea in town planning was the building of bypasses and 'arterial roads', and the Corporation decided to build the first stage of a ring road, with a new bridge. It designed a link from Long Lane, via Orford Green, to a

Rebuilding Warrington Bridge, 1913: the narrow early 19th-century bridge was replaced by one twice its width, but this was soon itself inadequate. In 1934 a second crossing, at Kingsway, was opened to take some of the through traffic out of the town centre.

Mersey bridge and then through Westy to Knutsford Road, which would also open up new areas of land for council housing. The key stretch of this new road, Kingsway and its bridge, was opened in December 1934. By this time, though, more ambitious schemes were contemplated. Lancashire County Council had just completed the East Lancashire Road, the most important trunk road scheme yet in the north of England, and was beginning design work on a new north-south trunk road which (when eventually built as the M6) was destined to help the transformation of Warrington in a way which nobody could have foreseen.

FURTHER READING: G.A. Carter, *Warrington Bridges 1285-1985*, gives extensive detail on the rebuilding of the bridge; see also G. Carter's *Warrington Hundred* (1947) for other material on the inter-war traffic planning of the town.

95. *The town centre and shopping before the 1940s*

A theme throughout this book has been Warrington's role as a commercial centre. As in most towns of any size, during the late 19th century there was major expansion of the shopping area. Prosperous traders went to live in the suburbs and their houses and yards were converted into shops, a process helped by the rebuilding and widening of Bridge Street, Buttermarket Street,

Warrington's last milk house, situated in Upper Bank Street (its site is now occupied by the market) and known as Warrington Farm. This view was taken in the early 1900s and shows the dairymaids with a gleaming churn for making butter. The farm (a misleading term, since there was no grass or fields – the animals were kept in sheds) and the milk business closed in 1911.

By 1914 the town centre was changing as multiples and chain stores opened

There were still numerous specialist craftsmen and tradesmen in the town

Corner shops and local stores were also very common

Hancock and Wood is now Warrington's oldest family-run retail business

Horsemarket Street, and parts of the market place which began in the 1880s. In 1890, though, Warrington was still a town of small and specialised shops, with many traditional traders. The trade directory of that year, for example, lists 49 bootmakers and shoemakers (and 15 clogmakers), 41 grocers and tea-dealers, 47 linendrapers, and 51 butchers. Even in the centre, shops were usually small and those selling foodstuffs were, by modern standards, unhygienic. Thus, the directory listed 19 milk-dealers, who fetched milk from farms around the town or kept cows in insanitary urban yards: they sold milk by the jugful, going round the streets with carts.

Scattered across the town, on just about every street corner, were the local shops, providing a service now looked upon with much nostalgia (though the reality was often less attractive). Warrington had over 300 corner shops in 1890. At the other end of the scale was the Warrington Equitable Industrial Co-operative Society, established in 1860 in a small shop in Cairo Street. The Co-op was a revolutionary form of retailing, pioneering features later common-place – bulk-buying, uniform pack-aging, standardised prices between branches – and developing the idea of departments, with a single store sell-ing a wide variety of products arranged in separate areas (now so

THE · WARRINGTON · EQUITABLE · INDUSTRIAL · CO-OPERATIVE · SOCIETY · Lᵀᴰ NEW · CENTRAL · PREMISES · SANKEY · Sᵀ · & · CAIRO · Sᵀ

The new premises for the Warrington Equitable Industrial Co-operative Society, built on the corner of Sankey Street and Cairo Street in 1908.

ordinary, then so radical). The WEICS flourished: its capital grew from £100 in 1860 to £75,000 in 1908, when it had 9,000 members and a turnover of £180,000. By that time, there were local branches in Winwick Street, Church Street, Lovely Lane, Stockton Heath, Latchford, Marsh Street, Bewsey Road and Penketh, and the main shop on the Sankey Street-Cairo Street corner was being rebuilt:

> 66 On the completion of these, there will be as a monument to what working men can do when combined together, a block of shops equal to any in Warrington and such as would not disgrace the movement anywhere … arranged to accommodate Grocery and Provision Departments, Boot and Shoe (including repairing), Drapery, Clothing and Outfitting, Millinery, Mantles, Furniture, Crockery, &c 99
>
> *Warrington Guardian Directory*, 1908

But signs of far-reaching change were visible in the town centre by 1914. The 1908 directory records that Messrs. Boots (Cash Chemists) had two stores, at 126 Bridge Street and at the Sankey Street-Bridge Street corner. In Horsemarket Street was the Home & Colonial Stores, in Bridge Street were Liptons Ltd and the Maypole Dairy Company. Some of these are now almost forgotten, but they were the pioneer national chains of multiple retail grocers: Maypole, Lipton and Home & Colonial could be found in every larger town, competing with local retailers who found it increasingly difficult to maintain their share of the market. The chains offered more competitive prices, a wider range of goods, attractive novelties, and a fashionable image. In this period began the process whereby, as people often now complain, 'all the shops look the same in every town'. The appearance, just before the First World War, of Messrs F.W. Woolworth and Co's hardware store in Sankey Street signalled another step along that road. Many smaller stores were forced out of business by these developments, but others adapted and met the challenge, seeing the changing nature of retailing as an opportunity, not a threat.

Hancock & Wood

In 1914 the well-situated town centre premises of Thomas Grime, general draper, and vendor of dress materials, mantles, jackets, hosiery and millinery, came onto the market when the owner retired. Next door was the shoe shop run by the Roberts family and they alerted Frederick Samuel Hancock (a travelling haberdashery salesmen who had married their daughter) that the well-established business was up for sale. He jumped at the chance and bought the shop as a going concern. Soon afterwards he went into the Royal Marines during the First World War, and during that time an elderly partner, David Wood, ran the firm. Frederick Samuel Hancock made a wise choice, of site, business and partner. As Hancock and Wood his firm has flourished ever since, adapting to meet changing times and surviving while most of the other familiar names of the town centre shopping streets disappeared. Though the store has altered beyond recognition – the filling-in of the old 'walk in' front being perhaps the most obvious change – this is now Warrington's oldest retail business, still run by the Hancock family as it has been for ninety years.

The 'walk in' front of Hancock & Wood's store in Bridge Street in the mid-1930s. The store has been a familiar Warrington landmark for nearly a century, and is still family-run.

FURTHER READING: the most important source for information about shops and retailing is the series of street and trade directories (published every two or three year from the 1870s onwards) and the Warrington Guardian Yearbooks from the first half of the 20th century. These give the names, addresses and other details of the businesses in the town, and also include invaluable advertisements and descriptions: sometimes there are photographs or engravings of the premises. See also C. Leach, *Decision and destiny: Warrington Co-operative Society Limited – the first 100 years 1860-1960* (WCS, 1960)

96. The Second World War 1939-1945

The Warrington area played a vital part in the military effort during the Second World War, and the impact of this role far outlasted the end of hostilities. Indeed, it was to be instrumental in shaping the town of the early 21st century. The most important single element was the construction, just before the war, of the RAF depot at Burtonwood which, in the hands of the Americans from

1942 to 1946 and again from 1948, was transformed into one of the largest military complexes in the western world. But there were other vital installations, such as the extensive RAF camp at Padgate, opened in 1939 and by 1943 'processing' 1,500 new RAF recruits each week. The camp closed in 1957. The vast Royal Ordnance munitions factories at Risley (later Birchwood) opened in January 1940, sprawled over two square miles of land, and employed at their peak several thousand local people. This site was chosen because it had excellent accessibility (a special branch railway was built into the site from Culcheth), was largely unpopulated and therefore safe for the production of ammunition, and was mainly undeveloped and unreclaimed moss so no farmland was requisitioned.

Warrington was fortunate to escape relatively lightly during the air raids of 1940-2 which devastated so much of Merseyside, Trafford Park and central Manchester. The worst single incident was the random bombing of the fetc at

LEFT *The aftermath of the only major air raid on Warrington during the Second World War: 16 people were killed at the fete in the grounds of Thames Board Mills in September 1940.*

RIGHT *Women munitions workers making shell-cases at the Fletcher Russell works on Wilderspool Causeway during the Second World War. The town's industries were switched to war production and women played a vital part in many heavy industries from which they had hitherto been excluded.*

the Mersey works of Thames Board Mills on 14 September 1940, in which 16 people were killed. Despite its importance as a major railway centre, and its range of key industries, Warrington was not targeted for significant action. It could easily have been otherwise, for in 1940 the Luftwaffe took an extensive series of reconnaissance photographs of the area, carefully annotated with the names of factories and industrial plants.

FURTHER READING: *The War and Thames Board Mills 1939-1945* (TBM, 1945: copy in Warrington local studies collection)

97. Burtonwood

The flat farmland of Burtonwood, close to major towns and hence a labour supply, and with good railway links, was chosen in 1938 for a new RAF aircraft and engine repair depot, part of Britain's rapid military build-up in the approach to war. The two-runway airbase, with headquarters and storage buildings, workshops and repair shops, became fully operational in the autumn of 1940. However, in the last months of 1939 the government had negotiated the 'lend-lease' scheme, whereby the United States provided aircraft for the RAF. American planes such as the Martin Maryland bomber were brought to Burtonwood and modified for European use, and by the summer of 1941 the base was at capacity. When the Americans themselves became combatants, urgent decisions had to be taken to establish US airbases in Britain. Burtonwood, by virtue of its size, location and safe distance from the Continent, was selected for massive expansion and in October 1942 was formally handed over to the Americans (US troops and airmen had begun to arrive in June).

During 1943 and early 1944 a huge reconstruction programme was completed. Burtonwood was chosen for the assembling of pre-packaged planes and by June 1944 had become the largest aircraft factory in Europe: over 10,000 people lived and worked on the base. As D-Day approached the activity became frenetic and the base grew inexorably. The statistics of this extraordinary place are awe-inspiring: at the peak of production, in December 1944, the population was just over 18,000 and, in July 1944, 269 aircraft rolled off the production lines in a single week. At the end of the war Burtonwood had 1,823 separate buildings, almost three miles of runway, 23 miles of roads, four million square feet of storage, and accommodation for over 17,000 people.

As is well-known, its impact upon Warrington, the nearest bright lights (not literally – the black-out was of course enforced) was tremendous. Within two months of the Americans moving in, the first marriage with a local girl had taken place. The tidal wave of newcomers meant a new and exciting element in the social life of the district. The US military police and the Warrington borough constabulary shared the task of keeping all under control, though it was an uphill struggle.

> 66 If, after the Yanks have departed England, Warrington Police Constables are heard to mutter such American colloquialisms as 'Okay, Buddy!', 'Take it easy', and 'Hiya', you can blame it all on the members of the Town Patrol of the 890th Military Police Company at Burtonwood 99
>
> *Warrington Guardian, quoted in Ferguson, 1986*

There were incidents of racism when the American authorities sought to impose a colour bar on the town's entertainment venues. Nat Bookbinder, owner of the Casino Dance Hall in Market Gate, refused to bar Herbert Greaves, a young West Indian war worker, and rejected the segregationist ban. Captain J.E. Lang of the US Army said

> 66 It is not our intention to dictate the policies of privately owned establishments but in the interests of eliminating trouble in which our troops may be involved we would appreciate your cooperation in prohibiting negroes from attending the dances 99
>
> *quoted in Toole, 1993*

Bookbinder replied that as long as a negro paid his admission fee like anyone else, 'the doors would be open to him and he would be welcome'. Indeed, he hinted that he might ban white Americans instead. The episode reveals the sometimes uneasy relationship with the peaceful invaders just up the road.

Burtonwood airbase made a major contribution to the Allied war effort 1939-45

At its peak it accommodated over 18,000 people

In the early 1960s it was the largest western military base outside America

It had a very important social and economic impact upon Warrington

After closure in the late 1960s the M62 was built along the runway

Today the huge Omega development occupies the site

Three images of Burtonwood and its impact on the town; from top to bottom: testing Pratt & Whitney aircraft engines at the BRD site in 1944 – when testing was in progress the noise could be heard two miles away; GIs and local people crowd the platform at Warrington Central Station in the early 1950s; an aerial view of a small part of the huge Burtonwood complex – in its heyday the base and its attendant facilities extended over more than three square miles.

In March 1946 the Americans handed the base back to the RAF and departed. Two years later they returned. During the crisis of the Berlin Airlift, Burtonwood was hastily reconstructed as a giant airbase and this time the Americans stayed much longer. It was decided to make this the main US military depot in Western Europe, and during 1953-8 it was doubled in size, despite local objections to the loss of farmland, road closures, and other inevitable intrusions. Burtonwood became the 'Gateway to Europe' and by 1961 was the largest military establishment in the 'Free World' outside America itself. For many thousands of American servicemen the first sight of Europe was the flat fields and grey skies of south-west Lancashire as they landed here: 25 million passengers arrived between 1948 and 1958 alone, and in the late 1950s there was an average of 30,000 flights a year from the base. Over 6,500 Americans married local girls, and the base became a piece of the USA transplanted, with American shops, baseball leagues and entertainment venues.

In the mid-1960s there was talk of developing it as a new international civil airport to replace those at Manchester and Liverpool, but this idea was stillborn and problems began to loom. The threat of colliery subsidence under parts of the runways, the switching of American attention away from Western Europe (especially during the Vietnam War) and schemes for motorway construction led to the gradual rundown of Burtonwood. By 1965 the USAF had largely pulled out; proposals to use it as the main US ammunition store for the European arena were dropped, because of very strong local protests; and in the late 1960s the M62 was built along the main runway.

The demise of Burtonwood was a major factor in the decision to create the Warrington New Town, so that the employment loss and the huge tract of derelict land could be dealt with. All that remains today is some warehousing and the RAF depot at Great Sankey, which is not part of the original site. But Burtonwood is being reborn with the 558-acre Omega project, which is transforming the former airbase into a complex of shops, office parks, residential and commercial areas, parkland, water features and new roads. This is likely to be the last major commercial development within the borough, and its completion will represent the fulfilment of the dream of the early 1960s in which the great tracts of military land would be reclaimed for commercial and community benefit, bringing employment, new landscapes and new population to Warrington.

FURTHER READING: A.P. Ferguson, *Burtonwood: Eighth Air Force Base Air Depot* (Airfield Publications, 1986) and *Royal Air Force Burtonwood: fifty years in photographs* (Airfield Publications, 1989); J. Toole, 'GIs and the race bar in Wartime Warrington', in *History Today* vol.43 (July 1993)

98. Housing 1945-1970

For thirty years after the Second World War successive governments insisted on the building of large numbers of council houses, and in Warrington completions reached a peak in the late 1960s. The earlier post-war estates were of traditional design, with semi-detached housing at relatively low densities, but there were some attempts to create new 'communities'. The earliest was the Dallam estate, with 620 houses, 24 maisonettes for single people and elderly couples, 12 shops, two schools and 20 acres of playing fields. This was followed by the new estates at Longford and Latchford and then the very large Orford estate, built in stages between 1955 and 1968 and with a total of just over 3,700 houses. This community, with a population in the mid-1970s of about 12,000, was the same size as the entire town 150 years before.

Slum clearance resumed in the late 1950s, but the figures of unfit houses continued to grow because standards rose. Nationally, large-scale demolition became the main policy. Warrington, to its good fortune, never experienced the wholesale destruction of entire communities witnessed by, for example, Liverpool, and the town therefore escaped the worst traumas of the 1960s' housing policies even though in 1965 it was claimed that 4,000 dwellings, 18 per cent of the town's stock, would have to be demolished. The 1991 census showed that clearance policies, the building of council housing and the new town estates, and the post-1975 strategy of upgrading older housing had been very effective. Only 0.3 per cent of houses were without a fixed bath or shower, and only 0.6 per cent had only an outdoor WC, both figures being approximately the national average, and substantially better than those for other larger towns in the north-west.

During the 1960s the government ordered local authorities to adopt 'industrialised building methods' (i.e. non-traditional forms of construction), allegedly because they were superior but in reality because they were cheaper, and they also encouraged high-rise schemes. Warrington was reluctant to obey, and thus managed to avoid the worst excesses of these disastrous policies, although industrialised methods were employed on the Houghton Green and Padgate estates in the late 1960s and early 1970s, and a few 'medium-rise' blocks were built. These projects were geared particularly towards rehousing people whose homes were demolished during the mid-1960s slum clearance programme. By 1972 there were over 9,100 council houses in the borough, 6,500 of them built since 1946. After that, council house-building programmes

Large numbers of new council houses were built between 1945 and 1970

Warrington avoided the main problems of high-rise developments

Slum clearance in the central areas was a significant part of housing policy

REFERENCE.
1. HAWLEYS LANE.
2. LONGSHAW STREET.
3. SCHOOL.
4. SHOPS.
5. MAISONETTES.
6. SITE for COMMUNITY CENTRE.
7. RECREATION GROUND.
8. DALLAM FARM.

After 1945 the borough council built large numbers of new houses on peripheral council estates. One of the first was Dallam Farm (1950-2). This plan shows how the estate was designed as a relatively low density housing scheme, with crescents and culs-de-sac of semi-detached properties, all intended to escape from the image of monotonous rows of uniform terraced housing.

At the centre of the estate was a group of maisonettes in Harrison Square. These were intended for couples and single people, but from the beginning many prospective residents had misgivings about the flats and serious problems eventually developed. These blocks have now been refurbished.

were rapidly scaled down and by the late 1970s almost ended. From the early 1980s it was the sale of these houses, not their construction, which occupied the column inches in the press.

FURTHER READING: There is no general account of housing in Warrington in this period. The minutes of the Housing Committee are a useful source, as are the brief descriptions of new housing in the various official guides to the borough. For individual estates, local newspaper reports are helpful but these are unindexed. See also the material on housing, in the Warrington local studies collection. The county volumes of census statistics give figures on housing quality broken down by ward, allowing comparisons across the borough: those quoted are from the 1991 Cheshire Ward Statistics.

99. Motorways, new roads, and their impact

The motorway network round Warrington was developed from the early 1960s

The M6 was a main axis of the new national system of motorways

Warrington became one of the nodal points on this network

This had a profound effect upon the town's fortunes and its potential growth

Within the town, expressways were built to link with new housing areas

In the 1930s the Ministry of Transport, observing with interest the rapidly-growing German *autobahn* network, began to plan a national system of high standard roads in Great Britain. Outline schemes of possible routes were prepared, all including a new road up the west side of the country from the Birmingham area into Lancashire and on to Scotland, with branches to connect with the Manchester and Liverpool conurbations. Also in agreement with this strategy were the highway surveyors of Lancashire County Council who, at first separately and then in conjunction with the government, planned a motorway network for Lancashire which could slot into any wider national scheme.

The Second World War prevented further progress but in 1949 the county council published *A Road Plan for Lancashire*, explaining its proposals in detail. The most important element was a north-south motorway from the Kendal area, via Preston and Wigan, bypassing Warrington to the east and crossing the

Building the second Warrington Bridge, 1985: just upstream from the existing bridge (which was built in 1911-15), this allowed the creation of a huge traffic gyratory system in an attempt to relieve congestion at this extremely busy interchange.

Mersey on a new bridge at Thelwall. Another motorway would link Liverpool with Manchester and Yorkshire, and improved trunk roads were to run from Prescot through Warrington to Irlam and Salford and from Warrington to Winwick and Golborne. The ministry accepted the main north-south motorway scheme in its entirety and as the M6 it became a main axis of the new network. The route was approved in 1953 and in 1958 the minister accepted the detailed plans for the Thelwall to Preston section. Work on the Thelwall viaduct (then the largest road bridge in Britain) began in September 1959, and on the main motorway 18 months later. The entire length of the M6 from the A50 junction to Preston was opened in July 1963.

During the late 1960s and early 1970s the construction of the motorway network was at its peak. The M62 was built from Liverpool to Hull, the section from Tarbock to the M6 at Croft being opened in 1973 and Croft to Eccles in the following year, while the M56 from Chester to Manchester added a parallel route on the south side of the Mersey valley. There were several other schemes for motorways in south Lancashire and north Cheshire which have not come to fruition, and perhaps never will, but the basic network around Warrington, as established in the mid-1970s, gave the town an almost unrivalled position as a focal point on the national network.

The most obvious benefit was the removal of most of the through-traffic which had clogged up the town centre. Although the subsequent growth of traffic means that congestion and delays have not been eliminated, without the motorway 'box' things would now be infinitely worse. Combined with the building of town centre roads such as Academy Way and the Midland Way expressway, the motorways allowed the town centre to be fully pedestrianised and enabled major environmental improvements to be undertaken. In the wider sense, the motorway has dramatically reinforced Warrington's role as a crossroads. Long-distance traffic bypasses the urban area, but the new roads have greatly extended the town's catchment area for retail and other business. In other words, it is not only easier to *avoid* Warrington but also to get *to* Warrington. This has been the main factor behind the remarkable success of the new town and the commercial activities central to its strategy. None of the business and retail parks, warehousing complexes or freight depots, would have materialised without the motorway system.

Motorways and new trunk roads in the Warrington area 1960-2000.

After the motorways had been completed, road-building was concentrated on the fast new links which tied together the residential districts of the new town. Thus, Birchwood Way, Cromwell Way and Midland Way were built between 1970 and 2000 as a part of a much more ambitious road network

The M6 at Appleton on a relatively quiet day (but with the traditional cones much in evidence!). The motorways have become one of the most significant elements in the geography, economy and life of early 21st-century Warrington.

designed in the late 1960s. Substantial parts of that network have not been built, and some (such as the link from Westbrook Way to Winwick Road) have been dropped from future plans. Today only the extension of Birchwood Way to Winwick Road, relieving the overcrowded and winding Long Lane, remains on the list. One very important project was the construction in 1985-6 of the second Warrington Bridge, just upstream from the older one, so that a huge roundabout could be created at this always-busy junction. The associated completion of Academy Way and dualling of Mersey Street required the removal of the old Warrington Academy building. It was winched painstakingly out of the path of the new road and then, sadly, found to be structurally unsound so that much had to be demolished.

FURTHER READING: J. Drake, *A Road Plan for Lancashire* (Lancashire County Council, 1949); H. Yeadon, 'The Motorway Era' and A.G. Crosby, 'Epilogue and Retrospect', in A.G. Crosby (ed.) *Leading the Way: a history of Lancashire's roads* (Lancashire County Books, 1998); the various New Town and Warrington Borough planning documents 1969-2002 discuss the road schemes which were proposed or built.

100. *Railways in the twentieth century*

The rail network was reduced by closures in the 1960s

The main lines through Bank Quay and Central stations were upgraded

Ideas for future improvements and reopenings are raised from time to time

The rail network of the north-west reached its maximum extent in the years around the First World War, and in the 1920s began to contract as passenger services faced competition from road transport and freight traffic shrank with the decline in key industries. In the Warrington area there were several closures, although most lines through the town remain open. The line from Widnes to Altrincham via Warrington and Lymm closed in 1962; from Glazebrook through Culcheth in 1964; and the 'direct' line from Padgate to Sankey in 1968.

The town is fortunate that its two main lines have been protected from threat of closure and have received significant investment in the last forty years. In 1974 the line from Crewe through Warrington and on to Glasgow was electrified and at the same time the old and run-down Bank Quay Station was partly rebuilt. With the major upgrade of services on the West Coast main line Warrington now had more trains, and faster trains, to London and to Scotland than ever before, and this level of service in theory continues today, though notoriously the reality is often different. Services to Manchester, Chester and North Wales from Bank Quay also improved. On the line from Liverpool to Manchester via Warrington Central there are now regular services to, for example, Sheffield, the East Midlands and East Anglia. On this route an entirely new station was opened in 1980 at Birchwood, serving the district centre and the eastern half of the new town.

Freight traffic from the Bank Quay area remains an important element in Warrington's role as a railway centre, and the line from Latchford and Arpley

via Bank Quay low level to Widnes is still open for freight, though passenger services ended forty years ago and the line is truncated at Latchford. From time to time suggestions are made for further development of the rail network locally, such as the introduction of new local services to Crewe and Preston and even, recently, the reopening of the line from Lowton via Culcheth to Glazebrook, but these always founder on the rock of money, or the lack of it. Nonetheless, more than 170 years after the first line in the area was opened the railway continues to play a useful role in the local economy and transport network.

FURTHER READING: G.O. Holt, *A Regional History of the Railways of Great Britain vol.10: The North-West* (David & Charles, 1986); P.A. Norton, *Railways and Waterways to Warrington* (Cheshire Libraries, 1984)

LEFT *A Nottingham to Liverpool train about to cross Froghall Lane Bridge on the ex-Cheshire Lines Railway, 3 November 1957.*

RIGHT *An atmospheric shot of 45252 passing through the recently-closed Arpley Station in the winter of 1959, with a permanent way train. The station buildings were demolished in 1968.*

101. Warrington New Town

Nothing in its recent history has had such a far-reaching effect upon Warrington than its designation by the government as a New Town in 1968. It is impossible to overstate the importance of that event, the impact of which has been felt widely across north Cheshire and south Lancashire. Warrington was already an old and large town, and the decision to expand it on a massive scale reflects contemporary planning philosophies which argued that, rather than choosing a largely green field site (as with earlier new towns, such as Skelmersdale), a substantial existing core would be more advantageous – there would already be an extensive infrastructure, labour force and sense of community. It might also avoid the fierce planning battles encountered in projects for new towns in green belt areas.

Warrington was chosen for several reasons. The first, prominent in the early thinking, was that expansion would remedy the major problems of the town itself, and in particular those associated with the running down or ending military employment at Burtonwood, Risley and Padgate. The second was that it seemed an excellent place for the reception of overspill from the Manchester conurbation. The project was conceived in the heyday of massive slum clearance and rehousing schemes and central to those was the principle that many residents of the inner cities would be 'decanted' to new communities

The designation of Warrington as a new town in 1968 was a key event

The town expansion resulted in a very rapid population increase in 1975-95

Huge investment in infrastructure and employment transformed the economy

The new town has been very successful, although national planning policies eventually turned away from the new town programme well beyond the conurbation. A third reason which emerged was less clearly defined but soon became the most important: Warrington was superbly placed to become a regional centre, where (in contrast to the fortunes of much of the north-west) economic expansion and population growth would continue. The rationale for the new town then became to ensure that development took place in an orderly fashion, with proper phased provision of transport and other infrastructure, housing, community and leisure facilities, and shopping and retailing, as well as the industrial estates which were the key to it all.

The designated new town was much larger than the existing borough (which had little undeveloped land because its boundaries were so tightly drawn). The borough had about 65,000 people, while about the same number lived in the adjacent rural areas included within the new town. The combined population of 130,000 was expected to increase to 200,000 by 1991 and perhaps 250,000 by 2001. This would be achieved in part by bringing in overspill, but it was certain that the commercial and industrial development of the town (specifically, an increase of at least 36,000 in the number of jobs in services and light industry) would draw in many new voluntary migrants. The basic design for the New Town was approved in 1968, detailed proposals were agreed in 1969, and work began in earnest in 1970. As in all the new towns of the 1950s and 1960s, the borough council was at first bypassed to some extent, because implementation was the responsibility of the Warrington Development Corporation, set up in March 1969. The objectives of the plan were defined as follows:

- to provide the widest possible range of opportunity and choice
- to make Warrington a good place in which to live and grow up
- to facilitate growth and change
- to carry out the development in a rational and businesslike manner

The development was to be based upon newly-created neighbourhoods and districts, focusing on district centres (providing a wide range of facilities and services) at Stockton Heath, Appleton Thorn, Padgate, Bewsey, and Birchwood. Initially the existing town centre, for which Warrington Borough Council continued to be responsible, was not expected to be much larger than the district centres, though with its older buildings and traditional layout it would be more distinctive in character. In the event, the borough council's effective strategy for expansion and regeneration of the town centre meant that it continued as the most important shopping and commercial zone within the expanded town.

The new residential and industrial areas were to be threaded together by a comprehensive network of new roads, woven within the existing framework of the M6, M56 and M62, and including urban motorways from Cuerdley to Martinscroft, Bewsey to Risley, and Padgate to Stretton. Huge new industrial areas would line the railways and cluster round road intersections, and a chain of parks and open spaces would follow valleys and wind among the housing areas.

Perhaps the most remarkable feature of this visionary plan is the extent to which it has been fulfilled, for Warrington is the most successful of the new towns of northern England. Development has been somewhat slower than in

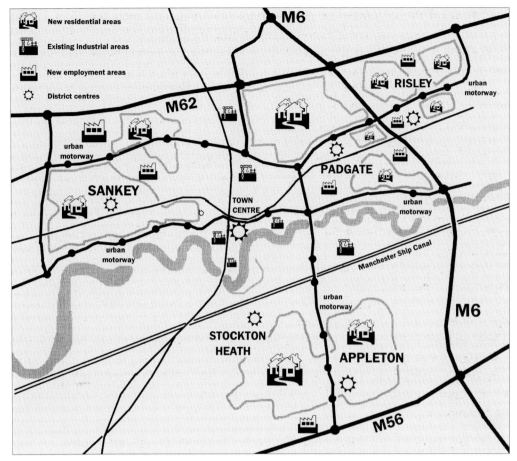

Legend:
- New residential areas
- Existing industrial areas
- New employment areas
- District centres

M6

M62

RISLEY

urban motorway

SANKEY

urban motorway

urban motorway

TOWN CENTRE

PADGATE

urban motorway

Manchester Ship Canal

M6

urban motorway

STOCKTON HEATH

APPLETON

M56

A schematic map of the outline proposals for the New Town, based on the plan drawn up in 1968-9. Note that only small parts of the urban motorway network have materialised in the subsequent forty years, and that there have been major changes in the planned distribution of housing, industry and employment areas.

the original timetable, and the most optimistic forecasts of jobs and population have not been reached, while the more costly infrastructure schemes have been dropped or scaled down, but a surprisingly large proportion of the plan has come to fruition. The Warrington project was a conspicuous success and the contribution of the new town scheme to the overall economic stability and growth of the town is fundamental. Of course, given Warrington's exceptional advantages in terms of communications and location, it would probably never have suffered from the depths of recession which affected other towns in the north-west, but the new town project represented a massive financial investment in the town and its future.

In the late 1980s the planning philosophy which lay behind new towns was no longer in favour, and the government wound-up the development corporations, transferring their assets to local authorities and the Commission for New Towns, and eventually to English Partnerships. By that time, though, Warrington's expansion had acquired its own momentum, and commercial and industrial development has continued ever since, given an invaluable kickstart by the strategy adopted in the mid-1960s.

FURTHER READING: The development of the New Town was preceded by a series of major and detailed reports and plans, notably the *Consultants' Report for the draft master plan* (1969). Warrington local studies collection holds copies of all these reports, together with other material produced by the Development Corporation, including various detailed social and economic analyses, reports on individual schemes and on the implementation of the overall plan, and assessments of its impact on the community.

102. Population since 1945

The population decline in Warrington town continued after 1945

The population of adjacent rural parishes rose rapidly in the 1950s and 1960s

After the New Town development began Warrington grew extremely rapidly

The population of the town is significantly younger than the national average

There is a lower than average percentage of people from ethnic minorities

The population decline which began in the early 1930s accelerated after the Second World War. In 1951 the county borough recorded 80,700 people but in 1971, as a result of deliberate and voluntary out-migration, it had fallen to 68,000. As the redevelopment of the town centre, the construction of new roads and further clearance of older housing changed the landscape in the 1970s, another exodus occurred – in 1981 the former county borough (the inner area of the new borough) housed 57,400 people, 25 per cent fewer than fifty years before. In contrast, the population of small towns and villages around Warrington was already increasing long before the new town was designated in 1968. Lymm, for example, grew by 43 per cent in just one decade, the 1960s, and the rural parishes in the present borough increased by 45 per cent over the same period. People were fleeing the inner areas and seeking pastures new, a process made possible by car, which gave mobility and flexibility, allowing people to commute from the villages and suburbs.

The development of the new town reinforced this developing trend. The population at the time of designation was 130,000. At the beginning of the 1970s the building of the new residential districts, including Westbrook and Callands, Pewterspear, Locking Stumps and Oakwood was getting under way, and the first major industrial and commercial estates were laid out, so by 1971 the population of the borough as a whole had increased to 136,000. During the 1980s and 1990s, though, these massive projects were completed and Warrington's fast-growing economy attracted large numbers of new residents, so population growth accelerated dramatically: in 1981 the new borough had 165,000 people, in 1991 there were 181,000, and by 2001 approximately 192,000.

The 1991 census, the latest for which detailed statistics are available, gave a valuable profile of the citizens of modern Warrington. The town was becoming a multi-cultural community, but the percentage of people from ethnic minority backgrounds was well below the national average. In 1971, when the first national information is available, 2.8 per cent of the population of the old county borough were born outside the UK, but of these half were from the Irish Republic. Warrington thus had one of the lowest percentages of Commonwealth migrants of any large town in the region. This reflects its economic structure in the 1950s and 1960s, since most migrants to the region from South Asia came to work in the textile industries, for which Warrington was not a major centre. Far fewer found work in the heavy industry, engineering and manufacturing sectors which were so important in Warrington. There were, however, significant communities of, for example, Poles and Ukrainians in

The population of Warrington in the later 20th century, showing how the old borough area experienced continued rapid decline while the surrounding rural areas, brought within the new town boundary, show extremely fast growth.

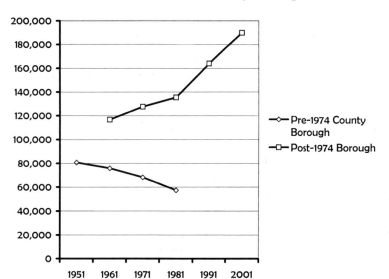

the town, who had come after 1945. In 1991 the same pattern was reflected in the fact that only 1.3 per cent of Warringtonians were from the black, Asian or Chinese communities, compared with a national figure of 5.9 per cent and a percentage in Preston, for example, of 10.5 per cent.

The impact of the rapid growth of the 1970s and 1980s was clear in another revealing statistic. In Warrington in 1991 only 5.9 per cent of the population was over 75 years old, well below the national average because so many younger people with families had been attracted to the town during the period of rapid expansion. Within the town the 'youngest' areas were invariably the large new residential districts, such as Oakwood and Birchwood, where the percentages of older people were less than a third the national figure. In contrast, traditional housing areas such as Stockton Heath and Latchford had proportions of elderly people well above that national figure. Figures such as these allow us to look ahead as well: in twenty years time, as the great influx of young people who came in the 1970s and 1980s reach retirement, Warrington may well have an unusually high proportion of *older* people, and the need to plan ahead for such a trend will be a major task of local health, social services and community organisations.

FURTHER READING: The Lancashire [to 1971] and Cheshire county volumes of census statistics chart the population growth of the borough of Warrington and neighbouring rural parishes. Statistics on the ethnic composition and age profile of the population in 1991 are given in the Ward Statistics for Cheshire [copies available in the Warrington local studies collection]. Population figures are also available in the economic and social profiles published from time to time by the borough.

103. *Town centre redevelopment: creating a new Warrington*

After the Second World War the multiples and the chain stores gradually pushed out many of the smaller retailers. They captured the market by their price and advertising policies, and could afford to pay the higher rents on prime town centre sites. One by one familiar names disappeared, though in 1954 Warrington still had, for example, three clogmakers and 21 private drapery businesses, including Hodgkinsons of Bridge Street and J. Leigh & Sons with their three shops in Lovely Lane, Mersey Street and Powys Street. Hodgkinsons made strenuous efforts to maintain a modern image and to diversify to offer the widest possible range – their 1951 advertisements, for example, announced that the premises at 18-22 Bridge Street were 'Warrington's Popular Shopping Centre', with a furnishing store, drapery store and fashion store, a ladies' hairdressing saloon [*sic*], and the famous fully-furnished model bungalow. But ultimately most of the 'old names' vanished, together with the shops themselves, as the redevelopment of the town centre got under way in the 1970s.

As early as the 1920s the congested crossroads at Market Gate was the subject of improvement schemes, following the widening of Bridge Street before the First World War and the rounding-off of the Sankey Street corner. The aim was to create a more appropriate centrepiece to the town, and the concept of a circus of buildings, first suggested before 1914, was adopted. There was to be to a uniform architectural style, to give a more imposing feel

In the 1950s and 1960s many traditional shops disappeared

The creation of the New Town in 1968 accelerated the changes

Comprehensive redevelopment of much of the centre followed

Today, plans for further expansion have been unveiled

to this focal point, but progress was faltering and confused. Buttermarket Street was rebuilt in 1912-15 but the widening of Horsemarket Street and completion of the roundabout at Market Gate had to wait until 1938. In the same year Wilson Patten Street was extended through to Bridge Foot, helping to take some of the traffic away from Sankey Street. Unfortunately, in the process of creating new townscapes, many of the most interesting and historically important timber-framed buildings of the town centre were demolished. Most people regarded this as progress:

> 66 The Corporation continued to pursue its street improvement policy, and in like manner the old Buttermarket, with its heterogeneous assortment of properties yielded to its purging enterprise, and became more worthy both in its proportions and appearance 99
>
> *Warrington Guardian Year Book, 1921*

By 1939 the general layout of Market Gate was complete, but widening Sankey Street had not yet begun when the war put an end to all such projects. Afterwards there was a long period when other priorities were found, and it was not until the late 1950s that schemes for central redevelopment were aired once more and the borough council gave serious consideration to the future shape of the town centre. At this point, though, the entire picture changed with the advent of the New Town. Plans for the town centre now had to be seen in the context of the extended urban area. The planners were very disparaging of the town centre and insisted that a 'comprehensive revitalising and restructuring' was necessary. While recognising that some historic buildings should be retained, and that some small parts of the town centre (notably around the Town Hall and Palmyra Square) had architectural merit, the basic view was that extensive redevelopment, with a brand-new road network, was essential.

The renewal of the town centre continued to be the responsibility of the borough council, which gave priority to the old market area and relieving the pressing problem of traffic congestion. Plans were drawn up in 1969-71 whereby most of the north-western quadrant of the town centre, around the old market place, would be completely reconstructed. Further extensive redevelopment was proposed for the Bank Street area and the derelict backlands behind Buttermarket Street and Bridge Street, and the whole of the Scotland Road-Academy Street area was to be comprehensively rebuilt. A new inner relief road would take traffic round the east side of the centre, linking with urban motorways and giving access to the relocated bus station and new multi-storey car parks. Elsewhere, piecemeal redevelopment of specific sites would be encouraged, though the more important historic buildings were to be retained. The regeneration of the town centre, and especially the new Golden Square shopping centre, was achieved by a very successful partnership between Warrington Borough Council and private developers.

The demolition of buildings on the north side of Sankey Street, opposite the Co-operative store on the Cairo Street corner, began in the autumn of 1973 and over the next two years a large part of central Warrington was razed to the ground. Great swathes were cut through the intricate fabric of the town, whole streets disappeared, and cranes and bulldozers became a characteristic feature.

FACING PAGE *The town centre in the late 1950s*

KEY

BH	Britannia Hotel [site of New Town House]
C	Cockhedge
Co	Co-op building [TJ Hughes]
CS	Central Station
E	Empire Cinema and Billiard Hall, a favourite haunt of Burtonwood GIs
GM	General market
HT	Holy Trinity church
MG	Market Gate
MH	Market Hall
M+S	Marks & Spencer
O	Odeon Cinema in Buttermarket Street
SEQ	South East Quadrant [future market site]

In 1975 new buildings began to rise from the dust and debris, with the completion of the new Golden Square shopping centre, the redevelopment of Scotland Road, the creation of the irregular Time Square on the site of the Bank Street properties, and the new market. Only two buildings in the old market place were spared – the black-and-white *Barley Mow*, dating back to the later 16th century, and the fine Victorian covered fish market.

Warrington was extremely fortunate to be spared the construction of a massive monolithic shopping centre of the Arndale variety. Such schemes were the ruin of several towns in the region and have been universally condemned ever since. What eventually emerged was unexpectedly in keeping with the scale of the town and the redevelopment of the market place was sympathetic. Time Square was satisfyingly irregular and human in scale. In contrast, New Town House, built by the Development Corporation as its own headquarters, is a typical piece of early 1970s architecture.

The redevelopment schemes, finished (it was thought) in the mid-1980s, created a shopping centre of regional significance, benefiting from good access via a new bus station and car parks, and with an environment which was potentially very attractive as pedestrianisation was extended. And it may change again, with plans to greatly extend and remodel the Golden Square shopping area by 2006, including a department store, a new bus station, improved car-parking and major enhancements to the townscape. This further emphasises that central Warrington is, as it has been for a thousand years, the retail focus for the whole of the Mersey valley.

FURTHER READING: For the 1950s and 1960s, information on town centre retailing and commercial businesses can be obtained from trade and street directories. The reports and master plan for the New Town (1969) include analysis of the town centre as well as proposals for its redevelopment. For the progress of the redevelopment, see Janice Hayes, *Changing Warrington* (1991).

FACING PAGE *The new town centre takes shape, late 1970s.*

KEY
1 Legh Street car park and bridge over Golborne Street [1973-75]
2 Golden Square shopping centre and Marks & Spencer [1973-79]
3 Golden Square shopping centre phase 3 [finished 1983]
4 New retail market [mid-1970s]
5 The site of Time Square
6 The Market car park [completed 1976]
7 Academy Way, phase 2 of the inner ring road [completed 1986]
8 Warrington Academy, awaiting removal to its new site on vacant plot to the left

104. Out of town shopping and its impact

In Warrington, which for centuries has been an important regional market centre, an even wider retail catchment has grown in the 1980s based not on the heart of the town but on new retail parks on the outskirts. The creation of the new town, preceded by the opening of key motorway links, made this an ideal location for 'out of town shopping', of which it was one of the English pioneers and is among the greatest success stories. The original plan, drawn up in 1965-6, long predated the idea. The retailing and commercial areas of the town were to be based on the series of district centres. Within a few years though, two new trends emerged. The first was an increasing interest in 'American style' out-of-town shopping malls and retail parks, and the second was the pressure from commercial and industrial interests to locate closer to major road intersections.

The new town plan was extensively altered to accommodate these ideas. A major catalyst to change was the building of a new distributor road, Cromwell Avenue, with excellent access to the M62 junction at Winwick. It had not been part of the original plan, but its construction was accompanied by the rezoning of the land northwards to the motorway, from residential use

Warrington was one of the first UK towns with major out-of-town shopping

This has become a key element in the local economy

The Borough Council has met the challenge by enhancing the town centre

The Gemini Retail Park, 2002, showing the great car parks around Marks & Spencer's and IKEA (the company's pioneering UK store), the new road networks which ring this part of the new town, and the widening work in progress on the adjacent M62.

and open space to commerce and retailing. The way was open for the development of the Gemini Retail Park, one of the earliest and largest such schemes in north-west England. It quickly achieved its objective when IKEA opened its first UK store there and by the early 1990s, as it attracted a range of other retailing giants including Marks & Spencer and Toys'R'Us, Gemini had become a focus of long-distance shopping. Indeed, so successful was it that traffic queues along Cromwell Way throughout the day now symbolise the powerful attraction of the 'big names and easy access' – though the latter is in consequence not always the case! The newest solution is the widening of the M62 and a new link road into the Gemini retail and business parks.

The effects of out-of-town shopping are very clear. Property rents at Gemini are among the highest in the region and the commercial expansion of the site is continuing. The impact on traffic levels in north Warrington is obvious, and the site has attracted, directly or indirectly, several thousand new jobs. The consequences for the older town centre, though, were less encouraging. Within a couple of years the borough council was urgently rethinking its policy towards the central area:

> 66 Car-owning shoppers now had a huge choice between Manchester, Liverpool, Chester and half a dozen major towns, plus several edge-of-town developments boasting stores from all the major national retailers. To lose our traditional trade to these rivals would not only cost income and jobs but threatened the town centre with a slow but remorseless decline. These were the challenges which faced Warrington Borough Council in 1994. The response was immediate: the appointment of a Town Centre Manager and the creation of the Warrington NOW Initiative, a multi-partner drive to ensure that Warrington was to have the best, the brightest and the most accessible shopping centre in the region. 99
>
> *Warrington Borough Council Official Guide, 1998*

The major environmental improvements and expansion of central area shopping which we see today were the result. The much-enhanced town centre of Warrington is a complement to the retail parks on the outskirts. Together they mean that the town is one of the foremost commercial centres in the region.

FURTHER READING: There is no general account of the development of out-of town shopping in the borough: some coverage is given in the planning documents produced by the New Town Development corporation and the Borough Council, and recent economic reports published by the borough highlight the significance of the sector for employment and commercial prosperity.

105. Industry and employment in the twentieth century

With its broad economic base Warrington met the challenges of the interwar period – characterised in the north-west by deep depression and the collapse of staple industries – better than many other towns in the region. From the late 1920s there were considerable problems in some of the town's major trades, but nothing resembling the wholesale disappearance of a single industry on which a whole town depended, as happened in the cotton towns. The really serious changes instead came in the 1960s and 1970s, when extensive restructuring of the older trades meant extensive closures of the town's factories. By this time, though, the arrival of new elements – service trades and light industry – helped to cushion the blow.

Some key industries declined catastrophically. The leather and tanning trades were threatened by cheap imports of leather and leather goods from overseas, by the development of plastics and synthetic leathers, and by the predictable problems of outdated methods and obsolete technologies. Most of the tanneries in the vicinity of the town centre and Winwick Road had gone by 1950, and the great riverside tannery at Howley closed in 1960. Similarly, Warrington's role as the outpost of the great Lancashire cotton industry came to an end in 1981 when Armitage & Rigby's Cockhedge mill, the last in the town, finally wove its last cloth. Its site became, in another symbolic change, the Cockhedge shopping centre based on the new ASDA supermarket (the structure of the building incorporates some of the beams from the old mill). Other industries were more able to adapt and withstand pressure.

The resilience of wireworking

The wireworking trades, so important to Warrington since the late 18th century, had already begun to diversify into other products. Within the wireworking firms there was a long tradition of adapting to new markets, and exploiting the opportunities presented by developing technology in other industries. This meant that the town's leading wireworking businesses did not suffer the large-scale contraction and obsolescence which were such a problem for many businesses in the region. Thus, Lockers (which progressively expanded its business empire and eventually became Thomas Locker (Holdings) Limited) developed new lines, manufacturing parts for aircraft and industrial plant, including equipment for brickmaking, cement-manufacturing and textile mills, and increasingly specialising in sieves, filters and filtration technology, industrial textiles, cable reels and drums, as well as the well-established woven wire cloths and products. By the early 1970s the firm was employing over 400 people in Warrington alone. The firm has continued to hold a large share of a highly competitive international trade, demonstrating its adaptability in the global economy.

The older wireworks, with their often-cramped sites and outdated infrastructure, contracted rapidly during the 1960s and 1970s, a process exemplified by the winding-down and (in 1986) closure by Rylands of their remaining Church Street site. Symbolic of the new age, perhaps, was the demolition of the buildings and their replacement by the Sainsbury superstore – the balance of employment in Warrington was switching from manufacturing

Warrington's broad industrial base was a source of economic strength

The depression of the 1930s did not hit the town as hard as its neighbours

In the 1950s and 1960s some traditional industries disappeared

Light industry and technological industries have replaced these

Service trades are now the main source of employment in the borough

Heavy industry has undergone large-scale restructuring

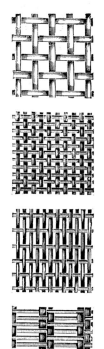

Examples of wire cloth and mesh woven by Thomas Locker's, from their early 1970s trade catalogue: at this date traditional products were still produced on a large scale.

The end of an era at Monks Hall steel works as Warrington Museum staff documented the traditional hand-rolling process at No. 5 mill shortly before its closure in February 1986. This view shows the interior of the mill taken from the overhead electric crane, with the furnace in the distance. The No. 4 Mill closed in March 1986 ending over a century of steel-making on the site.

to retailing and service trades. Rylands initially survived as a company, in 1971 becoming part of Rylands Whitecross Limited when it was bought by Sheffield-based Tinsley Wire Limited. This large group, with several factories in northern England, produced a wide range of steel and steel-wire product. In 1997 the name changed again, to Tinsley Wire Warrington, and in December 1999 the Warrington operation was sold to Carrington Wire Ltd. At present the 22-acre plant at Warrington produces over 100,000 tons of wire products annually. Thus wireworking and related metallurgical trades, one of the cornerstones of Warrington's industrial strength for over a quarter of a millennium, continue to be central to the town's manufacturing base.

Greenalls: the challenge of a changing market

The massive restructuring of the brewing industry not just in England but also in Europe in the years after 1960 could not fail to affect the town's oldest and most important brewery firm, Greenall Whitley. The switch from relatively small local breweries to huge plants, together with the increasing scale of the associated leisure and entertainment sectors, meant that the company had to rethink its strategies across the United Kingdom. The Greenalls Group had long ago diversified into tied public houses – this was one of its main areas of business as long ago as 1900 – and in the 1970s and 1980s this element in its structure was expanded rapidly. At the same time, and partly because of this, the group as a whole gradually shifted its focus from brewing to food, drink and accommodation retailing. By 1995 it had over 2,000 outlets across the United Kingdom and a turnover of over £1.1 billion. In 1991, as what in retrospect seems the unavoidable outcome of these 'seismic shifts' in one of Britain's fastest-growing business sectors, Greenalls finished brewing at Wilderspool, after more than two centuries. The decision to end the group's direct brewing activities meant that name was licensed to Carlsberg-Tetley and, as the company stated at the time, 'the transformation of Greenalls from regional brewer to national retailer was well under way'. In 1999 the process was carried to its logical conclusion when the group sold all its pubs and restaurants, the largest single purchaser being Scottish & Newcastle, leaving it focused on the hotel and leisure club sector. Thomas Greenall, back in 1762, chose to open a new brewery in Wilderspool – he recognised that the market was changing, and as a result a minor local trader became a business force to be reckoned with. Nearly 250 year later his name is still famous. That was a Warrington achievement.

Some new industries came to the town in the 1920s and 1930s. In 1937, for example, Thames Board Mills opened a northern base at the Mersey works, producing cardboard, packaging materials, cartons and boards. The works was noted for its early entry into recycling – by the late 1960s it was receiving almost 200,000 tons of waste paper a year for reprocessing. Other industry came during the war. In 1942 land at Lower Walton was purchased by Laporte for its new chemical works: a wartime factory, opened in 1943, was replaced in 1950 by a plant, the Baronet Works (named after the farm on which it was built, itself called after Gilbert Greenall, first Lord Daresbury, who owned the property) producing hydrogen peroxide, an essential ingredient in the manufacture of soap powders and related products.

This was a good example of local association between industries, for the Crosfield's site at Bank Quay (from 1919 part of the huge Lever Brothers group) was the world leader in the production of soap powders. Persil, the best-known of all washing-powders, was first manufactured at Bank Quay in 1909, when it was marketed as 'the amazing oxygen washer'. It was expensive (at 3½d. or about 2p for a half-pound), and had to be mixed with water to form a paste before use, but the popularity of the brand grew rapidly. In 1919 the factory produced 450 tons of Persil, and only three years later 2,800 tons. As the demand for consumer products grew, and washing machines appeared in middle-class households, the Bank Quay site was expanded to increase output: the 1934 figure was 19,000 tons. In 1939 the modern form of dry washing powder was invented, and in 1948 the introduction of fluorescers, giving that 'whiter than white' look, meant that the future was assured. In 1956 Persil from Bank Quay had a 35 per cent share of the British market.

Further, very modern, industries and businesses came in the 1950s with, for example, the arrival of what became the United Kingdom Atomic Energy Authority and British Nuclear Fuels at Risley and (just outside the borough boundary) the Daresbury laboratories. Since then the highly successful science and business parks at Birchwood and Westbrook have attracted numerous high-technology companies, research centres, warehousing and transportation firms. There has been a clear message in the second half of this book regarding Warrington's economic base and its industrial structure. In contrast to the experience of many towns in the region it was provided with a variety of industries, none of which so dominated the town that it was economically insecure as a result. The older established heavy industries did contract during the 20th century, but newer enterprises helped to cushion that difficulty. A favourable location meant that after the Second World War investment was attracted and diversification continued. The designation of the new town in the mid-1960s, and the resultant development of large industrial and commercial estates, ensured that Warrington again weathered recessions and depressions better than most of its rivals in the region.

In the last thirty years of the 20th century, the period of new town development, employment in the borough rose from about 65,000 to 95,000, a rate of increase which meant that Warrington was one of the few 'brightspots' in a region which generally saw a major economic downturn over much of the period. Within that increase, important structural changes occurred. There were originally few people employed in the primary sector (agriculture, mining and quarrying, and energy and water) but the latter groups showed a major increase as the employers such as the water and electricity undertakings grew – Warrington's role as a location for regional offices and headquarters was largely responsible. The decline in manufacturing in Warrington was even more dramatic than in the region as a whole, as firms such as British Steel,

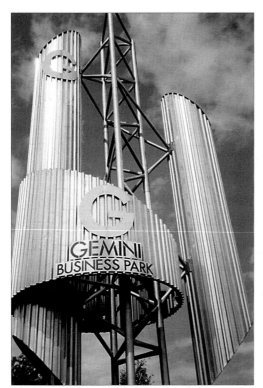

The new Warrington: office-based employment, now a mainstay of the town's economy, is symbolised by this futuristic sign for Gemini Business Park.

Cole Cranes and Firth Wire closed, and the borough council commented in 1999 that 'rationalisation and the introduction of new technologies [employing fewer people] exacerbated the decline'. However, the continued strength of Rylands Whitecross (Tinsley), Lever Brothers, Solvay, and the Thomas Locker Group ensured that a significant manufacturing sector does survive: it now employs about 15 per cent of the total labour force in the borough (compared with about 35 per cent in 1965).

The real growth has, therefore, been in the service sector, which covers a huge variety of trades and industries including office employment, retailing, transport, catering and leisure, banking and finance, and IT. Capitalising on its exceptional position as a transport hub, many firms have relocated in Warrington or expanded existing bases, a process encouraged for thirty years by the borough and new town authorities. The growth rate in the 1980s and 1990s was well over twice the national average and by the end of the century the service sector accounted for over three-quarters of all employment in the borough. Another significant element in this growth is that a high percentage of the new jobs created were taken by women, so that the female share of the labour force has also grown dramatically.

This has had a profound effect upon every aspect of the town, from its landscape to its social structure and, of crucial importance, its image. It has helped to create the sense of growing prosperity and 'shedding the legacy of the past' in exactly the way which the new town planners nearly forty years ago (and the borough council consistently since that date) have wanted. Warrington has shared in the ups and downs of the national economy, but today its unemployment rate is even better than that of prosperous Cheshire, and substantially below that of neighbouring parts of Lancashire. This key fact is a tribute to the success of the town in riding recessions and adapting to the challenges of the fast-changing economic circumstances of the later 20th century.

FURTHER READING: D.C. Johnson, *Industry and employment in Warrington 1820-1982* (unpublished University of Manchester MA dissertation, 1983: Warrington local studies collection reference ms.2797); Warrington Borough Council has produced, since the early 1980s, guides to the industrial and commercial opportunities in the borough, and these include many useful statistical profiles of employment, population trends and economic activity in the area (copies in the Warrington local studies collection); the 1971 *Borough Official Guide* has a lengthy section describing the industries of the town and their development to the early 1970s.

106. *Historic and natural landscapes*

Protection of Warrington's historic heritage did not loom large in the thinking of the Corporation or of many local people until recent decades. There were, it is true, influential people such as William Beamont in the mid-19th century, and Arthur Bennett in the forty years from the early 1890s, who campaigned for the preservation of historic buildings and opposed the wholesale demolition of the older townscapes of central Warrington, but their protests, although heard, went unheeded. Bennett, in particular, was a pioneer of many conservationist principles and, had his views been respected, much valuable historic architecture would have survived. Sadly, little did and we now have only the pictures of the half-timbered buildings of Buttermarket Street (swept away in the years before the First World War) or the 'oldest house in Warrington', a fascinating and very important medieval hall on the corner of Fennel Street (demolished in 1936), to show what used to be. During the 1950s and 1960s, and as the town centre was redeveloped, there was further loss of architectural and historical heritage – not dramatic buildings of national importance, but pleasant and locally valuable ones which gave Warrington a link with its rich past. Of the 52 buildings in the town listed in 1947 as being of special architectural and historical interest, only 26 now remain. Neither, for much of the 20th century, was Warrington's legacy of industrial archaeology regarded with much interest. Many earlier industrial buildings, such as the pinmakers' shops on the northern and eastern sides of the town centre, were cleared without any record.

In the past Warrington's historic buildings were not highly valued

Many were demolished in the earlier 20th century during redevelopment

The natural landscape suffered from industrial dereliction and pollution

More recently, strenuous efforts have been made to improve the landscape

Protection of heritage is now an important theme

More recently, protection of the historical legacy has become more prominent. The borough has 17 conservation areas, protecting townscapes of historical and architectural importance. Of these, seven are in or around the town centre – including Bank Hall and Park, Palmyra Square and Queens Gardens, Bridge Street and Church Street – while the others are mainly the old village centres of the district, such as Grappenhall, Stockton Heath and Higher Walton. Within these conservation areas, and scattered across the rest of the borough, are many listed buildings, and a recent report suggested that another 480 buildings could be considered as of local historic or architectural importance even if not candidates for national listing. These buildings are now relatively well protected.

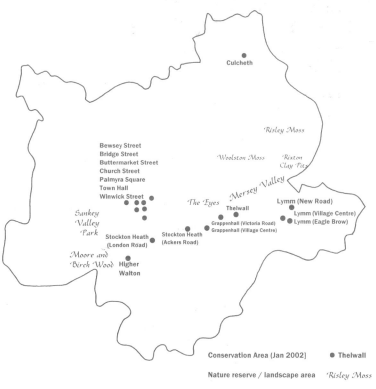

Conservation and heritage in early 21st-century Warrington.

Similar changes in attitude can be seen in policies towards the landscape of the borough, and its ecology and natural history. Many decades of industrial development spoiled and damaged the open land and countryside around the town. Dumping of industrial waste, pollution of air and water, and the proliferation of derelict land meant that by the 1970s there was a massive inheritance of degradation to be tackled. The new town strategy, which identified this as a key problem, planned to upgrade and improve the landscape, creating nature reserves and opening up streamsides and green wedges for leisure and amenity use. The borough already had a valuable asset in the form of urban and semi-urban parks, such as Victoria Park at Latchford and Orford Park, which had been acquired by, or gifted to, the town in the earlier 20th century. New projects included the creation of the Sankey Valley park in the later 1970s using the remains of the Sankey Navigation and the Dallam Brook as the axis of a new green space, and the setting aside of large areas around the new residential areas for parks and recreation areas – Birchwood Forest Park (transforming part of the site of the once-massive Risley munitions factories) and Woolston Park are examples.

The latest planning policies emphasise environmental conservation, with a general policy against adding further greenfield housing and commercial sites beyond those already designated. Protection of the green belt is paralleled by the enhancement or preservation of areas such as The Eyes at Thelwall and Woolston, where large tracts of marsh, scrubs, reeds and open water are now acknowledged as an important ecological habitat. This continues the pattern whereby some of the 'natural' landscapes, such as the surviving areas of Risley Moss and Holcroft Moss, have been designated as nature reserves, while opportunities for new habitats are afforded by man-made landscapes such as Rixton claypits and the lakes and woodlands between the Ship Canal and the old Runcorn & Latchford Canal at Moore.

FURTHER READING: The planning policies outlined in this section are discussed in more detail, with supporting evidence, in the first stages of the *Warrington Unitary Development Plan*, produced by the Borough Council in 2001-2. The local studies collection at Warrington library includes a full set of the reports, summaries, maps and plans associated with the UDP. For buildings of architectural and historical interest, see the *English Heritage Listed Buildings Schedules*, for Warrington Borough (copies in Warrington local studies collection); for the older buildings demolished in the 1920s and 1930s, see especially the books by Janice Hayes which are listed in the **Sources** section at the end of this book.

107. The Warrington bombings of 1993

On 20 March 1993 an IRA terrorist bomb exploded without warning at the top of Bridge Street, which was crowded with Saturday shoppers. Two children, three-year-old Johnathan Ball and 12-year-old Tim Parry, were killed. Another victim, 33-year-old Bronwen Vickers, died some months later as a result of her wounds. Many other people were injured, some critically. The bombing followed earlier attempts to blow up Warrington gasworks and the shooting of a policeman. These outrages, with their devastating and heartbreaking consequences, focused the eyes of the world on a town whose people were innocent victims of the political struggles of others. The events of March 1993 are etched on the memory of Warrington and produced an instant and profound wave not only of sympathy and outrage, but also of determination. In all the long and agonising history of the Northern Irish 'troubles', few terrorist deeds met with such universal condemnation, and the memorial service to the victims, attended by the Duke of Edinburgh and President Mary Robinson of Ireland, symbolised the hopes that from the suffering could come something more positive.

In retrospect, the Warrington bombing may perhaps be seen as a turning points, when the desire for peace and a political solution began to influence not only the ordinary people of Ulster but also politicians and even those organisations involved in violence over the decades. In Warrington itself the Peace Centre project, with its aim of bringing young people together to work towards a better future for all, offers hope for reconciliation and cooperation. And today the memorial to those who died or were injured on 20 March 1993 is not

The Secretary of State for Northern Ireland, Mo Mowlam [left], and Colin Parry [second left], father of Tim Parry, are joined by civic dignitaries and guests at the ceremony to mark the beginning of work on the Warrington Peace Centre.

only the inspirational, moving and much acclaimed sculpture and water feature, the River of Life, which snakes down the top of Bridge Street, but also, indirectly, the relative calm which, we may hope, prevails in Ireland.

FURTHER READING: The Warrington local studies collection has a large collection of material relating to the 1993 bombings, including news reports, video coverage and books.

108. *Warrington's future*

This book has charted some of the main themes in 2,000 years of the history of one of the most interesting and distinctive towns in northern England. It has covered many and diverse subjects – a Roman industrial town, a Norman power centre, a medieval friary, a 17th-century merchant, an 18th-century would-be university, dirty and insanitary Victorian housing, a late 20th-century

Warrington's future and past? The ten 'Guardians of Warrington' which now stand as sentinels at the town's heart, Market Gate. They symbolise the people who have protected and worked for Warrington over the past two thousand years, those who do so now, and those who will do so in years to come.

new city in the making. The thread linking these together is **location and accessibility**. From beginning to end, underlying Warrington's character, development and fortunes there has been a web of transport routes. For the past thirty years Warrington has been at a crossroads in both senses of the word – a nodal point in the national communications network, and a dramatic change of direction and character. The one certainty in its future is that these will continue to be the key to its development, dictating and shaping the way it grows and changes and the prosperity which it experiences and anticipates. The greatest of today's projects, the massive Omega development at Burtonwood, will succeed because of its location and its accessibility, just as surely as did Roman Wilderspool two millennia ago. The commercial buoyancy of the town centre is as much determined by accessibility and its ideal location within the region as was the good fortune of the medieval market. Future historians will enjoy the challenge of updating the story, and future Warringtonians will surely enjoy the knowledge of what has preceded them.

SOURCES & FURTHER READING

The Museum: Warrington Museum is an excellent starting place for any investigation into the local history of the borough, or any detailed aspect of its history. The Museum is itself of major historical significance, for Warrington was one of the very first towns in Britain to have a borough museum. Today, its displays give a rich and varied insight into the history of the town and its neighbourhood over several thousand years. There are many informative and lively exhibitions and displays that commemorate and celebrate special events, themes and occasions in the history of Warrington. The Museum is free, accessible and user-friendly and it is always full of interest. Don't miss it as your starting point.

The Library: Warrington Library is also historic in its own right – this was Britain's first municipal library funded from the rates. For over 150 years it has been serving the people of Warrington and today possesses a particularly fine local history and local studies collection. There are copies of just about every printed work which relates to the town and surrounding areas, together with many unpublished notes, theses, dissertations and compilations of information, and there are also excellent 'themed' collections, such as material on Lewis Carroll, and works by authors from the district. It also has a very comprehensive range of material for family history (including census returns, copies of parish registers and surname indexes) and a good collection of maps and plans. The Library and the Museum both have photographic archives.

Archive sources: The archives section of Warrington Library is the best place for original research into any aspect of the town's history, using original documentary sources. These go as far back as the early medieval period, though most date from 1700 or later. Warrington is lucky to have one of the best borough archives in north-west England, and its holdings include a very wide and diverse range of material – papers of local societies and organisations, the family and business archives of prominent (and not so well-known) Warringtonians, records of Warrington firms and businesses, property deeds and documents relating to land ownership, and notes and papers collected by antiquarians and historians in the past. There are two types of material which are especially noteworthy. The borough's archives include one of the most comprehensive and important collections of local authority records in the region – that might sound dull and boring, but in fact they are quite the opposite: the original records of, for example, the borough police, fire services, or sanitary department give a real insight into what life was like in Warrington in the 19th century. The other noteworthy material is the superb collection of poor law records from the 18th and early 19th centuries, perhaps the most outstanding in the north-west: there are excellent sets of accounts, workhouse papers, lists of paupers, detailed evidence for the 1832 cholera outbreak and much else, not only from Warrington but also from most of the other townships in the area.

Not all Warrington records are held locally. The Lancashire Record Office in Preston has among its collections a great deal of material relating to the town and adjacent parts of south Lancashire, including all the records of Lancashire County Council to 1974, the county quarter sessions courts from the end of the 16th century to the middle of the 20th (a key source for law and order, crime, the poor law and local administration) and almost all the wills and probate inventories of people from south Lancashire including Warrington town from the late 15th to the late 19th centuries. Cheshire and Chester Archives and Local Studies in Chester also holds important collections of archives relating to the Warrington area, including wills and probate inventories for all the parishes and townships south of the river for the same period as above; most original parish records; the records of Cheshire County Council and other local authorities; and many collections of papers from local families and landowners.

Further reading: Warrington has been fortunate with its historians, past and present. In the Victorian period there were several tireless and inquisitive researchers, including 'amateur' local historians and archaeologists who between them built up a remarkably clear picture of the town's history. Foremost among them were Thomas May, James Kendrick, Arthur Bennett and, above all, the 'father of Warrington history' William Beamont, who is now commemorated by a plaque on the building where he had his offices, next to the *Barley Mow*. More recently the research has been continued, and the existing published material on the town is a valuable asset to any researcher: in this context, mention must be made of *Early modern Warrington, 1520-1847: a definitive history*, by Ian Sellers, published in 1998. That book is exactly as its title suggests, and though not an easy read it is a mine of information about the town during those crucial centuries. The bibliography below gives general titles about Warrington (or in some cases Lancashire and Cheshire) which I have used in the preparation of this book. To avoid repetition these are not listed in the 'further reading' boxes which follow most of the sections in this book – those include additional titles specific to the particular topic covered – but the general titles below have been used throughout and all of them are recommended as background reading or as a source of general information.

General titles:

anon., *Warrington of Today: a souvenir in commemoration of the jubilee of the incorporation* (Robinson & Co., 1898)

W. Beamont, *Walks about Warrington, towards the beginning of the present century* (Warrington Guardian, 1887)

G.A. Carter and J.P. Aspden (editors), *Warrington Hundred: a handbook published by the Corporation of Warrington on the occasion of the Centenary of the Incorporation of the Borough* (Warrington Borough Council, 1947)

A.G. Crosby, *A History of Cheshire* (Phillimore, 1996)

A.G. Crosby, *A History of Lancashire* (Phillimore, 1998)

A.M. Crowe, *Warrington Ancient and Modern: a history of the town and neighbourhood* (Beamont Press, 1947)

J. Hayes, *Changing Warrington* (Warrington Borough Council, 1991)

J. Hayes, *Warrington* (Images of England series, Tempus Publishing, 1994)

J. Hayes, *Warrington Voices* (Tempus Oral History series, 2000)

J. Hayes and P. Williams, *Warrington in Camera 1850s-1950s* (Warrington Borough Council, 1981)

P. Williams and J. Hayes, *Warrington as it was* (Hendon Publishing Co., 1979)

Specific themes or more detailed analysis:

O. Ashmore, *The Industrial Archaeology of North-West England* (Chetham Society 3rd series, vol.29, 1982)

A. Bennett, *Warrington: as it was, as it is, and as it might be* (Sunrise Publishing Co., 1892)

W. Farrer and J. Brownbill, *The Victoria History of the County of Lancaster,* volume 3 (1907)

S. Grealey (editor), *The Archaeology of Warrington's Past* (Warrington New Town and Archaeological Surveys Limited, 1976)

C.B. Phillips and J.H. Smith, *Lancashire and Cheshire from AD1540* (Longman, 1994)

I. Sellers, *Early modern Warrington, 1520-1847: a definitive history* (Edwin Mellen Press, 1998)

D. Sylvester and G. Nulty, *The Historical Atlas of Cheshire* (Cheshire Community Council, 1958)

P. Tomlinson and M. Warhurst, *The Archaeology of Merseyside* (Journal of the Merseyside Archaeological Society vol.7, 1986-1987)

J.K. Walton, *Lancashire: a social history 1558-1939* (Manchester University Press, 1987)

H. Wells, *Walking into Warrington's Past: Church Street* (author, 1996)

H. Wells, *Walking into Warrington's Past: Bridge Street* (author, 1998)

H. Wells, *Walking into Warrington's Past: Sankey Street* (author, 2000)

INDEX